Gleanings from Rig Veda—
When Science was Religion

Gleanings from Rig Veda— When Science was Religion

Written by:

Choudur Satyanarayana Moorthy

authorHOUSE®

AuthorHouse™
1663 Liberty Drive
Bloomington, IN 47403
www.authorhouse.com
Phone: 1-800-839-8640

First published by AuthorHouse   10/19/2011

ISBN: 978-1-4670-2400-6 (sc)
ISBN: 978-1-4670-2401-3 (ebk)

Printed in the United States of America

Table of Contents

Part I

Part II

PART I

Foreword

Gleanings from Rig Veda is a comprehensive and condensed essence of pure supreme knowledge. Great rishis of ancient times have experienced this power of knowledge and practiced this religion of science and spirituality. The absolute truth transcends time and space. Scientific community derives the results based on experiments and research. There are prerequisites for any experiment to succeed and success depends on the level of skill of the observer. The oldest and the foremost Veda comprising thousands of hymns reflect on scientific and spiritual community to provide the utmost knowledge that enlightens the observer.

Sri C.S. Moorthy has done extensive research and thoroughly understood the dynamics and fundamentals of the science of Rig Veda. He made an offering of the pristine knowledge with all its glory, in the form of this book in such a beautiful and easy to understand language. He derived meanings for complex hymns that make it a wonderful read. This book is divided into two parts. The first part lays the foundation on Rig Veda. The Second part goes deeper into the ingredients that make up Rig Veda. This book is a scientific experiment, without any dramatization to highlight a point. Whether you are scientific or spiritual or both, Gleanings from Rig Veda present an interesting perspective of science that is when science was religion!

Badri Pidatala

Introduction

At the outset, let us make it clear, we are neither denouncing anything nor accepting anything either. We are trying to look at things as they are.

Rig Veda is the oldest compilation of knowledge in the world. No one knows when this happened! All other religious and other knowledge like Yajur Veda, Sama Veda, Atharva Veda, Puranas, Epics, Vedanta and other branches of learning called Vedangas and Upavedas came into being many thousands of years later and traced their roots to Rig Veda. Even Abrahmic religions arose much later. The compilers of Rig Veda, Angirasa Rishis had achieved the extraordinary feat of merging with Universal Consciousness. Hence, they could actually envision the grandeur of existence. Unfortunately, even during their time Rig Veda Samhitas was not properly understood by the scholarly class and thereafter it was increasingly less understood as time passed. Even today, in India, the Brahmin community trace their genetic lineage to one or other Angirasa Rishis.

What then is God? There are volumes over volumes written on what God is and what He is not. We are also told that He is indescribable and yet He is described in flowery language. The moment one describes Him there are others opposed to that description which results in a conflict. That way, different religions and sects come into being and divide humanity. There are also those who are opposed to the very concept of God. There are others who are indifferent to all these and pursue their so called self interest in this confusing society, even to the extent of involving the name of God to serve their selfish ends. In this context, do we have the competency to judge what is right and wrong? After all, right or wrong is a matter of opinion. On the contrary, fact is not dependant on opinion. In the jungle of opinions, God is irredeemably lost. Furthermore, judgment is always one sided based on man-made norms. The best judgment is limited by space-time constraint and therefore myopic, considering the fact that there are many other dimensions beside space-time in this universe, which are ignored. Balanced judgment is possible, only when all the dimensions are taken into consideration and we are able to look at facts and not opinion. Our life is influenced by both space-time and these other dimensions. About the other dimensions we know little. As we know only partially the factors influencing our life, we cannot hope to look at unalloyed facts. Angirasa Rishis transcended the entire dimension that are there in this universe and provided us guidance to achieve the goal pointed out in Rig Veda. The name Angirasa needs to be explored. At the root, "Ang" means fire and "rasa" means essence. Thus, they were essence of fire which is Consciousness. The Angirasa Rishis who are credited with the compilation of Rig Veda were persons who transcended all the dimensions we mentioned above. When they transcended all the dimensions that are there, they became one with Consciousness. They were thus, most competent to tell us the fact regarding God. This is wonderfully articulated by Rishika Vak Ambarni in Rig Veda Mandala 10 as described in Chapter 3. A word of caution though; merely learning about the fact and not acting on it could be deeply disturbing. Those lucky ones who heard late Jiddu Krishnamurti in his life time would agree that it is indeed deeply disturbing not to act on realization of the truth. He was indeed an Angirasa Rishi, even genetically speaking.

Even after thousands of years, Rig Veda the first book ever, remains an enigma many times in variance with the religious thoughts developed in subsequent ages but, surprisingly emerging that much more relevant for revealing the inherent Truth in a very explicit language, though, by some accounts, in a truncated form. Only, we have forgotten the idiom of that era. This is the fascinating aspect that prompted me to undertake this venture. We have only made a humble beginning. Much more research needs to be undertaken, to probe deeper into this way of looking at reality. Imagine that there is a scale. At one end is Rig Veda and at the other end is modern science with their latest discoveries, especially in physical sciences. We will find, astonishingly, great congruencies about some of which we talk in this book. And the scale tips in favor of Rig Veda, for exploring new frontiers of science! Incidentally, one should make a clear distinction between fundamental or pure science and applied science. We have steered clear of applied science altogether, as it is a totally different cup of tea.

The dichotomy of Spirit and Matter needs to be reassessed. Spirit is Matter. The whole universe is made of energy in different forms, but at the root one. On the one hand, this energy translates into spirit as it is intangible. On the other hand, it is now well established that matter, in the ultimate analysis is energy as discovered by Albert Einstein in the beginning of 20th Century. Spirit may not be tangible, but we do see, smell, hear, eat and touch matter. All these five sense activities are controlled by the mind which in turn is dependant on thought. Thus, thought drives the senses. We may say thought is responsible for the sensation. If I see a building in front of me, it is the response of the thought. Thoughts of others also concur with my response because thought has separated itself from rest of the world, uniformly for almost every one of us, as in the statement "I and the world at large." As it has been wisely said: There is no thought without a thing and nothing (no thing) without a thought! This dichotomy of me being different from the world is the foundation of thought. And thought also appears to drive the spirit. At its best thought gives a coloring to the Truth which is always in the present.

The foundation of thought fuels duality in the form of choice. There is only one truth. But the one is seen as many, the beginning of confusion. Reconciliation we presume takes time, perhaps many life times; and yet remain unresolved. The time element here is psychological in nature. Not only we are victim of thought, but we are also victims of psychological Time. Thought is a creature of Time. That is the reason it invents the concept of past, present and future. We largely skip the present. Past is dead and gone by and yet we cling to it; build enormous records to fall back on, why? It is because we want to whitewash the present with the past. This gives rise to untold conflicts and confusion. We then invent the future in order to conceal the problems of the present so that we can resolve them gradually. In due course of time we hope to resolve them. Unfortunately, new challenges deluge us so much that we forget about the past unresolved problems. On the contrary, we go on adding more issues to the unresolved category. These unresolved issues cause untold misery in our life. We may think we are making progress in time. But the fact is our confusion and conflicts keep on mounting.

We think that old gives place to new. It is a chimera. There is no such thing as old and new in reality. Old is new and new is old. When old is modified, so called new comes into being. It is only a change. Is it not old disguised in new garb? For the truly new to be, we have to rise above the thinking process and escape the time wrap. Then there is a transformation. This book attempts to make a humble beginning to highlight the fact that the oldest Rig Veda is all about this transformation. Rig Veda is also seized of the latest quest in fundamental physical sciences, that of a unified force in nature. It in fact did one better, in first identifying the unified force and relating all other manifestations in nature to that unifying force. As Rig Veda states at the very outset, there is but only one goal in life and that is to allow Individual Consciousness to lead us and merge with Universal Consciousness. The word 'allow' mentioned above should not be considered in the spirit of granting permission, an act of will. The 'allow' in this context involves restraining from performing those activities that impede the journey of Individual Consciousness towards the Universal Consciousness.

To sum-up in a nutshell, we may say that Rig Veda highlights three pillars of existence, which are:

Spirit of Consciousness

Spirit of Yajna or sacrifice

8

Spirit of Soma or Love

It is a well known fact that in the entire universe only earth is habitable and that is why we are here. We have been here for a very long time too. In 1970s two scientists Robert Dicke and Brandon Carter discovered a chilling fact and formulated what is known as Anthropic Principle. Most of the phenomena in the nature are so fine tuned as to make our existence in this planet possible. Even if one of the phenomena is tweaked even slightly, our life will cease to be and the planet will be as barren as rest of the universe. The ancient Rishis of Rig Veda were well aware of this fact. They went a step further to answer the question: What makes the phenomena remain so fine tuned? What is the motive? The answer was simple; it was the spirit of love and sacrifice. To bring home this point very clearly, they provided an apt illustration.

What was available for common observation was man himself. He has various limbs that act seemingly independently. But these limbs do not have any private programs of their own. They act only in the fulfillment of the object of the body whose limbs they are. They therefore sacrifice their private interest for the general good of the body and they love the body too, such that they would not willingly separate from it. This concept the Rishis projected on a vast canvas, so to say. They tell you to imagine that there is a Vishwanara (Universal man). He is in essence the Universal Consciousness. From him all the phenomena generate. The phenomena are there to fulfill only his objective and they love him ever so much.

Choudur Satyanarayana Moorthy
Navi Mumbai, India.
tathumoorthy@gmail.com

The Opening Invocation

This Mantra is widely used in the beginning of worship in many temples and homes. This is addressed to Ganapathi. In many temples where this Mantra is chanted may have deities other than Ganapathi. This mantra is of fundamental importance for spiritual progress.

The Mantra:

गणानां त्वा गनपतिᳵ हवामहे

कविं कवीनाम् उपम श्रवस्तमम् ।

ज्येष्ठ राजं ब्रह्मणाम् ब्रह्मनस्पत

आ नः श्रृन्वन्न् उतिभिः सीद सादनम् ॥

The Mantra occurs in Rig Veda 2.23.1. The Mantra drashta (the visionary) was Rishi Gritsamada.

We are not examining the conventional meaning. Since the mantra has a deep significance, there is more to it than meets the eye. We are going to look into this aspect.

The meaning: "We meditate on you Ganapathi, leader of the countable hordes, A seer superior to all other seers, who causes the hearing of the divine inspiration, who is the Para-Brahman and who is the presiding deity of the Mantra; May he hear us; May he be seated on the seat within, so that he increases our awareness.

Explanation:

Ganapathi is the consciousness—choice less awareness in every one of us. He is uncountable or immeasurable. Since he is the leader of the countable (Ganapathi), he has to be uncountable otherwise he will be one among us. What is countable is limited by space-time. Like life forms, atoms etc. These have a boundary, so you can count them. What can be counted can also be chosen from among many. So when as a countable, you, exercise choice, you are aware only by choice.

Ganapathi is able to directly see the Para-Brahman (Universal Consciousness) so he is seer of seers. He can make you hear Para-Brahman's breathing. This Ganapathi, the choice less awareness is seated within (at Muladhara Chakra) and he encourages us in becoming aware without choice.

This is the highest truth.

Chapter 1

Primacy of Consciousness

One of the cardinal principles of science is objectivity. Niels Bohr developed the Copenhagen interpretation of quantum mechanics. According to Bohr, the observer was very much part of an experiment. However, observer is always subjective. This is a fundamental departure in western scientific exploration. Subjective is consciousness in the final analysis. Read on . . .

It is illuminating to first understand the meaning of the word Rig Veda. Rig or Rik means eulogy or praise as distinct from prayer and worship. Veda is apparently knowledge. Did the great Rishis of yore merely concerned with transactional knowledge of the four dimensional world we live in? What is less apparent is that Veda also can mean 'to be.' The root of the word Veda is *vid* as per Vyakarna-Karika which gives five different meaning to *vid*. The first of the meanings is to endure, to stay or Astitva—the existence. If you are asked the question, 'how do you know that you exist?' You would respond simply by saying, 'I know that I exist.' And no further questioning is necessary. This clarity or awareness that one exists is the demonstration of what consciousness or awareness is, or has to be. This awareness, the Individual Consciousness is first and fundamental knowledge, everything else follows this knowledge. Without this awareness there is no existence. This knowledge has no beginning and therefore no ending. So it is eternal, or Anadi. This knowledge is also not tutored by anyone; it is synonymous with existence, so it is untutored or *Apaurusha*. Thus, Rig Veda is knowledge in praise of Consciousness and its manifestation in the cosmos. Rig Veda is Apaurusha (not compiled by man) because it was compiled by Angirasa Rishis, who were one with Consciousness and not by any poets are pandits. Furthermore, since Angirasa Rishis were one with Consciousness which has no beginning and therefore ending, it is the Eternal Truth, Rig Veda is Anadi. The Universal Consciousness assumes individuality after manifestation. To lead the Individual Consciousness towards Universal Consciousness and effect a consummation is the only objective in front of man. It is this transcendental knowledge that deserves the eulogy. Aptly, Rig Veda commences with the statement (RV 1.1.1):

अग्निमीळे पुरोहितम् यज्ञस्य देवमृत्विजम् ।

Meaning: I adore Agni, who is the leader of the journey in due season.

Agni, of course, is the light of Consciousness (Chidagni) in the individual and Yajna is the journey (for crossing the remaining lokas or layers) towards Universal Consciousness. Rishi Vamadevah Gautamah also explains his similar vision in Rig Veda Mandala 4 Sukta 58 Mantra 11 in the first part thus:

धामन् ते विश्वं भुवनमधि श्रितम् । अन्तः समुद्रे हृदि ।

Meaning: The life of all persons is sandwiched between two infinite oceans, the one below, individual consciousness, and the other above, the universal consciousness.

Consciousness is of paramount importance as Rishi Gristamada expressed in The Opening Invocation, we saw earlier. Hence, this opening invocation is chanted at the beginning of every religious occasion, to resolve in our mind at the outset, that we are aware of every act we are performing and are not a routine affair. If we are not so aware, our organs will be doing something and our mind will be involved in some other thoughts. It then becomes a futile activity. Perhaps this consideration prompted late J. Krishnamurti to coin the word "The Flame of Attention" as title of one of his books.

Consider, for example, cycling. Initially, let us say, you did not know cycling. Everyday, you set apart some time and practice balancing and riding the cycle. In due course it becomes a routine. Your riding performance keeps improving. You would not even be aware that you are exercising a skill. While riding, you may be thinking of many things, but your legs will not leave the pedal! You may become a star performer, but it is not a creative activity. With or without consciousness, you can do cycling. You will be 'down to earth.' In Sanskrit that is 'Bhu' loka. It means this cycling ability will not be useful in other realms or lokas. With earthly knowledge and skills, you will be able to prosper on the earth but will not be able to progress to higher lokas like Bhuvah, Suvaha etc. Earthly knowledge is limited by space-time constraint.

There are 14 Lokas or layers of consciousness—seven below and six above, the middle one being 'Bhu' Loka. We are not now considering the seven pathala lokas which lead to further regression, from earth's point of view. There is salvation only in the progression towards the remaining six higher lokas or layers of consciousness. The six higher lokas are: Bhuvah, Suvaha, Mahaha, Janaha, Tapaha and Satya loka. This Satya loka is made up of two parts. There is Brahma loka first and then the Satya loka proper. The Veda says that progress towards these higher lokas is the only goal in human life and not any other. It is indeed a very difficult proposition. God knows how many 'Janmas' (rebirths) one needs to take to arrive at the destination. To make progress one needs to leave the shackles of 'Bhu' loka. But so long as we are subservient to thought process we will not be able to break the shackle and take off.

We are predominated by thought process. Incessantly our brain keeps thinking something or other. A characteristic of this thinking power is orderliness and logic. What your eyes cannot see, what your ears cannot hear what your nose cannot smell or hands cannot touch, the thought can surmise. It could also device instruments for supernormal vision, hearing, tasting, smelling and touching. It can administer and organize. Modern science is replete with thousands of examples of this extended capacity of man. However, this thought process is limited by space-time constraint like any other organ of human body. Naturally, any instruments conceived by the thought process will also suffer the same limitation. Accordingly, if the thought conceives of star billions of light years away, the best space vehicle cannot cross the space-time barrier and reach the distant star.

First, we need to know what this space-time constraint is. We all know that space comprises the distance between two points A and B. Again when you measure a room, you look at the length, breath and height of the room. Similarly, if you have to locate a place on the map you look at the longitude, latitude and the height above the mean sea level. We cannot conceive of an object outside these dimensions. That is space constraint. Apparently, inseparable part of this space constraint is time constraint. It takes time to travel the distance from point A to B. Any aeronautical travel in space is limited by the speed of light, which we all know is 1, 86,000 miles per second. So to travel to a distant star one life time of a person is not sufficient. It will take centuries to reach the star! Somehow, if a man were to make the journey, when he returns back to earth he will be a stranger, as many generations would have overtaken him in his absence from earth. There should be some other way to circumvent the problem. Is it not a profound scientific issue? Modern science has only begun to address this issue in a fundamentally different way but only recently.

Some of the scientists have acknowledged that this new insight was gained from the established knowledge of the Eastern hemisphere. Perhaps they are reluctant to directly state that India is the pioneer in this break through. Only a hundred years back, Indians were considered as aborigines not capable of profound thinking by the Western Scholarship. They opined that whatever creative knowledge Indians possessed were those belonging to the Aryan race that migrated from western hemisphere, we were told! Even many enlightened Indians believed the western view. This myth has been laid to rest only recently. But habits die hard! Most modern educated Indians still cling to this misdirected view.

Ancient Rishis, great scientists that they were, took up the problem of limitation of thought in all its aspects and arrived at a remarkable solution. Even though thought is a very profound capacity, it is only a poor second to another faculty we possess that we share with other life forms. Thinking is not a faculty we share with other life forms in this universe, even like sense of speech and maybe smell. Unfortunately, this many times makes us very arrogant and vain, leading us to feel that we are superior to other life forms in this universe. We even think that the evolution of the species from the humble bacteria has produced man in the pinnacle of its glory. We appropriate the right to rule this universe. We don't mind trampling and destroying the other life forms for our enjoyment! Moreover, we also want to compete with our fellow beings to establish that we are more clever and intelligent than any of them. Our entire education system is designed to engender this competitive impulse in us. Thought is not only subject to limitation of space and time, it is also a material process. It is well to remember that 'Thought' and 'Thing' (matter) are inseparable twins. There is no thinking without a thing and there is no thing (English word 'Nothing') without thought. This is the threshold that modern science has arrived at. In Particle Physics, matter in the ultimate analysis is a wave of light, or a unit of energy which is interrelated to everything else in the universe. Matter so disintegrates in the presence of a still superior faculty in the life form of not only man but all other beings. Moreover, in Astrophysics or Cosmology also science has come to realize that the universe as we know it is mostly (The estimate is 95%) made up of Dark Matter, which we can say is an enigmatic 'nothing.' So there ought to be a superior force to thought.

Consider for example the currency of a realm. The currency of one realm is not valid in another realm. Rupee is valid in India. But in US, Dollar is the currency. So Rupee is not valid there. This is true for all other countries. Similarly, thinking is the currency in Bhu Loka. It is progressively less valid in the seven Lokas below and in the six Lokas above also it is not valid but, in all the Lokas 'Consciousness' is acceptable. That is a primary reason Consciousness is superior to thinking faculty in man. Consciousness

17

is superior in another sense also, in that; it is not limited by space-time constraint. Space-time we are told by our Shastras as well as Modern Science is but only four dimensions. There are six or seven more dimensions to deal with. Consciousness alone is capable of surmounting the obstacles that are likely to come in the upward journey. You can easily see this in operation in Bhu Loka, how consciousness surmounts the stumbling block of thought process, a product of space-time by mere awareness. We call the process "Meditation." Why do we need to be Conscious is the next question? Only when we surmount a dimension can we clearly see its working and not when we are under the influence of that dimension. Thus, when we surmount all the ten dimensions, we shall be able to see the full glory of this universe as a whole and not fragments of it as at present. Fragmentary view is distorting.

You are naturally conscious. It does not require anyone to teach you. Even a bacterium is conscious for that matter. The seven Pathala lokas we referred to earlier relates to the progress we made from rocks to bacteria, to insects, then plants, then animals and finally man. We do not know how many life times (Janmas) we spent in these lower forms. According to shastras, as we saw above, there are seven layers or lokas below before you evolve as a man! The progress was possible for many of the constituents of other species only because of consciousness. This progress has to be maintained because there are six more lokas to be traversed by man. It is consciousness that brought you up to this stage and it is the same consciousness that has to lead you further. The progression of consciousness is thwarted in man, by his thinking process interfering as 'choice.' Man imbibes the unique quality to choose between alternatives. At the root of this sense of choice are desire, security and fear. We will not go into this aspect here. This consciousness with choice is what makes us tethered to earth-Bhu loka. There is so much allurement here that we wish to be so tethered to the earth and we don't mind occasional suffering that we have to put up with. This, in short, is our lot.

It appears we don't mind wallowing in samsara sagara (the ocean of mortal living) even with all the troubles and tribulations in life.

No God will come and rescue man so that he can rise higher. The salvation lies in being aware without choice. This choice less consciousness or awareness is variously labeled in Veda as Agni, Brihaspathi, Brahmanaspati or Ganapathi. The Veda asserts that this Agni alone will appease all the Devathas (luminaries) with our offerings of love and sacrifice; fight the Asuras (inimical forces) on the way and surely lead us to the final destination. Not many are willing to make this onerous journey, though many talk about it in flowery language. Volumes over volumes have been written on this subject, especially in India. But the message remains in the books: to be read, appreciated and put back in the shelves!

Whatever practice man resorts to is always exercised after a choice. Let us say, my choice is to follow the precepts of A and your choice is B. Even if what they advocate is right, because it is founded on a choice, it will suffer the same malady: interference of thought process in the manifestation of consciousness. Please see this happening in you not only in this matter but any other matter with which you are concerned. The mere observation at all times will put to rest this choosing activity. When the choosing function is suspended, a silence descends and you are aware or conscious without choice. That is the highest form of meditation. Again, the moment you say to yourself that you will have this kind of meditation on a daily basis at a fixed time, you are back in choice making process so much so that it becomes a futile activity. When this wisdom dawns on you the choice less consciousness or awareness will come naturally to you. You don't have to do a thing about it. Perhaps this is what late J. Krishnamurti meant when he said that effort is contraindicated in the journey towards Truth. Consciousness is part of you as it is part of this entire creation as we mentioned while explaining the meaning of Rig Veda at the beginning of this chapter.

It is very interesting to observe that the Rishis of Rig Veda considered this issue regarding Consciousness as of paramount importance. Even the modern scientific community is laboring to discover a unifying factor that will take into account all their divorce scientific findings of all the energies and forces in nature.

The only difference is the Rishis of yore began with the unifying force and related all the energies and forces to this unifying factor, whereas the scientific community has identified the bits and pieces and trying to put them together. There is an axiom: Many parts do not make the whole! So the ultimate discovery still eludes modern science. What we are, however, concerned in this book is: Did the Rishis, at that ancient point of time, have a reasonable knowledge of all the "bits and pieces" that the scientists claim to have discovered, without the aid of sophisticated equipment and paraphernalia?

Every family group of Rishis that was involved in the compilation of the Veda had at least one member (Rishi) narrating his direct experience of Consciousness. Apri Hymns of Rig Veda are considered important not only in Rig Veda but more vitally so in the yajnas of other Vedas as well. The hymns appear in seven out of the ten mandalas (chapters) of Rig Veda, each hymn by a different Rishi. The first few mantras in each Apri hymn were outpouring of the Rishi as he witnessed the Consciousness (Agni). Astonishingly, they are also identical.

Chapter 2

Key to consciousness

Just as we need a key to open a locked door, Brahma or Mantra is the gateway to consciousness. Read on . . .

It is a cardinal principle of scientific exploration that every new observation has to be reduced to a formula in mathematical terms so that the discovery can be emulated and confirmed by peers for making the discovery a general law. This new formula may be discarded or modified with newer insights in science. This has been the hallmark of scientific discoveries. Exactly the same function is fulfilled by a mantra. However, there is a basic difference. For science, the phenomena are inanimate substances, whereas for ancient Rishis, the very same phenomena pulsate with life. According to ancient Rishis all the forces in Universe are related to Bijaksharas. Bijaksharas are those seed letters of Sanskrit alphabet that generate primal sound vibrations. Sound vibration is a rudiment form of life. The sounds of other letters are derived from these primal letters. The primal letters are associated, each with a luminary (Devata), and each devata is a force that radiates energy in the universe. For example, take the mantra Aum. In the mantra, 'A' stands for Brahma the repository of all energies; 'U' for Vishnu, the power that sustains (Electro-magnetic Force); and 'M' for Shiva the power that transforms one kind of energy to another (gravitational force). Thus, the primal letters are associated with various energy forms we encounter in the universe. A mantra is formulated using the Bijaksharas (primal letters). It is reviewed by Nawagwas or Dashagwas before accepted as common law. The man who develops the ability to deeply understand the Bijaksharas can certainly experience the forces behind each mantra, by realizing that the presence of energy as a cause happens in the Consciousness level. More important, the mantras are the key to Consciousness. Consider, you are busy at work whole day and return home tired. You take some rest; refresh yourself, and sit in a comfortable posture in front of the 'alter'. You meditate on a mantra; it could be OM or any other such scientifically formulated mantra. What happens? Your thoughts recede, and a silence comes into being. You are aware of everything but you are not part of it. Then the presence of our Individual Consciousness comes into focus. As a natural consequence, a perception of the powers other than our usual thought generated vision commences. Generally, however, in no time, a thought manifests and high jacks the silence and you are far away from that silence! We won't even know when we changed tracks. You therefore are unable to witness the universal forces at the root of the mantra.

However, a scientific formula and a mantra differ fundamentally. A scientific formula is concerned with matter (object) and its observation. It is therefore a material process dependent on thought alone. Thought cannot operate in infinity because it is finite, limited by Space and Time; so scientific formula also suffers this inherent defect. On the other hand, a mantra deals with the infinite forces which are not material in nature, but expressive all the same, for example vibration, and sound. One has to exit thought process to be able to progress in infinity. The mechanism available to us is mantra. Accordingly, in the Rig Veda, the Hymn 1.18 by Rishi Medhatitih gives an earliest indication that Mantra means Brahma. Thus, in 1.18.1, the Rishi appeals:

सोमनाम् स्वरणम् कुणुहि ब्रह्मणस्पते । कक्षीवन्तम् य औशिजः ॥

Meaning: O Lord Brahmanaspati or Brahma holder of key to mantras, make me, who pours the Soma (bestows love), come in the light (of consciousness), me who knows the mystery and who is born of luster.

Soma refers to the spirit of love most evident in the biological world that is in our body.

In the Veda, if we try to understand what a mantra is, we will have a good idea of who Brahmaji is. *Man* means mind and *Tra* means protection (The Dalai Lamas on Tantra-GH Mullin). Again, *Tra* comes from the root *Trayoti* which means liberation. Accordingly, Mantra would be an instrument that provides liberation of mind. Therefore, the Mantra provides liberation from the tyranny of thought, when it becomes the instrument of Consciousness. It is interesting to note that both Ganapathi and Brahma share the same labels Brihaspathi and Brahmanaspathi. Thus, Ganapathi as we saw earlier is Consciousness and Brahma as Brahmanaspati is the instrument of this Consciousness.

Mantra doctrine postulates that this tangible universe which we see around us is made up of only different kinds of vibration and energies working at different levels. The things which appear so solid and real are not what they seem. They are the result of interplay of different kinds of energies and consciousness. This appeared as a revolutionary doctrine in the beginning of twentieth century to the scientists. Till that time Newtonian physics prevailed. Matter was given an independent existence consisting of material and indestructible atoms. But the progress of science, especially of physics and chemistry during the remaining part of twentieth century, moved out of the above fixation and tended to concur with Mantra doctrine with the realization that matter and atoms are but products of a play of energy.

In the twentieth century, with the discoveries which have been made with regards to the nature of the atom our ideas about matter have changed completely so much so that we now regard the whole physical universe not as a mass of unyielding solid atoms but as an extraordinary play of different kinds of energies. What appears as a tangible universe to the senses has been found by the scientists to be mostly empty space. It has been estimated that if all the atoms in the body of a man (estimated at 10^{140}-that is 10 followed by 140 zeros in each cell and there are 10^140 cells in our body!) were collected together and all the empty spaces in these atoms were eliminated, we shall get a mere speck, so small, that a magnifying glass would be needed to see it. And even this speck of matter may be composed merely of energy according to the famous formula of Einstein, E=mc^2. It is now an established fact that physical matter is practically nothing but a multifarious play of different kinds of energies at different levels. Modern science has further determined that there are only four sources of energy in this universe which are: Gravitational, Electro-magnetic, Strong Nuclear and Weak Nuclear Force. So these, in fact, are the building blocks of our tangible universe. In India, ancient Rishis were very fond of symbolism which helps man to assimilate a concept of science. It is thus that our tradition depicts Brahma with four heads being the four forms of energy, Vibration/ Sound, Electro-magnetic, Strong and Weak Nuclear force. Further, Brahma is always shown sitting on a lotus. Lotus is the symbol of Gravitational force.

In Mandala 1, Sookta 40, Mantras 1-3, Rishi Kanvah Ghaurah gives an insight into the divinity of Brahmanaspathi or Brahma, thus:

उत्तिष्ठ ब्रह्मणस्पते देवयन्तस्त्वेमहे ।

उप प्र यन्तु मरूतः सुदानव इन्द्र प्रशूर्भवा सचा ॥१ ॥

Meaning: Rise up, Oh Brahmanaspathi (Lord of Mantras), we pray looking forward to the other divinities (Forces in nature) in your wake. May Maruts (Tachyons) come with auspicious gifts along with Indra (Atoms) promptly.

In modern science, Maruts represent Gravitational Force. Indra constitutes Electro-magnetic force, Stong and Weak Nuclear Force.

त्वामिद्धि सहसस्पुत्र मर्त्यं उपब्रूते धने हिते ।

सुवीर्यं मरूत आ स्वश्र्व्यं दधीत यो व आचके ॥२ ॥

Meaning: O Son of Strength, mortal beings invoke you for acquiring felicities (to progress towards Universal Consciousness). O Maruts, on praising you the auspicious power and might are bestowed on man.

Marut is the Son of Strength. Strength here is Rudra Shiva (the Gravitational Force in nature). Even modern science has found that Tachyons are a spin off of Gravitational Force.

प्रैतु ब्रह्मणस्पतिः प्र देव्येतु सूत्रुता ॥

अच्छा वीरं नर्यं पह्ङितराधसं देवा यज्ञं नयन्तु नः ॥३ ॥

Meaning: We look forward to the arrival of Brahmanaspathi followed by the divinity of Speech endowed with truth. May the divinities help all human beings in the journey (towards the Universal Consciousness) with the wealth (of enlightenment).

Speech is sound/vibration, the universal force that enables all action in the world.

The Rishis went deeper into this question of the constitution of this universe. They discovered that the intangible elements of the universe like thoughts and emotions have also a material basis. The subtle matter through which they work is also merely a mass of vibrations/sound and play of different kinds of energies. To them it became evident that all the manifested worlds are based on vibrations/sound and various kinds of energies and that all these vibrations/sounds and energies are connected with one another and can be traced from one stage of subtlety to another until they end in one primary, fundamental and all-embracing vibration from which all the constituent vibrations in the manifested universe emerge. This final abode is labeled Brahma Loka. The nearest modern science has been able to arrive at is the existence of sub-particles like phonons, theoretically that is. Science says there is a particle associated with every wave, including a particle associated with the sound wave traveling through the metal. It is labeled phonon. A phonon is not an elementary particle. It is certainly not one of the particles that make up the metal, for it exists only by virtue of the collective motion of huge number of particles that do make up the metal. But a phonon is a particle just the same. It has mass, it has momentum, and it carries energy. It behaves precisely the way quantum physics says a particle should behave. We say that a phonon is an ***emergent particle.*** No doubt this is a profound discovery in science. It establishes that sound also is a wave as well as a particle like light wave/particle.

There is only one way of knowing, fully anything of a subtle nature. That is by transcending it in our Consciousness. It is because Consciousness is not limited by Space-Time constraint. For example, in order to know what *Maya* is we must transcend its illusion. Similarly, in order to know the nature of this fundamental vibration which includes all other vibrations that lay at the basis of the universe, it is necessary to transcend the world created by it. This is possible only with the help of Consciousness and not by any amount of thinking, however profound it may be. It is only then that we can know the nature of this fundamental vibration which is called *Nada* (sound) and that aspect of Ultimate Reality which manifests *Sabda-Brahman.*

We will consider an example. You may look at any modern gadget that we see around us. Take, for example a refrigerator (fridge). It has three levels in which it remains alive like any other visible object in universe, including man. The first level is the body (cabinet) and the physical frame work. At the next level, the second, it has internal wiring and chemistry. At the third and final level it has the operating source or primary cause for its existence. Each level exhibits its own characteristics and limitations, but both the first two levels are dependent on the third level which hardly seems to have limitation. This is equally true of man. Thus, we function at three levels according to Vedanta. At the physical level (sthula sarira), we have various organs; skin covering them; with bones inside them; Then there is the subtle structure (sukhsma sarira) within the body, where blood is flowing all over the body; there is the network of nervous system; there are chemicals to masticate and digest food; enzymes to build muscles and maintain them and cell structure all over the body for protection; and also thought and mind that operate the sense organs. Sense organs are eyes, ears, nose, mouth (tongue), skin hands and feet. It is difficult to locate this mind. It appears to be all over the body, though thought can be traced to brain. As compared to the physical structure, which is very finite, the thought-mind is much less so. We see the first two levels which are finite in different degrees. There is this third level called the causal level (karana sarira) which is infinite within our body, the Individual Consciousness. It causes the other levels to function. Like a supervisor in a factory, it watches all the time the activity that takes place around it, but it never interferes. As a matter of fact, giving 'total attention' or 'being aware' means getting attuned to this causal level. The functioning at the two lower levels of gross and subtle body would be clearly understood at the causal level.

In the modern science, there are two branches namely, fundamental and applied sciences where applied science is dependent on fundamental science. Similarly, in the ancient times also there were two branches, Vedas and Tantras. Tantras were dependent on Vedas. Knowledge regarding mantras is a matter of prime consideration in Tantra Shastra (Science). Sabda or sound, which is of the Brahman, and as such, the cause of Brahmanda (this universe), is the manifestation of Cit-shakti (Consciousness) itself. The Visva-sara-Tantra says in chapter II that the Para-Brahman, as Sabda-Brahman, whose substance is all mantras, exists in the body of the jivatma (that is life form). It is either unlettered (dhvani) or lettered (varna). Dhvani is the subtle aspect of the jiva's vital Shakti (Energy). Further, the Prapancha-sara tantra states, the brahmanda is pervaded by Shakti (Energy), consisting of dhvani also called *Nada, Prana*, and the like. Moreover, the manifestation of the gross form (stula) of sabda is not possible unless sabda also exists in a subtle (suksma) form. Sabda is a guna (characteristic) of Akasa (vast empty space). However, Sabda is not produced by Akasa, but manifests in it. Sabda is itself the Brahman (the Unifying Force in science). As in the outer space, waves of sound are produced by movements of Vayu (air), so in the space within the jiva's (life forms) body waves of sound are produced according to the movements of the vital air (prana vayu) and the process of inhalation and exhalation. Sabda first appears in the Muladhara and it is this Shakti that gives life to jiva. The extremely subtle sound which first appears in the muladhara is called *Para;* less subtle when it has reached the heart, it is known as *Pasyanti.* When connected with *buddhi* (thinking) it becomes grosser, and is called *Madhyama.* Lastly, in its fully gross form, it issues from the mouth as *Vaikhari.* It is interesting to note that in the first two stages of para and pasyanti the association is with Consciousness and then Sabda move into the custody of space-time constrained buddhi and emerge as speech in vaikhari rupa.

We shall now consider the dynamical theory of Sakti (Energy) as Stress. The primordial "Sound" or Stress is the primordial functioning of the Brahma Sakti. What is Stress? Let us suppose that two things A and B are attracting each other. The name of the total mutual action is "Stress" of which the respective actions of A and B are the elements or components. Thus there may be Stress for three or four things and so on. Ultimately we reach Universal Stress which is an infinite system of correlated forces. A particular thing may be defined as a partial experience of this infinite system. The infinite system is, however, never really finitized by these partial experiences. Many parts do not make up the whole. When the stress between one such partial and another partial touches the normal consciousness, in either or both partial components, we may have, within certain limits, sensation of sound in either or both partial components. The Stress is Sabda and the sound is Dhvani. It is stress or Sabda which constitutes a thing.

The Lokas represent states or levels of Consciousness. Objectively considered, matter (thing) becomes more and more dense as one descends from the highest to the lowest Loka and thence to Talas (below earth); and as the veil of matter gets more dense, Consciousness gets dimmer too. The first five Lokas above, from and including earth are those of the five forms of sensible matter. That is to say, sensory functions predominate. The sixth Loka is predominated by thought/mind; the seventh Loka is the causal state of both thought/mind and matter, being *aham* (the ego).

Looking at it another way, Bhuh the Earth and the seven nether states are gross body; The Lokas from Bhuvah to Tapah are the subtle body, and Satya Loka is the causal body of the great Purusha. Thought, by its very nature, always looks at objects as away from itself. From thought (limited by space-time complex) point of view, each loka is far away from one another so much so that we cannot hope to reach even the nearest loka in one life time with our modest space vehicles. The lokas are bound by distance and time. Consciousness has no such space-time limitation. For Consciousness, the far is also near and it has no yesterday or tomorrow. It is always in the present. Also, it is thought/mind that diverts you away from Consciousness with lure of choice! In ordinary Bhuh experience, the object or "This" (Idam) is wholly outside and independent of, the Self, the two being mutually exclusive of one another. We may remain at this stage which is the basis of objective science or go within (inward) to the root of all experience. For, experience is always within. As the root is within us, introspection (Atma-Vichara) can alone discover the root. How? That which carries upward (from Bhuh Loka to Satya Loka) or inwards is the will-to-know of a nature ever more clarifying itself and thus gaining strength by its approach to the Almighty *Savitur* of all. But the object persists in experience until the attainment of the perfect Consciousness (Brahma-Swarupa) if inward journey or universal Consciousness (Brahma-Loka) if it is outward journey.

According to Tantra Shastra, Gayatri Mantra is the most important one. As we mentioned earlier, there is Earth and six Lokas or levels of Consciousness above, the Gayatri Mantra mentions only Bhuh, Bhuvar and Suvar. This is explained in Tantra Shastra. Bhuh is the place Earth we jivas (life forms) live in. Bhuvar Loka stands for five other Lokas, Bhuvar, Suvar, Mahar, Janaha, and Tapaha. Suvar stands for the sixth Loka where Sabda, as Vibration, and Energies predominates. Satya Loka, as the name itself signifies is the world of Truth. Let us turn to modern science for some knowledge regarding this Satya Loka. Science says, at the far boundaries of this universe there is what is known as dark matter and black holes. Nothing is known as to the contents of these dark areas. It is 90% of this universe! Only one thing can be said about them, they have in their entrance as it were, what is known as "Event Horizon". If any star, galaxy or for that matter a stray astronaut approaches it, he or it is drawn in and all his or its energies are sucked leaving only a mass to make the onward journey into the dark matter or black hole. This "Event Horizon" appears to be Brahma Loka as per Shastra. According to Shastra, the ego in some form subsists until one is able to reach Tapaha Loka. In mythology the enactment of Daksha yajna is symbolic of destruction of this ego. After Tapaha Loka, the ego is dissolved into the universal "I". Then one comes face to face with the Great Void, Nothingness: Shivam!

The inward journey we mentioned earlier commences from *Gandha* (smell) or Bhuh experience. This state is also known as *Parthiva* (concrete) Consciousness. From that state, through enquiry we reach what is *Rasa* (chemical constituents) or Apah experience. From there we reach *Rupa* (shape and form) or subjective root of Agni. Our inward journey continues and we attain to *Sparsa* (touch) or Vayu stana. This is not the touch produced by specialized form, for this is a sensation had after the production of Agni. The experience may be compared to the perception in ordinary life of the thermal quality of objects. *Sabda (sound) experience*, the subjective root of Akasa, is the seed of all externalized or externally located world phenomena. The root of externality-consciousness refers back to its origin the inner mind, the root from which the notion of externality arises as the tree from the seed. This internal root which grows into Akasa is the Brahma Consciousness as the internal root will, which lies at the root of all manifestation.

Tantra Shastra also recommends performance of Puja (worship) both in temples and in one's home daily. This Puja prescribes sixteen details to be carefully attended to in worshipping the idol or picture of God. It is called Shodasa Upachara Puja (16 steps of service). The thirteenth act is called Naivedya or what is known as Bhog in north India, symbolic offerings to God, of food or delicacies or fruits before they are distributed to devotees present.

All the Bhog items are on open display in front of the idol or picture being worshipped. Then a sloka is recited:

ब्रह्मार्पणम् ब्रह्म हविर्ब्रंह्माग्नो ब्रह्मणा हुतम् ।

ब्रह्मैव तेन गन्तव्यम् ब्रह्मकर्मसमाधिना ॥

Meaning: Brahma is the oblation; Brahma is the clarified butter, etc., constituting the offerings being made; by Brahma is the oblation poured into the fire of Brahma; Brahma verily shall be reached by him who always sees Brahma in all actions. This sloka occurs in Chapter 4 of Bhagwat Geeta as stanza 24. It is an allegorical statement Lord Krishna uses to advise Arjuna in the middle of the battle field (read Samsara—battle ground of life). This chapter is appropriately called "Brahma Vidya." Military *Forces (Stress)* are arrayed on both sides. Various *Powerful* armaments are on display. These armaments will discharge the four forms of energy in the ensuing battle. The conch shell heralding war is about to be blown (*Sound*). The presence of Brahma is quite evident! Lord Krishna says everything is Brahma. To get this message through he resorts to the allegory of Yajna of Yajurveda. In a Yajna there is the holy fire; there is an oblation; the clarified butter and other ingredients are poured into the holy fire along with the oblation and it is the Brahma in the form of Mantra who is performing the act and it is also Brahma in the form of holy fire who is receiving the offerings.

To help the aspirant called Brahmana to be focused, the ancients created a simple devise known as Yajnopavitam or Sacred thread. Yajna means sacrifice and Upavitam is thread. Thus the sacred thread is sacrifical thread. What is attempted to be sacrificed here is "ego". The strands of threads represent ego in different contexts. There are mighty forces acting as impediments in achieving the goal, merging the Individual Consciousness with Universal Consciousness. The blockages are represented in the form of three knots: Brahma, the repository of all the forces in nature; Vishnu, electromagnetic force that sustains life in this universe and Rudra, the gravitational force that transforms the energy. It is in this connection that the aspirant is advised that the only force that can enable him to transcend the powers of nature is "Tat Savitur," the Universal Consciousness as indicated in the famous Gayatri mantra. In fact the sacred thread is exclusively to be used for reciting silently and contemplating on the Gayatri Mantra. There are three strands of three threads each tied at the ends into a knot. Thus we have three knots. A single stand with three threads is to be worn by a Brahma chari a student of the Vedas. When he marries he becomes a Grahasta and will add one more strand to the one he already has making up two strands. On the death of his parents he gets the status of Yajamana who faces the world on his own terms. So he adds the third strand. He will wear the three strands till his death, or he becomes a Sanyasi, a monk. A Sanyasi wears no sacred thread because he has transcended his ego and wholly devoted to the contemplation of the Almighty. A single strand means the fire of ego stoked by one-self. Besides one-self, when the parents, wife and other blood relatives play a role in the stoking of the fire of ego, two strands are indicated. And when the aspirant takes the social responsibilities on himself on the passing away of his parents he takes on the third strand.

We have chosen the word Almighty over Consciousness deliberately. The world is full of mighty forces. Physics informs us that these forces are: Gravitational Force; Electro-magnetic Force, and Weak and Strong Nuclear Forces. However, ancient science adds one more and that is Vibration or Sound Force. The label Brahma refers to the convergence of these forces both in the microcosm and macrocosm. All these mighty forces are after all the manifestation of the Almighty force known in Vedas as Para Brahman. In man, the convergence as mentioned above takes place in what is known as "Swadistana Chakra," as observed by adepts in "Yoga" the science of convergence. "Brahma Yajna" is therefore contemplation on this convergence with a view to transcend their influence on our endeavor to reach the Almighty. The ancient Rishis therefore created a class of young aspirants called "Brahmins" whose only goal in life was to reach the Almighty. All their creature comforts were to be taken care of by the society. No doubt, in subsequent generations this noble ideal was diluted to such an extent that today only the label remains with the contents wholly forgotten. As we can see today, even in the scientific discipline a proficient scientist is funded by the government as he is totally focused on his subject of research to the exclusion of other social responsibilities. However, governmental influence and commercial considerations do derail the noble intent and the scientist is reduced to a spoke in the social wheel!

So long as universal processes operate, it is obvious that Brahma will be present. What are the universal processes? According to the ancients they are two. Modern science decidedly accepts only one process. Even though Isaac Newton's theory of gravitation showed that the universe could not be static, it was really Edwin Hubble, in 1928, who made a landmark observation, that wherever you look, distant galaxies are rapidly moving away from us. In other words the universe is expanding. Hubble's observation suggested that there was a time, called the big bang, when the universe was infinitesimally small and infinitely dense. Under such conditions all the laws of science, and therefore all ability to predict the future, would break down. Science accepts only the expanding phase. Ancient Rishis who were great exponents of Jyotisha shastra, a division of Veda, noted this fact long ago. They were clear and factual in stating that there is an expanding phase and then there is a contacting phase. They also noted that there would be a big-bang fusion before expansion commences and rapidly progresses to the point when there is a fission, thereafter contraction begins. According to the ancient Rishis, this process of expansion and contraction is a day and night in Brahma's life.

The Rishis also envisioned that the present life sequence, including that of man, consists of fourteen Manvantaras, also known as a Kalpa. We are now in Svetavaraha Kalpa (the period of white pig). Alternatively, we are in the seventh Manvantara named Vivasvata in which 195, 58, 85, 111 years have elapsed, that is roughly two billion years. The fourteen Manvantaras comprises of 1000 mahayugas. In turn each mahayuga is made up of four yugas having a total of 43, 20,000 years. Thus, Kretayuga is 17, 28,000 years; Thretayuga is 12, 96,000 years; Dwaparayuga is 8, 64,000 years and Kaliyuga is 4,32,000 years. We are now in Kaliyuga in which 5111 years have elapsed. All these amount to half a day in Brahma's life. Then there is the other half day consisting of night in his life. 365 such days amount to a year of Brahma. Brahma has a life span of 100 years. Thereafter there is total withdrawal of all forces in nature for a further period of 100 such Brahma years before another Brahma arises and the cycle begins afresh. When Brahma, the key to Consciousness (as we noted earlier in this chapter) is withdrawn what remains is only Consciousness by whatever name it is referred.

Chapter 3

Growth of Consciousness

A mother nurses her child for growth. Similarly, the universal mother helps her upasaka (devotee) to have growing consciousness until he becomes one with the universal consciousness. Read on . . .

Strictly speaking, there is no classification as male and female in the transcendental world. Only in the four dimensional mortal world, in which we are, we see this differentiation. For us birth of a child needs a male father and female mother. Hence from our point of view, depiction of a mother is essential for the new (baby) to be. Our two dimensional (space-time) logic presupposes that old gives birth to new. That this new is a modification of the old hence not new at all does not appeal to the senses. Transcendentally, the mother Aditi or Durga is also the same Para-Brahman or Universal Consciousness, as you will see in what follows.

Lalithambika-Tripurasundari

Shakti Cult is of great antiquity. We find prominent among the worshippers Rishi Agastya of Rig Veda fame. Both Agastya and his wife Lopamudra were great devotees of Lalithambika. In fact Brahmanda Purana states that Agastya was the recipient of the secret Lalitha Sahasranama (Thousand names of Lalithambika) from Mahavishnu. In Lalitha Sahasranama, at names 85, 86, and 87, Lalithambika is stated to be manifestation of three Kutas: a) Vagbahava (source of sound) Kuta; b) Madhya (central) Kuta; and c) Sakti (Energy) Kuta. Kuta means the highest, most excellent, first, the peak of a mountain, a heap, mass, and multitude. This is another way of stating that the three manifestations of Truth, the Savitur in Gayatri Mantra, as Bhuh: Shakti kuta; Bhuvah: Madhyama kuta and Suvaha: Vagbahava kuta. Shakti Kuta or Bhuh represents earth, The Madhyama Kuta or Bhuvah represents the windy and active vast mid-region and Vagbhava Kuta or Suvaha represents the heaven above (vast empty space) the abode of sound.

Lalithambika is otherwise known as Tripura Sundari. The word Pura needs a little clarification. Pura means in front, in the presence or before the eyes. We are facing, the three realities at all times. They are powerfully dazzling so much so that we cannot get away from the beautiful reality confronting us. They appear as Avaranas (Jewellery). We are ensnared. Be aware that this façade is the manifestation of the Supreme Power says Adi Shankara. We will deal with this aspect later.

Adi Shankara had taken up this theme to weave a beautiful poem to bring home the fact lucidly. The poem, in five stanzas is titled Lalitha Pancharatnam, to be sung with devotion in the early morning.

The Poem in Sanskrit:

The Vaghbhava Group: Saraswati

प्रातः स्मरामि ललिता वदनारविन्दम् बिम्बाधरं मृदुलमौक्तिकशोभिनासम् ।

आकर्णदीर्घनयनं मणिकुण्डलाढयम् मन्दस्मितं मृगमदोज्ज्वल फालदेशम् ॥१॥

I contemplate in the morning the beautiful lotus face of Goddess Lalitha—The exquisitely beautiful mouth, the delicate nose shining with nice pearl nose ring, the long eyes (extending upto the ears), the diamond studded ear drop adoring the ears, the graceful smile, and the forehead adorned with Kasturi fragrant and musk.

The Madhyama Group: Lakshmi

प्रातर्भजामि ललिता भुजकल्पवल्लीं रत्नांगुलीय लसदंगुलि पल्लवाढ्यां

36

माणिक्य हेम वलयांकृत शोभमानाम् पुण्ड्रेक्षु चाप कुसुमेषु सृणीद्धानाम् ॥२ ॥

Early morning, I worship the tender flowery soft, creeper-like hands of Goddess Lalitha. Adorned by resplendent bangles and arm-clasps (bracelets) studded with precious gems, with delicate fingers dazzling with diamond rings. These hands hold in them a bow made of sugarcane stalk, and arrow made of flowers and an ankush or goad.

<u>The Shakti Group: Uma</u>

प्रातर्वंदामि ललिता चरणारविन्दम् भक्तेष्टदान निरतं भवसिन्धुपोतम्

पद्मासनादि सुरनायक पूजनीयम् पद्माकुशध्वजसुदर्शनलांछनाढयाम् ॥३ ॥

The lotus feet of Goddess Lalitha, bearing distinguishing marks such as 'Lotus', 'the goad', 'the flag', and the Sudarshana Chakra are worshipped by Brahma, Indra and other luminaries. They grant the heart's desire of devotees and ferry them across the ocean of Samsara (ceaseless cycle of births and deaths). In the early morning, I bow down at these lotus feet of Goddess Lalitha. Lalitha refered here is Gayatri Devi (Cells in human body).

प्रातस्तुवे परशिवां ललितां भवानीं त्र्यन्तवेद्यविभवां करुनानवद्याम्

विश्वस्यसृष्टिविलयस्थिति हेतुभूताम् विश्वेश्वरीं निगम वाङ्मनसातिदूराम् ॥४ ॥

Goddess Lalitha who is the Supreme Power of the universe is auspiciousness personified and full of compassion to erring beings. She whose greatness is described by the Upanishads is however beyond the reach of Vedas, the mind as well as the words. She is verily 'Parasiva', the ultimate reality. Let me sing her praise in the morning.

प्रातर्वदामिललिते तव पुण्यनाम कामेश्वरीति कमलेति महेश्वरीति

श्रीशांभवीति जगतां जननी परेति वाग्देवतीति वचसां त्रिपुरेश्वरीति ॥५ ॥

Oh Goddess Lalitha, let me recite your holy name in the morning—names such as Kameshwari, Kamala, Maheshwari, Sri Sambavi mother of this Jagat and Vagdevi of speech and Tripureshwari. (Whether worshipped as Saraswati, Laxmi or Parvathi it is the same Gayatri Devi, the universal mother—Consciousness.)

Before we proceed further in understanding the concept behind Lalithambika a word of caution will be appropriate. The names of Devatas such as Ganapathi, Brahma, Vishnu, Shiva, and Lalitha etc. are mere labels. Consider an example; a number of identical packages are lying with you. What will you do to identify them separately? Would you not consider labeling them? Again, there are billions of people in the world. To separately identify each and every individual, we give a particular name to each person so that he will respond to the call of that name. Similarly, the world is made up of many dynamic forces some superior and others dependent on those superior forces. They are all, in the ultimate analysis, manifestation of That Supreme Force, Universal Consciousness. The Rishis labeled them for identification. In Rig Veda the Devatas (luminaries) are identified in order to be praised. In the other Vedas, Brahmanas, Puranas and Shastras they became prayer worthy. It is believed that, on praying to them, these Devatas (luminaries) will exercise a choice to bestow their munificence on man, an ardent devotee, as they have power to sway the welfare of man one way or other. On this belief, men develop an emotional attachment to the image of these Devatas (luminaries). The image is not the thing. Unfortunately, what is happening today? The image is everything, the bigger the better seems to be the clarion call. And the image is worshipped with great fanfare. Has it not become a tamasha (carnival)? The powers behind the image need only give their attention towards you, so praise. They need not be courted. Remember, these devatas (luminaries) are much more powerful than us, mere humans. Indeed, man is constituted of these very powers. Science says these Devatas (luminaries) know more about us than we do. Take atom for example, it is there in every pore of our body, it even pervades our every thought.

The labels that the Rishis gave to the dynamic forces of nature are different from that on a package or tagged to a person. The names assume the form of mantras. As we have already seen, there is what is known as seed syllables (Bija Aksharas). These seed syllables are associated with various energies in nature and converge in the Muladhara Chakra as Para Vak (Supreme sound). The names are identified with the energy component of the devata and the corresponding bijakshara. When you properly recall a bijakshara, you invoke the energy behind the syllable. That is the reason a mantra is very powerful unlike any other word in any language. Corollary to this principle is the fact that if you recall a wrong bijakshara or pronounce it incorrectly, it could cause more harm to you than good. One parallel may be considered. Electricity if supplied through proper channels will glow your lights, it will operate your computer, geyser, fridge, bell and what not. Carelessly if you bring it into contact with your metal chair, you can imagine the consequences.

Let us revert back to the first three verses of Adi Shankaracharya. The Lalitha Sahasranama, we saw, mentions three Kutas (heap or collection)—Vagbhava Kuta; the Madyama Kuta and Shakti Kuta. The heap or collection in each Kuta represents millions of cells. The area of operation of the Vagbhave Kuta is the face from head to neck; the area of operation of Madyama Kuta is from neck downwards till waist; and Shakti Kuta operates from waist down wards. There are 15 bija aksharas related to mother Lalithambika called Panchadasi. Vagbhava Kuta contains the bija aksharas Ka A E La Hrim; the Madyama Kuta contains Ha Sa Ka Ha La Hrim; and Shakti Kuta has Sa Ka La Hrim.

This Bhu Loka where we are now is a central place where all the forces and energies in nature converge. The repository is Bhudevi Goddess (Earth). She is like a mother who bears the child in the womb. She is Loka Mata (Universal Mother). When we are considering the external world or cosmology we call it Bhu loka. However, when we consider the inward working of a man, we say it is Muladhara—the foundation.

There is an interesting anecdote in the Puranas, to bring home the point that the Loka Mata brings into being the Individual Consciousness in man with the help of all the forces in nature. The Mother wanted to go into seclusion and she wanted to place a reliable security guard at the entrance of her citadel so that no one can enter the place without her permission. She creates such a person on her own! She labeled the person Ganesha, actually the Individual Consciousness. Consciousness knows no labels. Many Devatas (Luminaries) and Rakshasas (Dark forces) tried to gain access to the mother's abode but in vain. Ganesha acquitted himself well as a security guard. These Devatas and Rakshasas are in fact 'thought' forces. Then Lord Shiva himself wanted ingress but Ganesha the Consciousness strongly stood his ground. This is to highlight the fact that the Individual Consciousness is the Universal Consciousness, mightier than Shiva Shakti (might of Shiva or gravitational force). Here is also a clear hint that the Mother who is repository of the various forces of nature (composed as atoms) is the cells in human body and Ganesha is DNA, a creation of the cell. All the forces in the nature are traceable to an atom according to physics except gravitational and electromagnetic force, which, however, operate on the atom. Each cell in human body carries 10^14 (10 followed by 14 zeros) atoms. Cell itself is a minute organism, nevertheless most powerful! By a remarkable coincidence, the number of cells in a human body is the same as Atoms in each cell (10^14). What is the function of this DNA? DNA restricts entry into the cell. It is the holder of the genetic code of a person, and the vast reservoir of memory of the individual. In Sanskrit he is known as Jathavedas. Without DNA (Ganesha) there is no life! No Consciousness no life. The most excellent mother is roughly distributed in three groups: Saraswati as the creative group of cells; Lakshmi as sustaining group of cells and Durga as destroying and transforming group of cells in the human body. All are manifestations of the one Gayatri Devi, who in turn is that Savitur (Universal Consciousness).

In the Rig Vedic era, the Rishis had a vision of Gayatri Mantra which also focused on Savitur as light of lights or Cosmic Core. The early vision of Gayatri, perhaps, was not a female deity, but rather, the name of the poetic metre of the esoteric mantra. This mantra occurs in Mandala 3, 62nd hymn, as Mantra 10. The Rishi is Viswhvamitrah Gathinah and the Devata is Savitur. In the eyes of Rig Vedic Rishis the concept of 'male' and 'female' are irrelevant in spiritual journey towards the Universal Consciousness. It is only in later literature; Gayatri is identified as a female deity. It has also been suggested that the three Devatas Saraswathi, Laksmi and Parvathi or Durga are her manifestations.

Rig Veda in its entire contents mentions only seven female deities. Except Gayatri, the other six deities have very little resemblance to the female deities that were developed in the Puranic period. Saraswati is the goddess of the Word and divine Inspiration that comes from the *rtam* the Truth-Consciousness. Barathi (Mahi) and Ila are also different forms of the same Word. In Rig Veda Mandala 1 Hymn 3 Mantra 12 Rishi Madhuchchhandah Vaishvamitrah visualizes Sarasvati, thus:

महो अर्णः सरस्वती प्र चेतयति केतुना ।

धियो विश्वा वि राजति ॥

Meaning: Saraswati floods all our thoughts by awakening our perception in Consciousness.

Saraswati represents a special movement in Universal Consciousness by which the Truth makes itself heard. That is the reason, she is Goddess of Inspiration.

Usha is repeatedly described as the Mother of the Cows. Contrary to what most scholars believe, (Gow) cow in Rig Veda is not the four footed animal but Vedic symbol for light (in science we know it by the label Photons). Ushas is identified with the rays of this light that reaches us at early dawn. Psychologically, Aditi is the supreme or infinite Universal Consciousness, mother of the gods (luminaries), in opposition to Danu or Diti, the divided Consciousness, mother of Vritra and other Dhanavas (dark forces)—enemies of the Devatas (luminaries) and of man in his progress.

Even more interesting is the mantra which gave genesis to the concept of mother Durga. In Rig Veda Mandala 1, Hymn 99 has only one mantra. This is a peculiarity not found anywhere else in the whole of the Rig Veda Samhita. This mantra is addressed to Agni and the Rishi is Kashyapah Marichah. The Chandas is Tristup. Thus,

जतवेदसे सुनवाम सोममरातीयतो नि दहाति वेदः ।

स नः पर्षदति दुर्गाणि विश्वा नावेव सिन्धुं दुरितात्याग्निः ॥

Meaning: Agni, the one who knows of all births, we bestow Soma (Love), may he burn up completely the wealth and knowledge of the inimical thoughts in us. May Agni lead us to happiness; overcoming all grief and sin, may he carry us as in a boat across the river (Samsara sagara—the sea of finite existence?).

In a later era, Mahanarayana Upanishad came to be compiled. In the pages between 93 and 102 of the Ramakrishna Math edition of the Upanishad, Durga Suktam is stated in seven verses. The very first verse is the above mentioned Rig Vedic mantra. Only in the second mantra mother Durga is introduced. Thus:

तामग्निवर्णां तपसा ज्वलन्तीं वैरोचनीं कर्मफलेषु जुष्टास् ।

दुर्गां दवीं ॐ शरणमहं प्रपद्ये सुतरसि तरसे नमः ॥

Meaning: I take refuge in her, the Goddess Durga, who is fiery in luster and radiant with ardency, which is the Energy belonging to the Supreme who manifests herself manifoldly, who is the power residing in actions and their fruits rendering them efficacious. O Thou Goddess skilled in saving, thou take us across difficulties well, to you our salutations. Apart from the opening mantra there are three more mantras from Rig Veda in the Durga Suktam.

Sri Suktam (Rig Veda, after 5th Mandala) is amongst the more popular Vedic hymns. In fact its only rival in popularity is Purusha Suktam (Rig Veda 10, 90). "Sri" is conventionally the Goddess of prosperity, wealth or plenty; and is a synonym of Lakshmi, the consort of Vishnu who is one of the classical Hindu Triad. However, as the divinity invoked in the Sri Sukta, she does not appear in this narrow context. We have to bear in mind that the ancient Rishis were exclusively concerned with the transcendental world and the divinities (luminaries) encountered therein. Most of the transcendental world is beyond the four dimensional world of Space and Time to which we are confined. Only in the four dimensional world that we live in, wealth signifies property, ornaments and edible food and accrue great value. These have little or no value with other dimensions. So the wealth with which Goddess Laxmi is associated is Universal Consciousness with reference to Individual Consciousness which is characterized by Agni. Thus, Laxmi is identical with the Sun and the Moon and Agni, and adored by all the gods (including Vishnu and Siva); she is "Narayani" as well as "Triyambaka". That is why her appeal is universal. Sri-Sukta is now included in Rig Veda and is read as a khila-sukta after the fifth book (Mandala). It consists of fifteen verses, which the commentators describe as Riks (Standard Vedic Verses). But the verses are obviously post Vedic in character, and do not belong to the Vedic corpus. The fifteen verses are addressed conjointly to the mystic fire (Agni) and the Goddess of wealth. Agni, of course, confers on man the greatest wealth, that of Supreme Benediction.

In the preamble to Mahabhagavatha, the great Purana, we have this interesting narration of Suta (the narrator.) "High minded Maharshi Bhagavan Vyasa the speaker of endless Dharmasastras, chief of all men, learned in the Vedas, and proficient in spiritual knowledge, received no satisfaction from his work in compilation of the earlier seventeen Puranas. There are eighteen Puranas in all. He then thought to himself, 'How shall I narrate Mahapurana, than which no greater Purana shall exist on earth, and wherein the supreme Bhagavati is extolled exhaustively?' Failing to know the truth, about the Devi (luminary), his heart became agitated.

He thought, 'How can that supreme and most abstruse truth be known to me, which is not known to even Maheswara of vast knowledge?' So thinking and finding no other means, Vyasa set his whole hearted devotion to Durga; went to Himalaya; and there practiced severe austerities. The consort of Siva, who is ever fond of her devotees, was pleased with such devotion and, remaining unseen in the sky said, "Mahamuni Vyasa," go to Brahmaloka (As we have seen, this is the event horizon in the science of cosmology) where all the Srutis (four Vedas) incarnate live; there you will know my stainless supreme existence. There sung by Srutis, I shall become visible and do what is desired of by you." Hearing the message from above, Bhagavan Vedavyasa at once proceeded to Brahmaloka, bowed to the four Vedas and asked, "What is the supreme and undecaying Brahman?"

Hearing the Rishi ask this question with modesty and submissiveness, the Vedas at once replied.

Rig Veda said: "In whom are contained all things, out of whom appear all things and whom all describe as the highest Being, that Adya (Primal) Bhagavati is Brahman (consciousness) itself."

Yajurveda said: "The Ishwari who is worshipped in all yajnas and in yoga and for whose existence we (Vedas) are deemed the authority, that Bhagavati alone is Brahman (consciousness) itself."

Sama Veda said: "By whom this universe is moved, whom all yogis contemplate, and by whose light the universe is manifested, that world pervading Durga alone is supreme Brahman (consciousness)."

Atharva Veda said: "The Iswari of Suras (Enlightened ones) whom, all who are favored for their devotion see, that Bhagavati Durga all Sastras describe as supreme Brahman (consciousness)."

Suta said, hearing the incarnate Srutis thus express themselves: "Vyasa the son of Satyavati, became certain that Bhagavati Durga was supreme Brahman." After they had spoken as mentioned above, the Srutis further indicated to the Mahamuni: "what we have said we shall make directly visible to you." So saying, the Srutis began to sing in praise of that Parameshwari who is existence, consciousness and bliss, and holds in Herself all Devas and Devis (luminaries). According to modern science, all the energies are devolved in event horizon, thereafter giving way to a singularity.

The Srutis said: "Supreme universe-embracing Durga be pleased. The three Purushas Brahma, Vishnu, and Maheswara, are created with their individual gunas (characteristics) according to Thy will for the threefold work of creation, preservation and destruction. But, O Mother, Thou hast no creator in the three worlds. Who in the world can therefore describe Thy qualities, impenetrable by the intellect of the Jivas (ego-centric souls)?

"O Mother of the three worlds, it is by worshipping Thee that Hari (conqueror of darkness) destroys invincible Daityas (dark forces) and thus preserves the three worlds, and it was by holding Thy feet on his breast that Maheswara was able to drink deadly poison, Halahala (the initial outcome of the churning of the vast ocean by luminaries and dark forces) enough to destroy the three worlds (the physical; the subtle and the causative). How can we describe the force of that (incomprehensible) nature of Thine?"

"We bow to Thee, O Mother who art the body, the consciousness, the Sakti (power) of motion, and other Saktis (Energies), and the highest Sakti (Power), constituted of Thy own gunas (characteristics) by the instrumentality of maya (illusion) of the supreme Purusha (Paramatma), and Tho art She who resides as Consciousness in the bodies of Jivas, who, charmed by Thy maya (illusion) and with discriminating knowledge describe Thee as Purusha."

"Brahma-tattva is that aspect of Thine which is devoid of all distinctive conditions such as masculinity, femininity, etc. Next, Sakti is that primary desire of Thine which arose in Thee for creating the world. That Sakti appeared in one half as the supreme Purusha, so that both Prakrti and Purusha are but Sakti in different forms (Dynamic and Static). Both are but manifestation of Thy maya. Even Parabrahma-tattva (static character), therefore, is nothing but Thyself as Sakti (dynamic power)." Mother Durga appeared and in the lotus (gravitational force) at her feet was placed the Mahabagavatha. She directed Vyasa Muni to learn that and declare it to the world. She also said that Krishna (in the Mahabagavatha) is her avatara (incarnation). The name Durga means an impenetrable fort. Why should she be given this label by the Rishis? This fort is part of Satya Loka. As discovered by science, it would appear, it is the black hole with black matter within. At the entrance to the black hole is the 'Event Horizon,' what is known as Brahma Loka. The black hole is predominated by gravitational force, the abode of Shiva and Durga or Shive. Incidentally, our cosmos is 95% dark matter. Science says, if a planet, a star or an astronaut strays anywhere near it, it or he are pulled inside, first into the event horizon and then black hole itself. A person who strays near black hole, on being absorbed by the event horizon, will be sucked of all his energies and only the mass is pushed into the black hole. The mass is also denuded in the black hole. What remains is the Individual consciousness which then merges with Universal consciousness. Astonishingly, within this black matter, there is the region of Hiranyagarba—golden womb which is as bright as thousand suns! This golden womb is the origin of electro-magnetic force. We are lead to know that such is the place Vedavyasa attained by his Tapas before commencing to write Mahabhagavatham.

Even more explicit is the vision of Rishika Vak Ambhrni in Rig Veda Mandala 10 Hymn 125 Mantras 1-8. Rishika is the feminine gender for Rishi. It is a unique narration, in that; she is one with the Universal Consciousness when she explains her vision. Thus:

I walk with Rudras (gravitational force) and Vasus (particles in the gravitational field). I walk with Adityas (solar emanations) and also with Visvedevas (all light dependant luminaries). I pervade Mitra and Varuna (bonded hydrogen). Even so Indra and Agni (atom and individual consciousness) and Ashwin twins (proton and neutron) too.

I pervade the endearment of Soma, I am the basis of Tvashtr (carbon), so also Bhaga (delight arising in the presence of Universal Consciousness) and Pushana (progressive increaser of Universal Consciousness in man).

I am the Queen that disseminates the wisdom of Universal Consciousness. I am the Universal Consciousness, the first among the sacrificing luminaries who have found me everywhere.

The wise know that it is by my sole power that they are able to see, eat, breathe, and hear what is being said. I may as well declare, that those who do not so contemplate on my universal nature, run the certain risk of futile life, lost in hopelessness.

On the contrary, I declare on my own the universal truth that, one who so contemplates, whom I love, whether he is a luminary or man; I will elevate him as Brahman (The Universal Consciousness); a Rishi or a man of clear understanding.

The man who turns away from this supreme knowledge is condemned to annihilation (in the sub-atomic world). For Rudra (gravitational force) I spread the bow (gravitational wave) so that, in the sub-atomic world the particles equally enjoy the battle. I permeate the whole universe.

In the beginning I bring forth the individual (father-karta). Our body is the ocean (samsara-sagara). In the depths of that ocean I interact (as individual consciousness) with every creature of creation; literally billions upon billions (atoms, cells, bacteria and viruses and rest of the world). I reach the Universal Consciousness pervading all these creatures.

It is me that blows as wind in this universe. It is me that brings into being and sustains all existence on earth, heaven above and beyond. Such is my magnitude.

Western science is now awakening to the fact that Indian philosophy has many similarities with modern scientific findings. The ancient

Rishis had an aptitude of saying a great deal in a few words. The Mantra 'Om' is an instance. For this short syllable contains a whole philosophy, which many volumes would not suffice to explain. The Mantra "Om" is composed of three letters A, U, M,—of which the first two vowels coalesce into O. Over the Om is written the sign of Chandrabindu or Nada and Bindu, shown as a crescent with a dot or point over it. Nada and Bindu are two of many aspects of that which in India is called the Mother, or great Energy (Mahasakti). This is both the efficient and material Cause of the universe which is its form and body. Nada is the Mantra name for the first going forth of Energy which gathers itself together in massive strength (Ghani-bhuti) as Bindu to create the universe, and Bindu, as so creating, differentiates into a Trinity of Energies which are symbolized by A, U, M. Nada and Bindu thus represent the unmanifested "fourth" (Turiya) state immediately before the manifestation of the world, in which animate life exists in the three conditions of deep sleep, dream and waking. In the West, man calls the Creator the Father, in the East man anthropomorphizes into God. More aptly the Supreme Creative Being in the East and especially by the Saktas is called the Mother, for this Energy conceives in Its Womb, which is Consciousness, gives birth to and nourishes, the Universe. The first Mantra into which a child is initiated is Ma or Mother, for that is its first word, and Mother is often the last word on the lips of the dying.

There is no end to the praise of Lalithambika. In this context Lalitha means play. It is the play of the Infinite Consciousness as Energy we see in this world wherever we turn. So we can go on and on.

Chapter 4

Limitation of Knowledge

Knowledge is of two categories: Old and New. Experience and previous knowledge are obviously old. If we apply experience and previous knowledge to understand a new challenge, it is an act of modification of the old, as a response to a new challenge. There will always be some inadequacy. New response to new challenge is transcendental knowledge. Read on . . .

Brahma is the label given by ancients to the repository of all energies in the universe. In the ultimate analysis, everything is a manifestation of energy. Remember Einstein formula $E=mc^2$. Since Brahma holds all the different kinds of energy with him, he naturally becomes the source of creation in this world. Perhaps Rishi Atharvan was the foremost to grasp the fact of this reality. So, in the genetic linage, he is mentioned as the eldest son. In the same lineage are Rishi Bharadvaja and Rishi Angiras. These are rishis of Rig Veda.

The following slokas are from Mundaka Upanishad. There are 108 important Upanishads. Out of them ten Upanishads are considered more important and Adi Shankara had made his exhaustive commentaries on them. Of these 10 Upanishads, Mundaka Upanishads is one. It belongs to Atharva Veda. Mundaka means tonsure or the razor used for this purpose. This is indicative of the subject discussed in this Upanishad, and is important to a class of people called 'Sanyasins'. They are monks who have renounced the worldly pleasure and wander from place to place without seeking anything for themselves. It is more to do with the effacement of 'self'. The whole book is divided into three Mundakas. We are now considering only the first section of first Mundaka.

ॐ ब्रह्मा देवानां प्रथमः सम्बभुव

विश्वस्य कर्ता भुवनस्य गोप्ता ।

स ब्रह्मविद्यां सर्वविद्याप्रतिष्ठा-

मथर्वाय ज्येष्ठपुत्राय प्राह ॥१॥

Meaning: Brahma, the creator and protector of this universe, arose first, before all devatas or luminaries. To his eldest son, Atharva, he imparted the science or the knowledge of energy, the basis of all sciences.

अथर्वणे याम् प्रवदते ब्रह्मा-

थर्वा तम् पुरोवाचाङ्गिरे ब्रह्मविद्याम् ।

स भारद्वाजाय सत्यवहाय प्राह

स भारद्वाजोऽङ्गिरसे परावराम् ॥२॥

Meaning: What Brahma imparted to Atharvan, even that science of energy, Atharvan imparted to Angiras (sr.) in olden days. Angiras passed it on to Bharadvaja Satyavaha, and he in turn to Angiras (Jr.). Thus the science descended from the greatest sages to lesser ones.

शौनको ह वै महाशालोऽङ्गिरसं विधिवदुपसन्न पप्रच्छ ।

कस्मिन्नु भगवो विज्ञाते सर्वमिदं विज्ञातं भवतीति ॥३॥

Meaning: Saunaka, that famous householder, once approached Angiras (Jr.) in the manner laid down by the scriptures (in the modern sense, having suitable qualification and following

50

prescribed procedures.) and enquired (like a modern PHD student). "Sir, what is that, knowing which everything in the world becomes known?"

तस्मै स होवाच द्वे विद्ये वदितव्ये इति ह स्म यद्

ब्रह्मविदो वदन्ति परा चैवापरा च ॥४॥

Meaning: To him Angiras replied: There are two kinds of knowledge to be acquired, as indeed the knowers of Veda have said—one a lower and the other a higher.

तत्रापरा ऋग्वेदो यजुर्वेदः सामवेदोऽथर्ववेदः शिक्षा कल्पो

व्याकरणं निरूक्तं छन्दो ज्योतिषमिति । अथ परा यया तदक्षरमधिगम्यते ॥५॥

Meaning: Of these, the lower consists of the study of Rig-Veda, Yajur-Veda, Sama-Veda, and Atharva-Veda, phonetics, the code of rituals, grammar, etymology, metrics and astronomy. Now the higher Knowledge is that by which the imperishable is attained. (Obviously, in the ancient age, the other professions like book-keeper, trader, scientists, medical men etc. were not demarcated as there was no monetary economy then.)

What the above mantras highlight is the two categories of knowledge. There is the mechanical knowledge like knowing once name, address, riding a cycle, two wheeler or car, constructing a building or bridge or any other engineering activity. There is again the knowledge of diseases and their remedies of a doctor. There is knowledge of an architect, the knowledge of a scientist and a philosopher. There is knowledge that can be learnt from religious books and rituals. There are also the job of an accountant, banker, lawyer and salesmen which entail knowledge. These are outputs of the human brain—a natural and healthy function. It is only a matter of degree how much you remember in your field of specialization. For unremembered portion you can refer to books or computer data and carry on your profession. Then there is skill and proficiency. It is also a kind of mechanical knowledge.

These activities are necessary to keep the society healthy and prosperous. The knowledge in this area pertains to transactional aspect of man. Transaction means there is a giver and there is a receiver. Now-a-days transactional knowledge is available only for a monetary consideration. This is the Lower Knowledge as replied by Angiras.

Then there is what is known as transcendental knowledge. First we should understand what is transcendental? In the mechanical knowledge process we saw above, experience and skill plays an important part. It may be your personal experience or experience of others codified for your reference. That is past experience. That knowledge helps you to achieve good results. You may prosper in this world. But the scope of the transcendental knowledge is invariably outside the purview of past experience. The challenge is in the present and the response has to be spontaneous. No referring back to past experience or knowledge. Each experience during your transcendental inward journey is personal and unique. Past experience and therefore knowledge will not allow you to progress in your inward journey. The transcendental experience is always new. On the other hand, knowledge and past experience are always old. Even what you experienced a second back is past experience in this connection. The challenge is how we can avoid the transactional knowledge function to interfere in our progress in transcendental journey? This transcendental knowledge is Higher Knowledge according to Angiras.

Clearly, accumulated knowledge, tradition, gurus and the like have no relevance in the advancement of transcendental knowledge. You are a light unto yourself. It is well to remember that guru in its root meaning implies removal of darkness and not a teacher or trainer who imparts some knowledge or skill. One may even learn and follow the traditions and rituals. But one would realize for what they are worth. Then we will find some gems even in that tradition here and there! It is in this context that Adi Shankara created his immortal treatise *Viveka Chudamani.* The title means "Crest Jewel of Discrimination." Viveka (discrimination) is the rare jewel Chudamani. The discrimination between what is transactional and what is transcendental and pursuing the later assiduously is advocated in the book.

Our society (whether it is Hindu, Buddhist, Christian or Muslim) has cleverly manipulated the transcendental knowledge for transactional purposes and institutionalized it, in the form of organized religions. You find mammoth temples, mosques, churches which are awe inspiring; innumerable rituals; many classes of mediators to God; priests, soothsayers; gala functions and a long list of dos and don'ts, to uphold the tradition. We are enamored. From childhood, perhaps, we are exposed only to this aspect of life; our education also supplements this outlook. But clearly it is a grand illusion. God is not in the temples, mosques or churches. We are clearly informed so by the Upanishads. We are told that God is in our heart. Yet, we visit these places in search of peace of mind and the blessing of the benevolent God or his representative Guru. We are willing to spend ton of money on an idol or a ritual when thousands continue to starve; and these starving millions do not even have a roof over their heads. In short we have become insensitive. Hardly conducive for transcendental journey!

What we said above is beautifully summed-up by Isavasya Upanishad in the topic captioned Vidya-Avidya-Upasana. This Upanishad is also part of the ten important Upanishads on which Adi Shankara has written his commentary. This Upanishad is the last chapter of the Sukla-Yajurveda Samhita. In the Isavasya Upanishad at stanzas 9, 10 and 11 Vidya-Avidya-Upasana is discussed.

अन्धन्तमः प्रविशन्ति यऽविद्यामुपासते ।

ततो भुय इव ते तमो य उ विद्यायाँ रता ॥९॥

Meaning: They who worship Avidya alone fall into blind darkness, and they who worship vidya alone fall as though into an even greater darkness.

अन्यदेवाहुर्विद्यया अन्यदाहुरविद्यया ।

इति शुश्रुम धिराणां ये नस्तद्विचचक्षिरे ॥१० ॥

Meaning: One thing, they say, is verily obtained from vidya, another thing they say, from avidya; thus we have heard from the wise who explained that to us.

विद्यां चाविद्यां च यस्तद्वेदोभयँ सह ।

अविद्यया मृत्युं तित्वाँ विद्यय अमृतमश्नुते ॥११ ॥

Meaning: He who knows at the same time, both vidya and avidya overcomes death by avidya and obtains immortality by vidya.

According to Sri Madvacharya, in the 10th mantra above, 'cultivation of right knowledge of *Brahman*' is vidya. What we say transcendental knowledge. All other notions of knowledge are transactional and therefore avidya.

As we have seen, book knowledge and experience are necessary for acquiring transactional knowledge in order to live comfortably in this world. We also need to depend on knowledge of others to meet some of our challenges in life, such as those of doctors, lawyers, engineers, accountants and bankers. However much, such knowledge is made available to us; personal issues would not be addressed by the knowledge. Your anxieties, fears, hopes, aspirations, desires and relationships cannot be addressed by this knowledge. The knowledge in short is impersonal.

There are then books on personal aspects that promise to alleviate your anguish. They solve one problem, but bring in its wake many others. This is so because they follow a partial approach. Your total personality needs to be addressed in order to sublimate the problem. Since transcendental knowledge addresses the personal aspect of a person, it was found very convenient by religions, to use this transcendental knowledge through books, impressive speeches, stories and what not to convert people to a life long allegiance to their doctrine of personal development. It has been found that the religions maim you and you live a handicapped life thereafter. You live in an illusion thereafter. One example will suffice. You know the religious books advise you that the ego has to be sublimated. After reading such books and after some practices prescribed therein, many start feeling that they have eschewed ego, but it raises its ugly head when suitable circumstances surface. Not a single soul has so far done away with his ego after reading scriptures or religious books. As second best, some of the books suggest that your ego is so sharpened that it is ready for being obliterated by the Lord. Then there are those who tell that the best way is Sharanagathi; total surrender to the Lord along with the ego. Of course that is not the way of knowledge but denying it. Such people contend that knowledge makes you ego-centric. In a way, they are right. As knowledge is objective, it is not helpful to you personally except for earning a livelihood. Strictly speaking, knowledge is only transactional.

We are, in fact, speaking of two different things when we consider knowledge. There is' knowledge' and 'knowing.' Knowledge is an accumulation process. You gather knowledge and store it in your mind. When you find a need for it you retrieve it for application. It is a process pertaining to the mind and stimulated by thought. On the other hand, knowing is an ongoing process. It is also a process of learning. It needs only your attention. What is attention? Attention is awareness. You can be aware when you are conscious. It is also total attention, when your consciousness is present. When you give partial attention, as we generally do, the other part of your attention is taken up by thought. Thought high jacks the event into the knowledge field! See this happening in you, it is very interesting. How does the thought highjack? It will use the tools of comparison and judgment; analysis; likes and dislikes; agreement or disagreement; conviction and non-conviction before storing the information in memory.

The moment the thought encounters a challenge in the form of a proposition, it will compare the challenge with what it already knows on the subject and stored in the memory and it will reach a judgment to accept or reject the proposition. Even if the proposition is accepted, it will be subjected to a thread bare analysis. In the process of analyses, your own likes and dislikes has a part to play. Whether you accept or reject the proposition, for some strategic reason, you may agree or disagree with it. The new proposition is so forceful that you are convinced it is the right thing and you accept it. After some time, there is another new proposition more convincing and you transplant the old proposition with the new one in the memory. All these action take place very fast in fractions of a second.

For living in this world earning a livelihood; for decoration; earning acceptability in the social ladder; boosting one's ego; knowledge is very handy. For seeking the inner Truth-the Paramatma (The almighty); only the process of 'knowing' is necessary. We live in a delusion if we think that transactional knowledge will help in realizing the inner Truth.

How the limitation of the knowledge is overcome by consciousness needs to be examined more elaborately. The materialists, especially of the western world, start the analysis with the world. To them matter exists and exists independently in the universe. The world is other than me. At least up to the time of Newton this was an indisputable issue. Even the Samkhya system in India was wedded to this premise. Put another way, what we are saying is this: While on your way, if you encounter a person or see a big building, would you not normally say that it is independent of you? We are saying that this is not unconditional. "You" are encountering a person or seeing the building. So, existence of consciousness cannot be denied. So a need to explain the relationship of matter and consciousness arises.

When the analysis starts from me 'the self', the outlook is different. We don't assume anything. The self who is making the enquiry being consciousness, it already exists. The only question then is: Whether the matter and therefore universe also exists? This is very logical. How do I know that anything other than me exists? In other words this is nothing but asking how man knows the world. How is the knowledge obtained?

The knowledge of an object is said to involve three ingredients, the knower, the knowledge process and the object that is to be known. The knowing process acts as the connecting link between the knower and that which needs to be known. This simple phenomenon of knowledge has aroused great systems of philosophy of which the prominent phases are known as idealism and realism. These words were coined by Western thinkers, though they are not wholly applicable to the way of thinking in India. Still they have impacted the contemporary Indian thinkers. We shall first examine the Western schools of thought.

Concerning the theory of knowledge, as we already saw, there are two prominent schools which go by the names of rationalism and empiricism; one holding the opinion that knowledge arises from within by the very nature of the reason of the individual, the other holding the opposite view that knowledge arises by the contact of the senses with objects, i.e., objects cause the knowledge. Over the centuries, it has been found very difficult to reconcile the two opposite views both in the west and the east. We may count Descartes, Spinoza and Leibnitz as protagonists of realist school. On the other hand there were equally great people like Locke, Bishop Berkley and Hume, the protagonists for empiricist school. But all differed in their manner of presentation. It was left to Immanuel Kant to bring the two schools together in reconciliation.

Till the time of Isaac Newton, the western society was of the firm conviction that matter exists independently in the universe. It was believed that, however much matter is analyzed and probed there will still remain a minute particle of matter. This misconception was exploded with Einstein's discovery in 1905. Newton's physics was thereafter labeled mechanistic materialism. The Church was very much in agreement with Newtonian outlook, and even today adheres to the principles. This doctrine of mechanistic materialism, which thinks all reality is matter, cannot even dream that knowledge can arise spontaneously from the reason of man, or the mind of the individual. To them, knowledge is what is known as epiphenomenon, a secondary effect that is produced by a primary reality which is quite different from knowledge. In other words something produces knowledge. It cannot arise of its own. Even though knowledge is material in essence, it cannot be the nature of reality. There is some defect basically in this doctrine, because, if matter, which is regarded as ultimately real, is to be all-in-all, and there is nothing to be outside it, there would not be an object of awareness for anyone. There would be nobody to know that matter exists, if it were the only reality. If you consider the other view of empiricism doctrine that knowledge arises by the contact of the senses with objects outside, which has some association with materialism, though not wholly, it cannot be regarded as entirely true, though there is some truth in it.

In the example quoted earlier, we posed the question; you encounter on your way a man or a building. Is the encounter real? Do the man and the building exist independently? Till now we examined the question with reference to the man and building outside. It is inevitable that we have to examine the other aspect of the event, "I" who encountered the man and the building. This 'I' the individual is a complex structure. There have been many schools of thought, each taking a facet or feature, which is revealed when understanding is focused on that particular aspect only. Man is never accustomed to think in a total manner. Vedanta says this problem arises because man himself is not a totality; he is a partiality. He is an abstraction from the total whole. Thinking being a part of man's personality, all thoughts are partial in nature. A part cannot comprehend the whole (Totality). To say that rationalism is wholly right may not be entirely acceptable, nor can empiricism be said to be wholly right. Both the doctrines stick to one aspect of the truth, and ignore the other ones.

The individual belongs to the world in one way and maintains his own individuality distinct by isolating himself from the world in another way. This duality is man's reality. Man does not know what he really is. Subjectively, man has an inborn capacity to know, but objectively he has not got that knowledge—he has to receive that knowledge from outside. Therefore, man is both a subject and an object. As a subject he is a free man. But as an object, he is dependant and not free. This is called the conflict between the doctrine of determinism and free will. Man is free to some extent and he is bound also in some way. As a subject, man is one thing and as an object, he is another thing. Here is a humorous twist to this problem. We are inside the universe as an inseparable part of it and yet we do not seem to be that. We seem to be paying taxes to two governments, because we seem to be citizens of two realms. While we seem to be receiving support from the two governments to which we appear to belong, we also seem to be rejected by both; each government saying we belong to the other! This predicament defines man. Man is ever unhappy though he has the right to be eternally happy.

But in the eastern culture, down the ages, they look at the above problem differently. We say that rationalist character in man arises on account of subjectivity that he is, and the empiricist character arises on account of objectivity which, he also is. Being a part of this universe, man is bound by the nature of this universe. A being of the universe cannot be separated from an awareness of this being. Being is awareness or Consciousness. Knowledge arises from within man, because his being is inseparable from Consciousness. In this respect rationalism would appear right. On the other hand, man has broken away from the connection that he has with universe. He stands outside it as an object. Since he stands as an object, he is affected by the space-time limitation. He is deprived of the inborn knowledge and he is subject to the law of gravitation; the law of physics and astronomy. When he becomes an object, a body maintaining individual identity, man is determined by the law of nature and has no freedom, whatsoever. Yet, man has an inward connection with the pure subjectivity of the cosmos (Universal Consciousness) and, therefore, he is free to that extent. One does feel sometimes that one is free and at other times one feels bound. One is in hell and heaven at the same time! We say, human being is mortal but there is God within. Thus, the Vedic dictum '*Tat Twam Asi*'.

If you look at it from purely a materialist stand point, knowledge would be utterly impossible, because knowledge is not the nature of the object. The object is matter, it is not conscious. One cannot therefore, extract knowledge from an object and bring it within the perception of the mind so that the presence of the object could be noticed. If somehow you manage it, the knowledge so obtained should be compatible to the individual's perception. This individual perception must have some prior knowledge, such that both match. This line of argument was in vogue even from Socrates' time prompting him to declare his famous dictum "Know thy self." Man has to know himself, and then he knows all things. Empiricists don't agree, hence the conflict. We also feel that both are partly right. The conflict remains unresolved, because it is one set of thoughts in conflict with another set of thoughts. There cannot be an end to it.

We now arrive at the subject matter of Mandukya Upanishad, again one of the ten most important Upanishads. In the west it goes by the label of epistemology. The way we know that an object exists. We are here concerned with the process of knowledge. Even though we do not bestow attention to it, it is a daily activity in our life. How does the process begin? The process involves three functions, cognitive, co-native and affective. Consider the daily ritual of sleeping at night and waking in the morning. We would generally not notice it, but we daily pass through three steps. When we go into sleep we slowly arrive at a point when we know nothing. We are in deep sleep then. We do not know our own existence. We are then woken up. Initially, we are not aware of the world outside. We are out of sleep yet sleepy. There is a momentary indeterminate consciousness. We are merely aware. In the next stage there is self consciousness. One feels that one is. We are not clear of things. The duties, anxieties and worries of the world are yet to take over. A little later the full impact of your personality asserts. The indeterminate awareness of things around has now become a determinate perception.

When this concrete knowledge of the nature of objects around is obtained, another process sets in. Sage Patanjali calls it

Aklishta Vritte—there is a modification of the mind, a psychosis of non-pain-giving; in the sense that it is a mere awareness of the presence of the characteristic of an object and nothing more. Subsequently, the emotion or the feeling aspect is associated with it. The object becomes lively with the feeling of "mine and not mine," "like and dislike," and "love and hatred" attached to it. This is a further development. Let us consider an example. At first one may see something standing in front of oneself. This is an indeterminate perception of the object. It turns into a determinate perception when it becomes clear what is standing in front is a man. But a mere awareness of the fact of a being standing need not necessarily get associated with love and hatred. This Aklishta Vritti or mere perceptive act can suddenly transform into the consciousness of a person who is liked or disliked. If he is liked he is welcomed and if he is disliked, we turn away or shrink away from meeting the individual. This psychosis is called Klishta Vritte by Patanjali—a condition of mind which is pain-giving. The object itself does not give pleasure or pain, but when it is associated with a feeling, it arouses likes and dislikes. Our attitude towards the object gets conditioned by this process of perception which is associated with the effective involvement of likes and dislikes. Consider: you see a building in front of you. It is a building that belongs to you is something that follows from the mere act of perception of the building.

All activities can be regarded as reaction of psyche depending on the particular phase of its functioning such as cognitive, co-native, or affective; understanding, will and feeling. But these functions happen so rapidly that one appears inseparable from the other. One may say, 'I know there is such a thing in front of me, I feel something about it and I decide upon a course of action with reference to it at once.' This 'At once' is only a way of saying. A series of processes have taken place within the mind, in a fraction of a second, which prompts us to feel that it happened at once. It is a highly conditioned way of looking at things. Man is not seeing things as they really are. We are living in a world of appearance. A partial world conditioned by the reactions generated by our individuality. This aspect was frequently emphasized by late Jiddu Krishnamurti in almost all his speeches.

The universe as we see it is not only conditioned by the space-time complex but also by our internal conditioning. It is obvious that all objects are seen as they are in space and time. The question arises: why there should be a compulsion to be aware of things in space-time complex only? We are brainwashed, so intensely and to such a logical perfection that no one can think except in terms of space and time. It is as though we are made to put on a spectacle over our eyes, with one glass of space and the other of time. Perhaps if we use different, glasses we shall see differently. Alas, man cannot remove the space-time spectacle he is fitted with. It is because; man is made of their very stuff. Man is a spatio-temporal phenomenon. It would appear we are a born prisoners. The Rishis of Rig Veda are distinguished from us because they were able to transcend the limitation of space-time dimension and see the universe at once, in all the dimensions that are there. In modern times late Jiddu Krishnamurti was able to do so.

There is more trouble in store for man. Just as senses can see only through space and time and in no other way, the mind can think only in certain given ways and in no other way. What are these conditions to which the mind is subject and in terms of which alone it can think always? The psychological spectacles are *quantity, quality, relation and modality, says Immanuel Kant.* We cannot know anything unless it is defined with reference to the four facets mentioned above.

Every object has certain features that can be defined. These characteristics are what are called qualities of the object. There could be many characteristics which could not be counted, like color, height, weight etc. A particular object could be named in terms of its qualities, which are associated in turn with its quantity. Quantity and quality go together, they cannot be separated. Thus objects are measurable. In Sanskrit it goes by the nomenclature *Nama-Rupa.*

Everything is related to something else. If you recognize the presence of an object, it is due to the relation that it has with something else, a thing which no one is able to ponder upon. When a person says, "here is a pink wall', it is implied that there are no other pink walls around. If all the walls around were pink, then there is no point in saying, 'here is a pink wall'. So there is a relation between the pink wall and non-pink walls in this case. Everything is depending on something else, so that no one knows one thing unless the characteristics of another thing are assumed at the same time. Nothing can be known in isolation. It would appear, no one knows where one is and what one knows. The objects which are assumed to be quantities and are defined by qualities are also known through relations that obtain among things—also known as the principle of relativity. Further, every object exists in a condition, a situation, a circumstance, a state of affairs, which is called a mode. Everything is in some mode. These are the four ways by which mind can think and no other. Even when we think of God, one can think only in terms of quantity, quality, relation and mode. Therefore, it is an inadequate representation of the Eternal Principle, known as God. So we say God is immeasurable.

There is another faculty in man, *reason*, regulating sensory perception, the function of understanding and the assumptions of the intellect. Reason itself is, an offshoot of the categories of the understanding. What can reason argue about except things which are conditioned in the manner as mentioned already? In an argument, even about God Himself, there is this conditioning of the mind, so much so, we are not sure that we are arguing about a real thing. The God which is in our mind is a part of the phenomenon of the universe of the categories. Therefore, everyone is in a world which is nothing but phenomena, and reality cannot be known. No one can see it, because it is not an object of the thought or of the senses. We already know that mind is conditioned to look at the world from within the four walls of quality, quantity, relation and mode. It cannot look any other way. God being an unconditioned entity, it is outside the scope of the mind to comprehend it. What mind comprehends in the name of God is its own bias. Late Jiddu Krishnamurti use to lay great stress on the fact that we never tire of creating images. A husband has an image of his wife and children and they have also an image of their husband or the father as the case may be. We establish our relationship with these images and carry on life. We are thus never in touch with reality.

There is, however, something in man which is not merely the mind which thinks. There is what is known as will, and also feeling. Our will decides that we should do the right thing. The feeling comprehends that there is something which is inscrutable in this universe. Whatever be the argument of the mind which is conditioned by the four categories, and whatever be the difficulties felt by the senses which are restricted to the operation of space and time, the operation of will and feeling cannot be abrogated wholly. Generally the will is the deciding factor. This action of will is also known as ethical consciousness. Man is somehow impelled to do the right and not the wrong thing.

How is it that we are impelled to do the right rather than a wrong thing? We cannot say this urge arises due to the operation of space and time or the operation of the four limiting categories. It stands as something unique in itself. In the Rig Veda, it is in this context that Rishi Atri says, addressing Indra at Mandala 5, Hymn 35, at slokha 8:

वयं शविष्ठ वार्यं दिवि श्रवो दधीमहि ॥

O Indra, may we hold in thought the inspired knowledge that is the supreme good. Then there is feeling, which plays an important role in our life. Apparently, man lives more by his feelings rather than his understanding, or any other psychic function. Quite frequently, man decides upon a course of action on account of a certain feeling in him; notwithstanding logic or no logic. What is feeling? One is liable to accept that it is a deeper and more profound faculty than the logical intellect or the theological reason. Logic seems to be poor and inadequate equipment which man is wielding, in the light of a more forceful urge within him called feeling. When feeling begins to operate, logic fails. It is this feeling that takes the concrete form of desire, and when it becomes vehement it turns into passion. For example, beauty and its appreciation is a feeling and defy logic.

In the knowledge process, there are three ingredients, as we mentioned earlier: the knower, the object of knowledge and the process of knowing. The knower comes in contact with the object of knowledge through the medium of knowing process. What do we mean by these three items,-the knower, the knowing process and the known object? The knowing process is the illuminating link connecting the knower and the object of knowledge. It has to be an illuminating or illumined process, because knowledge is always an illumination. It is a light of a peculiar nature, not like others such as sun light. It is a movement of self-consciousness.

It will be little difficult to explain what consciousness is. We have to think that it is clarity, because there is no other word to explain it, and everyone knows what consciousness is. We are aware that we are and one need not ask for an explanation of what that phenomenon is. We know that we exist and no further explanation is necessary. If anybody wants to know what consciousness is, he only need close his eyes for a few seconds, and feel how he knows that he is. This intriguing experience of one knows that he is, is consciousness operating. In this consciousness of one's being there is also the root of the urge to know that other things are also there, apart from one self. As we saw earlier, when we wake up there is first self-consciousness and then a general consciousness. For self consciousness, consciousness of other things is outside of it.

There is also a thing called mind in man. It cannot be located, but we know it is there. This mind is charged with consciousness; similar to a copper wire may be charged with electricity. Like the wire becomes live when electric energy passes through it, so, the mind becomes live and we are inclined to say the mind moves. The wire is not electricity; even so, the mind is not consciousness. Yet, when we touch the live wire, we suffer a shock, because the force and the medium cannot be separated from each other. The same can be said of mind and consciousness. It is as if life is induced into an inanimate object. The mind is an urge within to move outwardly. It is also not a thing or substance. It is a faculty which pushes everything outside. There is a permanent impulse within everyone to move outside oneself; to go beyond the limitation of one's body, and man is more an object than a subject in the practical field of the world. For this reason, he is so much concerned with things outside rather than his own self within. Everyone are worried about the world, and there is no other anxiety. The mind pushes itself beyond itself. So, when consciousness operates through the mind, it looks as though the consciousness is also drawn towards an external object. What, however, moves is only the mind and not consciousness? This movement of the mind attended with consciousness is the knowing process.

According to Vedanta, the mind assumes the shape of the object. This form that mind assumes is called *Vritti*. Thus, when a form is known, or an object is contacted, the mind is supposed to envelop that object. This process of enveloping of the object by the mind is called *Vritti-Vyapti*. *Vyapti* is pervasion. The pervasion by the mind of a particular location called the object is *Vritti-Vyapti*. However, it is not enough if the mind assumes merely the shape or form of the object. It has to be aware that the object is there. This awareness that illuminates the form of the object is due to the presence of consciousness in this moving process called the mind and called *phala-vyapti*. Thus, a two-fold activity takes place when an object is known, the mind pervades the object and the consciousness illumines the form. It is only because of the consciousness attending on the mind that the object is perceived.

Now, the object cannot be wholly material. If it is so, consciousness cannot illumine it, since there would be qualitative difference between the object and consciousness. Vedanta says that the object cannot be wholly material, because the consciousness knows that the object is there. Since consciousness is able to come into contact with the object because there is some similarity with the object. This leads to the conclusion that the principle of consciousness is somehow inherent in the object. In Vedanta it is called *Vishaya-Chaitanya*. *Vishaya* is an object and *Chaitanya* is consciousness. However, *Vishaya-Chaitanya* does not mean consciousness of the object, but object which is itself a phase of consciousness. It is as well to remember that consciousness is everywhere.

Consciousness is infinite. It is indivisible. There can be nothing outside it. This infinitude implies that externality is anomalous. It cannot be finite, as the very knowledge of the finitude of consciousness would suggest the infinitude of it. Since it is infinite, no object can be external to it. No object can exist outside consciousness. Thus the object which the mind perceives is a phase of the consciousness. It is a formation of the consciousness itself. The Self collides with Self! In Brihadaranyaka Upanishad, Sage Yajnavalka says that this is the reason why we love the things of the world. We love things of the world because we see ourselves reflected in it. That is also the cause of relationship. Otherwise, nothing can attract anything else.

In conclusion we may say, the knower and the object of knowledge are linked by the flow of consciousness, the knowing process. God himself is in front of man as it were.

Thus, Purusha Sukta of Rig Veda tells us that all these things that are seen are the limbs of the One *Purusha*, the all being. Every atom, every particle, are all energies, every location or point of objectivity, is the head of the Cosmic Being. God alone is. The absolute is the only reality. Things are not what they seem.

Chapter 5

Divisive Thought

On the one hand, thought is material. There is no thought without a thing. There is nothing (No-Thing) without a thought. On the other hand, thought is also dependant on consciousness. No consciousness, no thought. Consciousness is not material, a thing limited by space and time. Consciousness is infinite. Read on . . .

In the Rig Veda at mandala 1 hymn 164, mantra 20, sage Dirghatamah Auchathyah expounds the following parable.

द्वा सुपर्णा सयुजा सखायासमानं त्रिक्षं परिपस्वजाते ।

योरन्यः पिप्पलं स्वाद्वत्त्यनषनन्नन्यो अभिचाकशीति ॥

Meaning: Two birds with graceful wings, close companions, perch on the same tree. Of them one eats the sweet fruit. The other, not eating, simply looks on.

This verse is quoted in Atharva Veda (9.9.20); Mundaka Upanishad (3.1.1) and Shvetasvatara Upanishad (4.6). It is a very significant parable.

This mantra beautifully brings out the relationship between individual consciousness and thought. The tree symbolizes the human body. On this tree perch two birds, while one, the thought, eats the fruits of labor, the other bird, consciousness watches on, not partaking the fruits of the tree. The thought is thoroughly involved in all worldly activities, whereas consciousness is a mere witness to the frenzied activities we involve in.

At every moment of life we are driven by thought. Except in deep sleep, thought pervades us in various ways. It appears, our progress and recognition by society is dependent on the development of thought. This is the reality in life. Managing our affairs with the help of thought gives us a great sense of belonging and security. We are afraid to step out of this grip of thought. Anything outside this grip of thought is viewed by us with disdain and considered foolhardy. But thought is totally dependent on consciousness. No consciousness no thought.

According to Indian system of philosophy, there are three separate faculties *Manas, Buddhi, and Chitta.* Manas (Mind), controls and coordinates the activities of *Pancha Indriyas (Five sense organs).* The Pancha Indriyas are: two eyes; two ears; nose; mouth and the body including both hands and legs or skin covering all organs. The Indriyas (Sense organs) gather sensation through seeing; hearing; smelling; tasting and touching. The sensation is transmitted to the brain (the instrument of Buddhi) through the mind. In return the mind receives instruction for response from Buddhi. For adequate response Buddhi may seek information from memory or *Chitta* which is under the control of DNA. This cycle is a mechanical activity in a normal healthy person. Consider the example: You see a person on your way. The moment you see the person you recognize him as your friend and act accordingly. In that split second your system has undergone all the steps mentioned above.

So long as these three faculties operate we are not disturbed. There is this fourth faculty *AHAM ('I')* which converts the purely mechanical function to one of personal function. 'I' enters in the picture. In fact this 'I' is the first thought in us. This thought drives us through out our life. All we have to do in our life is satisfy its wants; allay its fears and secure it from real or imagined danger to its survival. This 'I' thought sees itself as separate from the world. I AM different from everything else around me is the beginning of a distortion and an illusion. Since it has divided itself from rest of the world around, the 'I' has a tendency to divide everything it comes across. 'I' as we said, is a thought, which drives our world. We begin our life with a drawback, so to say. 'Viveka' (discrimination) is being aware of this distortion at all times.

To depend on the distorted thought entirely is unreliable because it gives a lopsided view of the world. If the first 'I' thought is sublimated, the same distorted thought becomes divinized, meaning, it turns into Individual Consciousness. Thought is entirely light based. Whereas, a full 95% of this universe is outside the ken of light, being dark matter with black holes! Like electromagnetic force propagates light along with atoms and particles dependant thereon, vast space and dark matter propagate gravitational force, which also influences thinking. The two forces could work at cross purposes at times! Yet all the scientific discoveries; profound philosophies; religious books; great kingdoms; great monuments, things of desire and wants; means of entertainment; are all based on the thought alone. Where will it lead? It will lead to division, confusion and conflict as we see around us and never towards lasting values in life. This is the moral lesson Mahabharata teaches us. Mahabharata war took place 5100 years ago. You can visualize that there were great people of Sanskar (great traditional knowledge-Dharma) on both sides like Bhisma Pitamaha; Dhronacharya; king Jayadratha and Kripacharya on the Kaurava side; and there were Dharmaraj and Krishna on the Pandava side, besides Veda Vyasa, yet the war was inevitable because the divisive thought was at play in every instance. There was therefore a need for Krishna (Electromagnetic Force) to impart the knowledge of Bhagwat Geeta to Arjuna (son of Indra the atom) in the battle field.

The legacy of religion and philosophy left behind by our ancestors is what we call Sanskar (Tradition). Whether the Sanskar is a day old or a thousand years old, it is the same thing. It is the 'Establishment' as coined in the modern social context, in the west. This Sanskar or tradition builds a psychological enclosure of four walls within us and would attempt to make sure that we are imprisoned within the four walls for rest of our life. We are so used to this imprisonment that even if we rebel, we will fall into the trap some other way because our thoughts are oriented only for a traditional outlook in life. We can never hope to be free, in the true sense of the word. The phrase in Sanskrit is, we are forced to float in Samsara Sagara (the ocean of finite social values) and not enabled to come out. It is also comfortable. It gives many opportunities, so why will one wish to come out? Freedom on the other hand is very adventurous and reward uncertain. If we consider this Sanskar (tradition) whether it is ancient philosophy and religion on one hand or modern science on the other, it is an edifice built on belief. It is another matter that you find a belief no more valid and replace it with another one. It is yet belief. We give a flavor to it by calling it as Faith. The whole of Islam and Christianity to a very large extent is based on faith. After 12th Century AD, even Hinduism is largely influenced by faith.

What is belief or faith? Consider an example. Let us say, I accost you and ask you whether there is God? What will you reply? Will you say, I don't know, which the correct reply is. More often, you will not say that. You will say yes, I know there is God. If you are an atheist you will say there is no God. Now what is this knowledge? This knowledge is based on books of theology or atheistic literature depending on your stand. The book is a dead thing. You give life to it by reading it and accept the contents thereof to arrive at the conclusion. The book may be a latest one or it may be the oldest Veda. Alternatively, religious authorities and your parents accepted the proposition that there is God because their parents believed so in a hierarchy that goes back to thousands of years. Yet it is a belief and not a fact. Both the thesis that there is God and its antithesis, that there is no God is defective, in as much as, they both are belief based. We also do not have time to impartially investigate the matter on our own so we accept the line of least resistance! Moreover, the man who has seen God will not say so because he becomes Bhagwan (God)! Seeing God is same as the Individual Consciousness merging with Universal Consciousness. Thereafter, Individual Consciousness is not available to confirm the merger as an experience. Any other experience, short of total merger as mentioned above, howsoever conclusive or convincing it may be, is an illusion and a cunning enactment of thought.

Interestingly, there is an all inclusive analysis of the world cultures. According to this analysis, there are two world traditions which have formed the cultural and ethical basis of the world as we know it. Both have an unbroken history going back thousands of years. A 5000 year old tradition known as Judaism is the mother of the western civilization. Judaism was the basis of later Christianity. Sanatana Dharma is the older of the two with a literature going back to the beginning of the recorded history.

The ancient civilizations such as the Roman, the Greek, the Egyptian, the Sumerian, and the Babylonian have all but vanished, even the Jewish culture as we see it today has undergone many fundamental changes since its inception 5000 years ago—yet the Sanatana Dharma endures as the Hindu civilization continues as a vibrant and living testimony, virtually unchanged for over 6000 years.

These two streams of tradition have shaped two different thought systems that can be broadly classified as Vedic and A-brah-mic (also known as Semitic). Here it is important to note that the Vedic tradition should be more appropriately called Brah-mic as opposed to A—Brah-mic (Semitic). Why so, will be clear little later. Believe it or not, any one person in this world, consciously or unconsciously, must belong or been influenced by one of the two thought systems, language notwithstanding. The main difference between Vedic (Brahmic) and Abrahmic are typical of the difference between Eastern and Western religions in general in contemporary terms.

The Vedic tradition or Brahmic tradition is a group of religions that have originated from Indian subcontinent. They consist of Hinduism; Buddhism; Jainism and Sikhism. Even other Asian religions such as Taoism, Confucianism and Shinto have their roots in Tantra a branch of Brahmic religion. The category of Abrahmic religions consists of Christianity; Islam and Judaism which claim Abraham or Ibrahim as a part of their sacred history. These two streams represent two very different world views. Their respective thought systems are fundamentally different at almost every point of comparison.

Fundamentally, there is a vast difference between Brahmic and Abrahmic religions; with the Vedic goals being unitary and introspective while the Abrahmic goals being dualistic and extroverted. The Vedic mind tends to see God everywhere and in all things and consider them sacred. The Abrahmic mind considers it heresy to believe that God pervades all things, and make a strong difference between what is sacred and what is profane. This contrast is no where more evident than in the field of physical sciences. It was a foregone conclusion that the world was dualistic; 'I' and the world of matter were two different and independent entities. Up to the time of Isaac Newton science was hand in hand with Abrahmic religion, but it took a u-turn after Albert Einstein's discoveries and tended towards Brahmic religion. There appears to be no turning back. There is another aspect to this shift in orientation. As we said, till the time of Newton, it was believed that matter has an independent existence. No matter, however much atom was split, and the individual particles that make up the matter are analyzed, there would still be an irreducible element of matter. This belief was shattered by Einstein irrevocably. It raised a basic question for Abrahmic religions. Einstein showed that, in the ultimate analysis, everything is energy including matter. Matter has no independent existence. This is a basic postulation of Brahmic religions.

The basic difference in the outlook between Brahmic and Abrahmic religions can be restated differently. It is with reference to consciousness. Brahmic religions unequivocally state that 'I' and 'Consciousness' are two different and distinctive faculties in man. 'I' is a product of thought, rather the first thought, which is limited by space-time. It is finite. 'Consciousness' is infinite and it transcends thought. But this 'I' also termed 'Ego' is dependent on consciousness. Therefore consciousness is alone God otherwise known as Brahman, later identified by various functional names in Brahmic religions. 'I' a limited and dependent thing cannot be divine in any sense. Abrahmic religions consider consciousness an inseparable part of 'I-consciousness' well articulated by Sigmund Freud. Therefore in the west, study of thought is a solely material activity. Even though the knowledge gained is profound, it explains only the process of thought and nothing more. The process does not explain the cause. For knowing the cause, one need to transcend thought process, that is what Brahmic religion is all about.

One is reminded of Rudyard Kipling the great English poet (1865-1965) who composed a beautiful poem, the first part stating the questions a man ought to seek answers in any matter or situation in life:

'I keep six honest serving men, (they taught me all I know) What and Why and When, How and Where and Who.'

The western definition of thought answers the three questions, How and When and Where; but does not address the questions, What, Who and Why adequately. All these questions were addressed by ancient Rishis of Brahmic religions exhaustively. Modern science is trying to follow suit in the last four hundred years under the label of science.

In the west, thought or thinking has been defined as mental activity which enables humans to model the world according to their own goals, plans, ends and desires. Thinking is manipulating information, as when we form concepts, engage in problem solving, reason and make decisions. A thought may be an idea, an image, a sound or even an emotional feeling that arises from the brain. No distinction is made between thought and thinking process.

Further, in the perception of the westerners, the word thinking encompasses diverse psychological activities. In its extended definition thinking is inclusive of, sometimes "tending to believe," especially with less than full confidence ("I think that it will rain, but I am not sure"). At other times it denotes the degree of attentiveness ("I did it without thinking"), especially if it refers to something outside the immediate environment ("It made me think of my late teacher").

Sri Aurobindo provides a very clear picture on this issue based on Rig Veda. Indra (Atoms) is the Mind-Power that is freed from the limits and obscurations of the nervous consciousness. It is this clear intelligence that fashions thought or of action not distorted by nervous impulses of the senses. If we look at it from modern science point of view, atom is a primary light source that is involved in thought formation. This clarification arises from Rig Veda Mandala 1 Hymn 4.

A mechanistic view is conceived by Biology. Thought is outcome of Neuron (Nerve cell) activity. Neuron is an excitable cell in the nervous system that processes and transmits information by electrochemical signaling with the help of axons. Neurons are the core components of the brain, the vertebrate spinal cord, the invertebrate ventral nerve cord, and the peripheral nerves. A number of specialized types of neurons exist: sensory neurons respond to touch, sound, light and numerous other stimuli affecting cells of the sensory organs that then send signals to the spinal cord and brain. Motor neurons receive signals from the brain and spinal cord and cause muscle contractions and affect glands. Axons connect neurons to other neurons within the brain and spinal cord. Neurons respond to stimuli, and communicate the presence of stimuli to the central nervous system, which processes that information and sends responses to other parts of the body for action. Is thought purely mechanical as is made out? It also involves understanding, willing and feeling. These are not purely mechanical processes. The neurons are called Nadi in Sanskrit. In ancient times, the Rishis made considerable progress on this subject. They even calculated that there were around seventy two thousand nadis in each human being distributed all over the body. They had precise knowledge of the functions of the principle Nadis and the means to control and redirect their movements with mantras and swara yoga. Neuron cells are only a part of the overall cell structure in a being. There are billions of cells in our body and each of these cells contains billions of atoms. We may say that all cells are actuated by atoms. Neurons are no exception.

Thinking is in the present. There is a difference between THOUGHT and THINKING, clearly brought out in Rig Veda Mandala 1 Hymn 171. Thought (Indra) is a product of light as we saw earlier, whereas, thinking is actuated by gravitational wind (Maruts), or Tachyons of science. Thinking is a fundemantel and incessant activity of the organism called brain. Thinking has a movement and Thought is static, embedded in the past. The Thought may have arisen the last second or many years back, it does not matter, the effect is same. Thought consolidates the ego. It uses the Thinking process for its mobility from past to the present and into the future. The Thinking mechanism is used as a vehicle to bridge the past with future. Future is unborn yet. At best one can make a projection into the future. The projection is the outcome of Thought. Thought seeks continuity, from past through present into the future. Thinking has no past or future. It is here and now. But Thought influences the Thinking all the time. Thought process is ever overshadowed by EGO ('I'), the very first thought. What is more important to realize is, that, attending to Thinking, and being an integral part of the Thinking is Consciousness which is not EGO based. As we said, Thinking is the activity of the brain. It is a purely mechanical process. When you see an incident; a scene; or undergo an experience, you are in a state of experiencing that vision or deed. At that moment (perhaps a fraction of a second) there is no thought. Actually, you are in the present. Then thought makes an entry with a choice as to whether the experience is a pleasurable one or a painful one, based on past knowledge and experience of the event as stored in the memory. If it is not able to relate the new experience to any past knowledge or experience, it computes other possible solution to deal with the event, again based on past knowledge and experience. For example, your ego (Thought) will say 'what a satisfying experience, I should have more of it, let me return to same place and time to have more of it.' The event has already become a past experience. Mind you, all this happens in a split second. You will not be able to observe these things happening unless you are watchful. Past experience whether generated in the last moment as we saw above or some years back; or improvised from the knowledge gleaned from texts of authority, all suffer the same defect. We are trying to apply the past to a present event. Past is crystallized and the present is fluid. The principle just demonstrated applies to thought process also. So long as you are thinking, you are in the present, but the moment you stop and act, you bring in the past. The secret is at the point of action. If you revert back to ego based action (of thought) you are in the trap of the past, but, if at that point your consciousness takes over, you are acting independently. Figuratively speaking, you should reprogram the 'default.' A parallel can be drawn in the use of computer. Every time you are done with an application, the system 'defaults' back to operating system. This is a vital function in the computer. This reverting back ought to be to consciousness and not thought process. That makes a world of difference.

Using the thinking process, the ego is able to imagine that it has a unique characteristic (thinking) as a human, which gives superiority over other species. Even among humans, often ego projects its individuality as superior to other humans. In the process, it creates a virtual reality which leads to limiting our personal world. The thinking process is woefully underdeveloped and grossly overvalued. Only 10% of our brain capacity is utilized in a lifetime!

Virtual reality plays a major role in our life. Whether it is one's spouse, children, near and dear ones, or friends, we have an image of the person in our mind. You cannot do without an image. This image is a thought construct. Similarly, others have an image of us. Life is all about these images interacting with each other. Thus we live in virtual reality.

Most of the time our mind is so crowded with wishful thinking, grandiose plans for future; our idiosyncrasies; our imaginary fears or phobias; psychological security concerns that there is no room for creative thinking. The mind has to be relatively empty, quiet and relaxed to receive creative ideas. Such creative ideas do come to all of us. But we miss to cash in as our thinking is otherwise busily engaged in frivolous pursuits. Only awareness or alertness can help us root for such opportunities.

It will not be incorrect to say that our thoughts create our reality. 'Think and grow rich' is the catchy phrase made popular by Dale Carnegie with his book which carried the phrase as title. The question arises whether there is any scientific basis to the above phrase? But commonsense prompts us to think that it is unrealistic, for example, for you to imagine a million dollars in your briefcase all of a sudden. Yet such things happen around us most of the time! Only we are not aware.

When you switch your cell phone, radio or television, sound and pictures appears to come apparently from nowhere. Is it not unrealistic too? There is certainly nothing connecting the cell phone, radio or Television to anything else. You just switch them on and you get light and sound. They certainly appear to be 'things' that appear at your beck and call.

We have arrived up to a level of knowledge that we can explain this phenomenon with reference to an objective matter, but not in our subjective thought process. Thus, we say these devises are powered by electricity and there is liquid crystals and cathode ray tubes projecting photons and other electrons bombarding the screen, releasing energy to create the images we see. At the other end, somebody used some electricity or some other energy, to power the transmitter, caused some electromagnetic waves and your cell, radio or TV catches those signals and converts them to your delight.

What we have not yet grasped is that our thoughts are waves too. We don't have full knowledge as to how our brain works. However, it is apparent that our brain acts as a transmitter and receiver of sound waves and converter of particle bombardment into images that we project for ourselves and to world at large with the help of other energies from our own body. When we transmit a thought, the receiver at the other end some how converts those waves into matter, and if thought results in the creation of actual matter, will it not be *thought creating matter?* Theoretically, in science this is called teleportation.

Science says that matter vibrates and has a wave function too. That would mean that everything in this world is interconnected. If our brains are sending wave after wave of thought, who can say what effect they are having? Consider Electromagnetic radiation. It does not get lost in space. Once it is sent out, it can travel millions of light years and return centuries later. Perhaps thought waves also have the same capacity. This possibility arises because atoms are always entangled with electromagnetic force. Thought is also entangled with gravitational force through what are known as Tachyons, a sub-particle of Mesons. In Rig Veda, Tachyons are known as Maruts children of Rudra Shiva (Gravitational Force) and they are closely associated with Indra (Atoms) the substance of thought. Considerable research is going on in this area. For example, Phil Callahan says that Tachyon is a theoretical particle, which travels faster than the speed of light. A nice limerick describes the property of Tachyons:

There was an young lady named Bright

Who's speed was much faster than light

She left home one day

In a relative way

And returned home the previous night.

His conclusions are:

Tachyons do exist.

As predicted by Dr. Cope, they occur in conjunction with weak magnetic poles.

They are easily detected by living plants.

Therefore living plants are super conductors.

We read in the Puranas, that sages had powers of telepathy. We are prone to dismiss such claims of supersensory perception as myth in keeping with our western upbringing, but now science is coming round to the realization that there is substance to such claims after all. To sum up, if you send out (transmit) thought waves it would be natural for some one tuned in to be able to receive it. Until the transmitted wave is received by someone else, it will keep going. Not only that, any other thought wave transmitted with the same wave length will add to the volume. This realization is not something new. It was contemplated in the Rig Veda at some length as we shall see next.

The thought-forces were given the nomenclature of Maruts, sons of Rudra (Gravitational Force). They do not enjoy the status of luminaries for the simple reason that they are not dependant on light source, they depend on gravitational force which Rudra represents. Agni and Indra have by far more hymns dedicated to them than all other deities in Rig Veda. Maruts rate next. For understanding the function of Maruts, we have to turn to Ramayana. In this epic penned by Rishi Valmiki, we are introduced to a unique character popularly known as Maruti. All the epithets and virtues attributed to Maruti (also known as Hanuman) equally apply to Maruts. Incidentally, all the principle Rishis figuring in the Rig Veda have a role in Ramayana. Just like Maruts help Indra in Rig Veda, Maruti helps Rama in the epic. We shall not go into it. We are here concerned with thought-force. In modern science the scientists have discovered a particle that answers to the description of Maruts. The credit for this discovery is due to Dr. Sudershan. He found that the neutron in the nuclei of the atom contains a particle known as Meson. In turn, this Meson contains Tachyons which travel at a speed faster than light. It was Einstein who had stated that light travels at the fasted speed and no other substance can approach this speed of light. This belief was laid to rest.

The Vedic Rishis made a distinction between thought and mind. The mind collects the information given by the five senses and the information stored in the memory along with earlier sense contacts with the help of DNA. Recent scientific studies throw more light on this aspect of memory aided by DNA. For example, Dr. Vladmir Poponen has done experiments with laser beams passing through DNA in what is known as "Phantom DNA effect." The experiments conclusively proved that there is a non-physical template in DNA which is also attached to the vast space in the universe where our memory is in fact stored. There is growing scientific evidence that vast space itself can store information. This was the basis for experiments by Dr. Walter Schempp. His explosive discovery about quantum memory set-off the most outrageous idea of all. Short-term and long-term memory does not reside in our brain at all, but instead stored in the 'zero point field' or implicit order as David Bohm puts it. After Pribram's experiments in this connection, many scientists including systems theorist Ervin Laszlo would go on to argue that the brain is simply the retrieval and read-off mechanism of the ultimate storage medium. Thoughts are mental entities formed, released and retrieved by the mind. Every one of us forms such thoughts and releases them. Once thoughts are released, their life is independent of the mind that formed them and they travel around depending on Maruts or thought forces by gravitational law. Each thought has an idea at its core. During its travel, the thought may be caught by other minds of persons who offer a welcome to it and the thought deposits the idea it carries to the mind of the recipient. The power of thought depends on the power given to it by the originator. A thought released by a person, joins with similar thoughts released by others and they form a group or a flock like a flock of birds. This is articulated in Rig Veda by Rishi Kanvah Gaurah with reference to Maruts at mandala 1 hymn 37 mantra 9 as follows:

स्थिरं हि जानमेषां वयो मातुनिरेतवे ।

यत्सीमनु द्विता शवः ॥

Meaning: Their source are indeed firm (thought), they as mental energies (birds) are able to exist from the world of life energies (senses). Thought's luminous prowess follows as a double everywhere (with Maruts).

After acquiring more and more power from other kindred thoughts, these thoughts may return to the originator with redoubled vigor. The originator of thoughts need not always be human beings of earth. In the Vedic psychology, there are three lower worlds of matter (Anna); life-energy (Prana) and the mind (Manas). The beings of these worlds are called typical beings since they are not subject to evolution as the beings on earth. These other beings can also radiate thoughts or mental movements which can impact on the minds of the earthly beings. Maruts the thought-Gods help Indra in his battle against the demonic forces. They are therefore called as the younger brothers of Indra (Indrajestha RV 1.23.8). Maruts begin the work of Indra in introducing the harmonious thoughts and mental movements in man.

The Maruts are particular divinities who set a divine pace to the mental movements of fierce speed and brilliance. All the divinities have two births as it were. The first birth is in the collective creation in their designated function. Their second birth is their birth in man when their faculties find expression in man. The first step in the manifestation of the divine mind of Indra is the birth of mental movements of fierce speed and brilliance which are needed to counter the influences put forth by the demonic forces. The biological definition of thought examined earlier postulated that thinking is the outcome of neurological activity. The neurons are cells like other cells in human body. We have seen earlier that an average human body contains about 10^{14} (Ten followed by 14 zeros) cells. Each of these cells in turn house 10^{14} Atoms. The count of cells includes 72 million neurons in our body. These cells also contain Atoms of the same magnitude as in other cells. Thought in effect is the activity of Atoms in the human body. Rig

Veda identified the right thinking as the power play of Indra ably assisted by Maruts.

In the formulation of Quantum Entanglement Theory, the new science states that it is wrong to simply assume that our entire world exists independently in one form, irrespective of our measurement of it. There is no such thing as an object fixed in space, just information. We can only gather information about our world and order it as we see fit, so that it makes sense to us. The universe is a sea of information. What is this activity of gathering and floating information but the activity of Maruts?

Enlightened thinking of Indra is opposed to dark and depressive thinking encouraged by the demonic forces that thwart our progress towards universal consciousness. In this function Indra is ably assisted by Maruts. What are these demonic forces? They emanate from the dark matter including black holes about which science is deeply concerned at present. The dark matter constitutes over 95% of the known universe. The dark forces emit anti matter, the demonic forces. We depend for our existence on the luminaries like atoms and particles. Illumination is absent or obscured in dark matter, and therefore with the dark or demonic forces the present form of existence is out of question. In 1928 it was Paul Dirac who created an equation that suggested the existence of antimatter. For every atom or particle in the universe there is its counterpart in the form of antimatter. If matter and antimatter collide there will be an explosion, so that only energy is left behind.

In the Rig Veda we frequently come across sooktas narrating that Indra secured the light of consciousness (indicated as gow in Sanskrit) from the dark forces. In a very superficial level, we may say, our otherwise bright thinking undergoes bouts of depression and laced by dark and pessimistic thoughts. Indra restores that lost brightness.

PART II

Invocation

I ask you to look both ways. For the road to a knowledge of the stars leads through the atom; and important knowledge of the atom has been reached through the stars—*Sir Arthur Eddington, 1928*. This is what ancient Rishis realized! Read on . . . .

In science there is the concept of Standard Model. It is towards the end of 19th century that electrons, protons and neutrons were etched out of the classical atom, which until that time was considered as the smallest form of matter. In the 20th century these components of atom were further split to reveal a plethora of many more tiny particles. A 'standard model' was mooted by bringing together the entire particle zoo in a single family tree. The notable exclusion was gravity. This is not a unique attempt, though.

The ancient Rishis conceived such a standard model most conclusively for all time to come inclusive of gravity. In an Indian household, even after many thousands of years that have passed, such a model is worshipped even today with greatest reverence. No wonder, this model is regarded as the quintessence of Veda. We are talking of the depiction of mother Gayatri. The very first step was taken in this direction by Rishi Vishwamitrah (universal friend) Gathinah in the 3rd mandala—62nd hymn-10th Mantra of the Rig Veda. It is addressed to Savitur (universal consciousness):

तत् सवितुर्वरेन्यम्

भर्गो देवस्य धीमहि

धियो यो नः प्रचोदयात् ॥

Meaning: We meditate on the divine splendor of Savitur, who is supremely desirable and is That One (Universal Consciousness). May he activate our thoughts towards wisdom. Over the ages, additions were made to this basic Truth so that the full splendor of the standard model stood revealed.

When we make a scientific investigation, there are two ways of doing it, top-down or bottom-up. In top down form of investigation, you begin with the top most Truth and arrive at the details that manifest from such a Truth. It was an extremely arduous job. This was the regimen pursued by the Rishis down the ages. On the other hand, the scientific community took up the visible objects in the world for investigation and proceeded to determine the next higher level of manifestation and so on. They did penetrate quite deeply towards the one single unifying force at the top, but till date have not succeeded in their endeavor.

There is another fundamental difference between the two ways of looking. Scientific community is motivated by a desire to seek explanation of the natural phenomena and a vision to utilize the extraordinary power to serve man in his never ending appetite of wants and comforts. On the other hand, the ancient Rishis realized that the Truth alone exists. Our reality is at best a virtual reality, an illusion. No doubt, in the two dimensional world (space-time) we live in, what we see is a tangible reality, but the world is multi dimensional. When you take into consideration other dimensions that exist, Truth begins to unfold and our two dimensional reality begins to fade. Truth is the only manifestation and the manifested. We as the manifested become ignorant of the Truth which is the manifestation and revel in that ignorance. The Rishis were motivated to resurrect man into realizing his true nature. For this job, they recognized that merely knowing the existence of more powerful phenomena than man was not sufficient. Also, channeling the powerful elements of nature into sub serving man's greedy appetite is ignoble, they felt. These phenomena need to be courted to help man in realizing the final goal of unraveling the Truth. These elements of nature are ever willing to help, because in the ultimate analysis, they are the constituents making up man.

There is also another angle to be considered. It will be easily appreciated that not everyman can become an able scientist. It needs an aptitude and the effort to back the aspiration for becoming a scientist. We may appreciate the marvel of a standard model when explained to us. But the same standard model is a vital tool in the hands of such a research scientist. Similar considerations made the Rishis create a class of people called 'Brahmins'. The primary goal of the Brahmin class was to discover the fundamental Truth and in turn educate others in this pursuit. This class has all but vanished today. To be sure, there are Brahmins even today but they are not the class originally contemplated by those Rishis. Down the ages, other Rishis reclassified the Brahmin function to exclude scientific enquiry in order that the Brahmins conform to the tenets of Brahmanas (a subsidiary book of Vedas). For the original class of Brahmins, Gayatri Mantra was an indispensible tool to reach greater heights in their spiritual flights, since it was the standard model. For even the later Brahmins, Gayatri Mantra is important, but it is part of a bigger litany, seeking prosperity and comfort in this virtual world. Today, everyone uses the Gayatri Mantra as though it is some voodoo; even rendered into carnal music for mere entertainment.

The great contribution to science by Richard Feynman, the charismatic Californian Particle Physicist was the unique diagrams that depict particle interactions using a series of arrows to show the paths of the particles involved. Even in this matter, the ancient Rishis forestalled the modern scientists, with a difference though. Whereas the scientific diagrams merely trace the movements and action of the particles in nature in order to explain their function, the ancients made the same diagrams as a means to secure the cooperation of these forces in helping man to advance in his spiritual goal. The name by which these diagrams were identified is "Yantra". Tantra-raja-Tantra says the Yantra is technically called "Mandala". Mandala is defined as a collection of energies. The origin of the Mandala is the Center (Bindu). The diffuse, and therefore feeble, forces are gathered up from all the sides, rendering them powerful by the very act of gathering up. Thus the forces of the universe are concentrated in the Mandala. A best example of such a mandala is Sri Chakra. Mandala gave inspiration for pictorial presentation. Raja Ravi Verma created many such pictorial presentations of Hindu deities (luminaries). We are concerned here with such a presentation of Gayatri.

The original three lines of the mantra we indicated above got an additional first line in Vajasaneyi Samhita (36.3) and Krishna Yajur Veda Taittiriya Samhita (4.1.11.1):

ॐ भुर्भुवः स्वः ।

Meaning: May we become aware of the three planes in us. The Consciousness is denoted by prefix Om, which is present in all the three planes. This Om is called *Pranava*.

The three planes in us are the physical, subtle and causal. This is not unique to man alone. If you reflect, the mechanical devices invented by man also have three planes. If you consider man, physically, there is the outer casing of bone structure and skin, like the cabinet in a mechanical device. This plane is known as 'Bhu', the physical or earthly plane. Then there is a sophisticated inner network of nerves; glands; cells; blood; chemicals; atoms and particles; the mind and thinking that pulsates life, even like the internal wiring of a mechanical device. This is the subtle body (Bhuvah). However, both these two planes suffer the space-time limitation in different degrees. The third causal plane (svah) is beyond the space-time limitation in man alone and not shared by the mechanical devices invented by him. The causal plane for a mechanical device is the elemental forces predominating in the universe e.g. electro-magnetic force.

Vedas inspired Tantra Shastra and Yoga Shastra. We have already seen the introduction of the most important symbol of tantra, Aum in the Gayatri Mantra. Yoga shastra also found a place in the Gayatri Mantra with mention of four more planes after Bhur,

Bhuvah and Svah. Together the seven planes or lokas are called Vyahritis. Vyahriti means a perfect utterance. Loka means world or simply plane of existence. Thus each plane is a world in itself.

ॐ भूः । ॐ भुवः । ॐ॒ सुवः । ॐ महः ।

ॐ जनः । ॐ तपः । ॐ॒ सत्यम् ॥

We have briefly considered the three internal planes which Gayatri Mantra mentions. If we are aware of internal planes, then we should also be aware of the external planes which are the four other lokas. Before we consider the other planes, we are vitally concerned with the eternal link connecting the internal and the external planes. Here a little clarification would be in order. There are two ways of looking at the lokas. In the first perception, within man there are the internal, gross; subtle and causal planes and the external planes, such as the four other lokas in the form of chakras. In the second perception, man exists in the first three lokas. These three lokas are the bhu or earth; bhuvah or the atmosphere around us and svah or the troposphere, stratosphere, mesosphere and thermosphere above which protects the life on earth from space bombardments and ultra violet rays. Man looks at the physical universe as external in what science calls astronomy or cosmology. Man stands on earth and looks at the universe. Here a famous Vedic dictum comes to mind. Whatever the universe contains is in man and what is not in man is nowhere in the universe!

Whichever way you look at it, the link between the internal and external planes is 'Breathe.' Man is born with his breathe. Only on death breathe departs his company. Breathe is flow of surrounding air through the nostrils. Western science has considered the contents of the air such as oxygen, nitrogen, carbon and other gases and their characteristics and properties, but not the impact of breathing. The subtle 'Prana' is also part of breathe. Breathing continues day and night, twenty four hours round the clock, whether one is aware of the process or not. If you ever take the time to observe the breathe and the manner in which the air flows in and out of the nostrils, you will notice that most of the time respiration takes place through only one of the two nostrils, alternatively. We apparently think that we breathe through both the nostrils simultaneously, but it is not so always. Physiologically, it implies that the alternating flow must have particular effect on the nervous system, producing a certain type of stimulus. Moreover, it must have a specific influence on the brain which requires very systematic regulation. In Yoga, they say there is a Swara (Rhythm). The breathe rhythm is based on the biorhythm, the energy rhythm of the body, and it is also related to the two hemispheres of the brain. When the left nostril flows (Ida in Sanskrit), it indicates that the mental energy is predominant, and the pranic energy is weak. When the right nostril is flowing (Pingala in Sanskrit), pranic forces are stronger and the mental aspect is weak. When both the nostrils operate together (Sushumna in Sanskrit), it indicates that the spiritual energy, the force of consciousness, is in power.

Scientific investigation has shown that the atmosphere is charged with electromagnetic energy which is vital to the preservation of life. Yoga says that where there is life, there is prana; and what science has found is that wherever there is life, there are electrical properties. In the Yoga texts, prana is equated with lightning, thus inferring that its properties have some similarity to electrical energy. Prana is also described as being magnetic as it has positive and negative aspects. Pranayama (control of the movement of prana) involves techniques to redirect, store, control, and regulate prana. Pranayama also means 'length of prana'. Why should prana be manipulated thus?

The aim of pranayama is to extend the prana into previously dormant areas of the body, brain and personality so that various inherent faculties are awakened and our perception gets highly sensitive. We saw that there are three ways we breathe; through the left nostril Ida; through the right nostril Pingala and through both the nostrils Sushumna. A key objective of pranayama practice is breathing retention in order to activate sushumna. Breathing involves inhalation, exhalation and retention of breathe each of which have a specific significance and effect. Inhalation draws vital air into the body. Exhalation eliminates the impurities both at physical and subtler level from the body. At the subtler level it removes negative mental impression. Retention within limit generates more vitality. By regulating these three aspects, control and balance is gained. Normal inspiration and expiration come and go in unequal proportions. Either inspiration is not full and expiration very long or vice versa. This leads to imbalance of prana in the nadi (nerves).

The human body is divided into two definite divisions or zones according to flow of energy and magnetic pull of positive and negative forces. The positive and negative forces are represented by Pingala and Ida. In the central axis where the two adjoining sides meet, the positive and the negative energies get neutralized and create a neutral energy field running up and down the central axis. This pathway is called Sushumna Nadi. Sushumna emerges from the base of the spine, the same as Ida and Pingala, but without swerving to right or left, it travels directly up through the center piercing the main Chakras and plexus along the route. Sushumna unites with Ida and Pingala at Ajna Chakra in the region of medulla oblongata. It thus corresponds to Cerebra-spinal Nervous System (CNS). At man's present stage of evolution Sushumna lies dormant. Hence the Yoga practices leading to the opening of Sushumna passage. With Ida or Pingala operations only half the brain operates in turn. When Sushumna flows, the whole brain operates and Karmaindryas (physical organs of action) along with Gyaneindriyas (mental organs) function at peak. Man gets to be super sensitive whether in spiritual or mundane life.

Within the subtle structure of pranic network in the body, every nadi has a specific route. At certain points groups of nadis come together forming centers of pranic and psychic energy, known as *chakras*. In Sanskrit chakra means a wheel, a circle, which is round and capable of spinning. They are in the energy circuit of the body. They receive energy from higher levels and distribute it through out the body and mind. The chakras are arranged in an ascending order of subtlety. The lowest chakra vibrates relatively slowly. As we go up the chakra ladder, the chakras vibrate faster as compared to the immediate lower chakra. The chakra vibration affects the glands and organs to which they are connected, thus influencing the entire body structure as well as the metabolism.

First to be counted is the lowest energy centre called Mooladhara. It is at the base of the spine. Moola means root and Adhara means support. This chakra is the foundational support to the human system. All the animal urges arise from this centre. In fact this chakra, next chakra Swadhisthana and Manipura in a crude form are found in animal kingdom also, but not the remaining higher chakras. It is also the place from which man's evolution begins. Mooladhara influences the excretory and reproductive organs and glands. It is connected with nasal cavity and sense of smell and can therefore be stimulated from the point of the nose. Two fingers above Mooladhara in the sacral plexus is where Swadhisthana chakra is located. Swa means self and sthana means place. Awareness of self and ego is aroused here. Swadhisthana also influences reproductive organs and glands. It is closely attached to Mooladhara. Again Swad in the name of this chakra refers to taste. Tasting is the sensorial faculty associated with Swdhisthana chakra. Behind the navel in the solar plexus is Manipura chakra. Mani means jewel and pura means city. It is the city of jewels. At this centre nadis gather, radiating immense light. Since it radiates light, it is also the seat of goddess Laxmi, the consort of Mahavishnu. Manipura contains the fire element. It is also known as seat of digestive fire. Manipura is concerned with digestion and absorption of food and prana. It is also considered as the mid-point between earth and heaven. In the two lower centers, awareness is oriented towards gross experience but from this point onwards higher ideals develop. So it is the point from which we move from gross to subtle. These three chakras thus represent, Bhu, Bhuvah and Svah respectively in the Vedic Gayatri mantra.

The next centre is Anahata chakra. It is the heart centre found in the cardiac plexus. Anahata in Sanskrit implies sound generated without two pieces being struck. It is here that Sabda Brahman (consciousness as sound) is heard. It is where the pulse of the universe and the pulse of human existence can be experienced. It is also residence of Jivatma or soul of an individual. According to Veda, the abode of Sabda or eternal sound is vast space or the Mahar Loka (A world of vast open space). Late Carl Sagan in his book "Cosmos" says Earth is a place (in the universe), but is by no means the only place and it is not even a typical place. The typical place is within the vast, cold, universal vacuum, the everlasting night of intergalactic space. According to Veda and Yoga shastras there is a correspondence between the heart centre and the vast open space explained by science in the above book.

Vishuddha chakra is in the cervical plexus or throat region. Vishuddha means purified in Sanskrit. Thus, this chakra prevents toxins from circulating through out the system. It has a direct influence on the throat, tonsils, vocal cords, thyroid and parathyroid glands. At this chakra the Jiva (individual soul) is purified in preparation for onward journey to remaining two chakras. Thus, it is considered as the gateway for liberation. The man who attains this chakra becomes "Triloka Darsi," meaning he conquers time concept as past, present and future. Normally, man is limited by space/time. The time constraint does not apply to the yogi. In the Vedas this is the Jana Loka or greatly populated world. A Swiss scientist named Hans Jenny experimented with the effects of sound waves deeply.

This aspect of science was named *Cyma tics*. His experiments demonstrated that sound waves projected into various mediums such as water, powder, paste, or oil produce different patterns with remarkable similarity to forms found in nature, such as spiral galaxies, cellular division in an embryo, or the iris and pupil of the human eye. The yogis who were able to attain this chakra were able to observe the vast spiral galaxies that are billions of light years away. Today scientists, with very powerful telescopes, are able to confirm their existence. However, man cannot hope to approach any of these galaxies because of space and time constraint. Continuing his exposition of the universe, Late Sagan says that from an intergalactic vantage point we would see, strewn like sea of froth on the wave of space, innumerable faint, wispy tendrils of light. These are galaxies. There are some hundred billion galaxies, each with, on an average, a hundred billion stars. In all the galaxies, there are perhaps as many planets as stars.

Ajna chakra is located at the top of spinal column. This centre is associated with pineal gland. Ajna means command. Intuition is transmitted to the lower centers and mind. It is the medium between higher consciousness (the guru) and the lower ego or jivatma (disciple). Ida and Pingala nadis merge with Sushumna nadi in this chakra. The place where the three nadis converge is a very powerful energy centre which awakens the higher creative force in man. The role of ajna is associated with the functions of pineal gland. The pineal enables the extra-sensory perceptions like clairvoyance, clairaudience, telepathy, etc. A yogi who has arrived at this chakra gains liberation from both space and time constraints.

Yoga shastra says the yogi sees sparks of fire distinctly shining. In the Veda this centre is Tapo Loka, which means flaming world. Else where in his book, Late Carl Sagan says that during the life time of a galaxy, about ten billion years, a hundred million stars will have exploded. The suicide rate among galaxies is very high. We have to go by distinct but tiny specks to record such events which occur on the boundary regions of the visible universe, rather frequently in the constellation hunter.

The last chakra Sahasrara is not a chakra as is often thought. It acts through nothing and yet, it acts through everything. An enigma! The word sahasrara means a thousand. The number simply implies that its magnitude and significance is vast—in fact unlimited. It transcends logic, for logic compares one thing with another. Sahasrara is the totality, so what is there to compare with?

It transcends all concepts and yet it is the source of all concepts. Concepts such as I and you; past, present and future; here and there; up and down, light and darkness etc. It is the merging of individual consciousness as prana with universal consciousness.

There is then only total awareness. This is the ultimate Truth. Such is the state that the Rig Vedic Rishis were witness to, so that they could become eligible for inclusion in the ancient text of Rig Veda. The groups of families who did get included thus, narrated their realization in what is known as Apri Hymns. In the Veda, the Sahasrara is known by the label Satya Loka, meaning the world of Truth. Interestingly, this Satya Loka has an appendage known as Brahma Loka. The yogi who attains Ajna chakra is drawn into Brahma Loka and denuded of all his energies so that what is left is only his mass. Beyond Brahma Loka it is total darkness and in the middle of such intense darkness is a world of bright light the Hiranya Garba (the womb of golden hue). At this point, even the mass is denuded, and what proceeds to merge in the Great Void or Universal Consciousness is the Individual consciousness. There is a renewal and return but what or who returns we do not know. Science also has arrived at similar conclusion and the research is ongoing. Theory of relativity states that nothing can travel faster than light. Accordingly, if light is obstructed and cannot escape in space, neither can anything else. Everything is dragged back by gravitational field. In observations in deep space, the scientists do come across a set of events, a region of space-time, from which it is not possible to escape to reach a distant observer. This is a black hole. It does not emit light. Its boundary is called an event horizon. Anything or anyone who falls through the event horizon will soon reach the region of infinite density and the end of time. The intruding object will be denuded of all energy and what proceeds into the black hole is only a mass. Eventually, this mass will be returned to the universe but it would be different from the mass that went inside the black hole.

Gayatri mantra proceeds to make another statement, in the last sentence. Hitherto, we considered the macrocosm. The microcosm also needs to be represented in the standard model. What constitutes the microcosm? Thus,

ओंमापो ज्योती रसोऽमृतबह्म भूर्भुवस्सुवरोम् ॥

Meaning: Consciousness is also present in hydrodynamics; thermodynamics and chemistry as immortal Brahma (the repository of all energy in nature) as is present in the gross, subtle and causal planes of the body. Everything ultimately is Consciousness alone.

Even though the Gayatri Mantra is completed with the above statement, a Brahmin is required to recall another related Mantra which describes mother Gayatri. Thus,

मुक्ता विद्रुम हेम नील धवल छायैमुखैस्त्रिक्षणै

युक्तामिन्दुनिबद्धरत्नमुकुटांतत्त्वार्थवर्णात्मिकां ।

गायत्रीं वरदाभयांकुशकशाः शुभ्रं कपालं घदां

शङखं चक्रमथारविन्दयुगलं हस्तैवहन्तीं भजे ॥

Meaning: I meditate on the (five-faced) Goddess Gayatri, whose faces are of the hues of the pearl, coral, gold, sapphire, black, and white, of three eyes, with jeweled diadems set with the crescent moon, with scientific significance representing the Great Truth, and holding in the (ten) hands, the poses of offering refuge and boons, goad, whip, white skull, rope, conch, discus and a lotus.

What is the scientific significance (Tattvartha)? The faces, in fact represent the five particles of physics. They are the photons, quarks, leptons, Higgs boson, and gluons. These are crowned by atoms and the three eyes are protons, neutrons and electrons. The ten hands are of course the ten dimensions in the cosmos. This succinct description covers almost the entire field of physics and some of chemistry as jewels are basically chemicals and chemicals are, after all particles of physics, depending on the number of protons in their structure.

Where does gravity get included? In will be clear from the answer to this question the depth of scientific knowledge of the ancient Rishis. They noticed that of all the objects that can be observed in nature, the lotus demonstrates an explicit evidence of gravity at work! Lotus leaf doesn't repel the drop of water on its surface. The self gravity of the water molecules is greater than the gravity between the water and the surface of the leaf. In this scenario, water tends to be together because there is nothing else attracts it more than itself to break the sphere of water. This made them include lotus in the pictorial depiction of the standard model.

Summation of description: Gayatri has at the top of the crown a tilak to indicate the presence of Savitur, or Truth; there is a bright disk of sun behind her indicative of electromagnetic force; then the atoms crowning the five particles. In the centre of the crown with the jeweled diadems is the Satya Loka indicated by another tilaka. Between the eyebrows there is another tilaka to mark the Ajna chakra. She has ten hands that indicate ten dimensions. She wares gold ornaments of different size with pendants at the middle of each that are placed at neck, heart, and navel levels to represent vissudha, anahata and manipura chakras respectively. She wares an ornamental waist band which has a tilak mark in the middle to indicate swadhistana chakra. She wears a garland whose middle coincides with muladhara chakra and is marked by a tilaka. She sits on a full blossomed lotus. In the back ground is bio-diversity with lot of greenery, water source and smaller lotuses. Pranayama is symbolized by a swan in the picture shown. Gayatri herself is the embodiment of a Cell in a living system

The Invocation

ॐ भूः। ॐ भुवः। ॐ॒ सुवः। ॐ महः।

ॐ जनः। ॐ तपः। ॐ॒ सत्यम्॥

तत् सवितुर्वरेन्यम्

भर्गो देवस्य धीमहि

धियो यो नः प्रचोदयात्॥

ओमापो ज्योती रसोऽमृतब्रह्म भूर्भुवस्सुवरोम्॥

Chapter 6

Agni—The Leader

We are familiar with Albert Einstein's formula E=MC^2. He revealed that mass itself has an associated energy that can be released if the matter is destroyed. So mass and energy are equivalent. The ancient Rishis saw this phenomenon in a more comprehensive way in their Formula AUM. In this formula 'A' stands for all the four forms of energy; 'U' stands for conservation of energy and 'M' stands for transformation of energy. The universe is only a play of energy. Read on . . . .

The ancient Rishis realized that this dynamic definition of AUM is nowhere more eloquent than in the vision of the burning flame labeled Agni (fire) in the Rig Veda. Agni occupied the most important position in the outpourings of the Rishis. Out of the 10552 mantras in Rig Veda Samhita more than 2000 mantras are directly addressed to Agni. There are many other mantras which indirectly relate to Agni. Rig Veda, in fact, begins with praise to Agni. Agni basically means fire or flame. Agni is a visible form of energy (in plasma state) in nature. Three manifestations are identifiable in a flame; the energy that kindles the fire, the visible flame (photons) that sustains light and the process of gradual release of the energy (gravitational action) that takes place. The ancient Rishis realized that the fire or flame is merely a physical representation of the mighty force that drives this universe.

Have you ever wondered what is our knowledge about what is inside the Earth, strangely, very little. Modern scientists are generally agreed that the world beneath us is composed of five layers-1) the upper surface; 2) a rocky outer crust; 3) a mantle

101

of hot, viscous rock; 4) a liquid outer core and 5) a solid inner core. The distance from the surface of Earth to the middle is 6370 kilometers. Between 650 and 3000 kilometers a kind of churning processes goes on giving rise to convection currents. Scientists have also observed that the pressure at the centre of the Earth is high—something over three million times those found at the surface. They also know from the Earth's history that the inner core is very good at retaining its heat. No one knows how hot the Earth's core is but estimates range between 4,000 degrees to over 7000 degrees Celsius—about as hot as the surface of the Sun. Even less understood is the outer core which is fluid and therefore the seat of magnetism. This magnetic pole plays a vital role in keeping us alive. In the Puranas, they name it Mahavishnu (Electromagnetic Force). We seem to live on fire. It is not only at the foundation of this Earth that there is fire, even on the surface we are exposed to Sun which is another kind of fire. We shall also proceed to learn that the intermediary region also is pervaded by fire.

To an anthropologist, the discovery of fire was the first basic step of the civilized man. Discovery of fire was a most important discovery in the right direction and nothing more. All that was left for subsequent generations of mankind was the more dynamic utilization of this fire for well being of man. The ancient Rishis not only recognized this utilitarian value of Agni (fire) but were able to perceive much more significance in it. In fact, they realized that the very life force of man is dependent on fire. In a way, Agni was the visual image of God. Thus, in Brhadaranyaka Upanishad in Chapter V, ninth Brahmana, we are told to meditate on Vishvanara, the universal man, the Agni in every one of us. In this connection it is very pertinent to note the power of heat in combustion and radiation are the most important factor in the sustenance of all forms of life on earth. The rain water which sustains life is obtained from clouds formed by the evaporation of the waters of the ocean by the radiant heat of the Sun. It is the heat that makes the food edible. It is the heat in the body that digests the food. The confirming sign of the death in a human body is the absence of heat, coldness all over. The Vedic rishis went far beyond this knowledge. In their intuition, they realized that the physical power of fire is only one aspect of Agni. Agni's influence prevails in every aspect of human activity including those connected with mind and life-energy (prana). Even more, Agni is very important in achieving perfection in all human activities and attainment of the ultimate goal.

In Rig Veda two Rishis are credited with the discovery of Agni (fire).

Thus, at Mandala 5, Hymn 11, Mantra 6, Rishi Sutambhara Atreyah says:

त्वामग्ने अङ्गिरसो गुह्वा हितम् अन्वविन्दञ्छिश्रियाणं वनेवने ।

स जायसे मथ्यमानः सहो महत्त्वामाहुः सहस्पुत्रमङ्गिरः ॥

Meaning: O Agni, the Angiras sought you by their meditational power in the silence of the forest region and realized the mighty power that you are; the Son of Force they call you, O Angiras!

According to this mantra, it was Rishi Angiras who discovered fire, and the Agni was born an Angiras in him. This is more significant. Here, it is not a mere physical fire Rishi Atreyah is talking of but the fact that the visible Agni represents a mighty force—the Universal Consciousness. The Angiras Rishis and their descendents play prominent role in the exposition of many mantras in Rig Veda. The word Angiras is associated with Agni in a more basic way. The root 'Ang' for Agni is the same as the root for Angiras in the formation of the respective words. It would appear that the Rishis that went by this appellation were intimately connected with the esoteric aspect of Agni. This is evident in the Veda elsewhere, when Usha the Dawn is praised for 'Angirasahood', the quality of Angirasa (Rig Veda 7.75.1 & 7.79.3). The Angirasa Rishis have been even invested with Godhood as Nawagas and Dasagwas for their steadfast attention to Truth—Universal Consciousness.

Incidentally, explaining the word *chit (consciousness or choice less awareness) Mantrartha Manjari* distinguishes the Supreme

Spirit (bhagavach-chit) as pure and transcendental Universal Consciousness from the soul (jiva-chit) or Individual Consciousness. The former is Godhead while the latter is the deity (Agni) who resides in us.

Then, at Mandala 10, Hymn 46, Mantra 2, Rishi Vatsaprih Bhalandana says:

इमं विधन्तो अपां सधस्थे पशुं न नष्टं पदैरनु ग्मन्

गुहा चतन्तम् उशिजो नमोभिः इच्छन्तो धिरा भ्रिगवोऽविन्दन् ॥

Meaning: They (followers of Brighu) worshipped him in the session of the waters (as water contains Agni in the form of Hydrogen). They followed him by his tracks (residual in a forest conflagration), as if tracking the cow (light-rays—photons) which is lost. After meditation, Brighu the wise thinkers desired and found him (fire), hid in the secret cave (of the heart). Sage Brighu, his clansmen and descendants worshipped the physical fire (Agni) considering it a visible form of God. Sage Brighu plays a prominent role in Yajur Veda and other brahmanical texts where rituals are prescribed as means of welfare and well being of man.

Incidentally, we have to consider an important aspect regarding Rig Samhita here. According to Yaska, the samhita is the first form of Vedic corpus, because the mantras were directly and transcendentally seen by the sages as so many samhitas. It is also in samhita form it was communicated to their disciples. The import of samhita cannot be adequately or satisfactorily be ascertained merely by examining the nature, form and modification of the words. A meaning apparent to grammarians need not necessarily be the import of words in samhita. The word *Manma* used in Rig Veda 1.162.7 is very relevant in this connection. An imaginative construction by which the words become not merely articulate but eloquent with reference to the context is envisaged. It is to be noted that seers who profit by this 'manma' are described as 'viprah' (those who are especially equipped with unusual insight, transcendental vision and extraordinary intuition.) With this background we should consider Rishi Virupa Angirasa's mantra 8.44.12:

अग्निः प्रत्नेन मन्मना

शुम्भानः तत्वं स्वाम्

कविविप्रेण वावृधे ॥

Meaning: Agni the first and the foremost of the devatas (luminaries), pervading all the realms and identified with the very life of all the creatures, is described here as materializing his own form and growing in splendor, by the ancient 'manma'. He is the Kavi (seer) and he grows by each illumined 'viprah' (sages, who had a vision of Consciousness). It is quite obvious; the Rishi is not talking of kindled variety of fire here.

There are ten Apri Sooktas in the whole of Rig Veda. Each Apri Sookta has 5 to 6 Mantras in the beginning, dedicated to Agni in almost similar vein. These Apri sooktas are the vision of the respective Rishis. We have choosen in this instance the vision of Rishi Agasytah Maithravarunih as revealed in Mandala 1, Sookta 188, Mantras 1-5, thus:

समिद्धो अद्य राजसि देवो देवैः सहस्रजित् ।

दूतो हव्या कविर्वह ॥१॥

Meaning: O passionate flame, shining, you conquer along with luminaries, thousands. O seer, O messenger, convey the offerings (to the luminaries).

तनूनपात् ऋतं यते मध्वा यज्ञः समज्यते ।

दधत् सहस्रिणीः इषः ॥२॥

Meaning: Agni (individual consciousness) goes to the Truth (universal consciousness), the goal of the journey. He is united with the yajna (journey) along with love (Soma). He establishes (in the aspirant) the impulsions in thousands.

आजुह्वानो न ईड्यो देवाँ आ वक्षि यज्ञियान् ।

अग्ने सहस्रसा असि ॥३॥

Meaning: O Agni (individual consciousness), who is invoked and adored by us, bring the luminaries of the sacrifice (journey). O Agni you are a giver of thousands.

प्राचीनं बर्हिः ओजसा सहस्रवीरम् स्तृणन् ।

यत्रादित्या विराजथ ॥४॥

Meaning: An ancient seat of grass is spread (The space of wideness of other divinities) by the might of thousand horses. There the (Adityas) protons shine.

विराट् सम्राट् विभ्वीः बह्वीश्च भुयसीश्च याः ।

दुरो घृतानि अक्षरन् ॥५॥

Meaning: The divine doors (within) are anointed with Light. Light that comes into being like an emperor, in all his royal might, as ruler (over subjective and objective existence) in great abundance, and all pervading.

If the Angirasa Rishis identified Agni with Individual Consciousness that has an eternal tendency to merge with Universal Consciousness, the Brighu Rishis saw Agni as a Purohit (leader in the forefront) in a ritual called Yajna. The word Yajna means a sacrifice. The Yajna is an elaborate process performed in a sacrificial ground; there is a sacred alter in which the holy oblations are offered through the instrumentality of the sacred fire; there is the blazing fire in the alter in the holy atmosphere of the sacrifice; and there is a substance offered, the sacrament. Certain ideas are entertained in the mind of the Yajamana (the organizer) which are conveyed through the recitation of *Mantras*. It is believed that Agni will deliver the offerings to the respective deities invoked in the progress of the Yajna. On completion of the Yajna, it is believed all the deities are pleased and they bestow their blessings on the organizers. Besides this physical aspect, the word Yajna has a more significant and deep connotation in the Vedas. This connotation has been elaborately dealt with in Chhandogya Upanishad in the 5th Chapter, sections 3 to 24. The Upanishad tells us that the whole universal activity of creation may be conceived as such a kind of sacrifice (Yajna) in what is known as Panchagni Vidya, or knowledge regarding five fires.

First the philosophical background governing the Vidya implied in Chandogya Upanishad. If we are unable to visualize the internal connection involved in a particular process of creation, we would not be free from the clutches of those forces which are responsible for this creation. Also, unless we have a practical living knowledge of the various factors that are involved in the process of manifestation, or creation, we cannot be free from the law of manifestation. Births and deaths are part of this universal process. What we call the universal process of manifestation is inclusive of every event that takes place anywhere, in any manner, including the experiences we have in our life. The Upanishad makes out the point that no event or experience is isolated from other experiences. Just as every performance or every item or ritual in a sacrifice is connected to every other item, the whole *Yajna,* or the sacrifice in a single comprehensive act of which the various items are only parts internally connected, the whole universal manifestation is a single process. If we can contemplate the internal connection that obtains between the effects that are visible with the causes that are invisible, then we would be free from the clutches, or the harassments, of these laws which are operating outside us. Everything is interconnected, interlinked in an organic manner, so that everything becomes as important as the other. It is interesting to note that modern science also has arrived at a similar conclusion.

Classical physics that prevailed in the west till close of 19th century supported the world view of determinism. Determinism—the world view that nature and our own life are completely determined from past to future—reflects the human need for certainty in an uncertain world. In a way the projection of that need is God, a creation of man's fertile imagination! According to the classical physicists, the universe was like a perfect clock. Once we knew the position of its parts at one instant, they would remain specified forever. Of course, human beings cannot know the positions and velocities of all the particles in the universe at one instant. But the perfect mind of God would know the configuration of all the particles, past and future. With Max Born's statistical interpretation of Broglie-Schrodinger wave function, physicists finally renounced the deterministic world view of nature. With the arrival of 20th century, the world changed from having the determinism of a clock to having the contingency of a pinball machine. Physicists realized that the concept of the perfect all-knowing mind of God has no support in nature. Quantum theory-that replaced classical physics—makes only statistical predictions. In Quantum theory, only probabilities are precisely determined.

In 1927, Werner Heisenberg realized that quantum theory contained some strange predictions. It implied that experiments could never be done in complete isolation because the very act of measurement affected the outcome. He expressed this connection in his Uncertainty Principle—you cannot simultaneously measure both the position and momentum of a subatomic particle (or equivalent its energy at an accurate time). If you know one the other is always uncertain. This uncertainty, he argued, was a deep consequence of quantum mechanics—it has nothing to do with a lack of skill or accuracy in measuring. The better we know the position, the hazier will its momentum be and vice versa. The fundamental importance of the uncertainty principle is that it expresses the limitation of our classical concepts in a precise mathematical form. In short the physicists have realized that at atomic level matter (particles) are both destructible and indestructible; where matter is both continuous and discontinuous, and force and matter are but different aspects of the same phenomenon. At the atomic level matter manifests itself in ways which seem to be mutually exclusive; that particles are also waves, waves are also particles. The subatomic world appears as a web of relations between the various parts of a whole. Our classical notions, derived from our ordinary macroscopic experience, are not fully adequate to describe this world. To begin with, the concept of a distinct physical entity, like a particle, is an idealization which has no fundamental significance. It can only be defined in terms of its connection to the whole, and these connections are of a statistical nature—probabilities rather than certainties.

What we are about to learn regarding the phenomena according to the ancient postulates have also been researched by modern science extensively and the results are, as usual, astonishingly similar. Two elements and a molecule are under consideration here, Hydrogen (Varuna), and Prana (Oxygen) and Apas (water). In the Panchagni Vidya, the first three postulates refer to Hydrogen as fire. The remaining two postulates being entrenched in the atmosphere, Oxygen acts as fire and Water as the base. In the ultimate analysis they are all Atoms, only the proton numbers in the nuclei vary.

We shall now revert back to Chandogya Upanishad as mentioned above. The Upanishad says there are various stages of manifestation. As an example a specific type of manifestation is under contemplation. The birth of a child is considered. We only think that the child is born from the womb of the mother. This knowledge is the least type of knowledge that one can have about the birth of a child. It is a tremendous process that takes place throughout the cosmos. The whole universe vibrates with action even if a single child is to be born somewhere in the corner of a house. It is not a private affair of a little child coming out unknown somewhere in a nook and corner of the world, as people ignorantly believe. The whole universe feels the presence and the birth of a single child anywhere. What produces the child is not the father or the mother; it is the whole cosmos that produces the child. The offspring maybe a human baby, a sub-human one or a super-human form it does not matter. Whatever is the character of that offspring, even if it may be an organic production, an atom, or an electron, or the composition of a molecule, the birth of it is regarded as the birth of a child, and it is made possible by the operation of cosmic factors. As we saw earlier everything in this universe is interconnected. Our two dimensional finite mind and senses are incapable of comprehending this interconnectedness. Evidently, there is no such thing as private act in this world. To say that the new born baby is my son or daughter in the above example is not appropriate. It is the baby of the universe. It belongs to where it has come from. It has come from every cell of the universe. It has not come merely from the seminal essence of the father or the womb of the mother, as we generally believe. It is the quintessence of every particle of the whole of Nature. That is why Sastras say, the Brahmanda (the universal egg) is in the Pindanda (lumpy egg—man). The macrocosm is in the microcosm. Therefore the nature which produced the child will take care of it and withdraw it for reason best known to universal law alone. This then is the philosophical background of the *Vidya* Known as *Panchagni-Vidya*.

Panchagni-Vidya makes a grand point. Things are not what they appear to be. Behind every process of activity in nature, there is a deeper significance. This deeper significance is the invisible aspect of every phase of our visible practical existence from day to day. We cannot claim that events suddenly develop and become visible to us, as if by magic in a single stroke. Take the event of a thunder. We do not know the sudden development of a thunder, except when it is visible and heard. There is an immediate rainfall followed by winds. We feel the dampness and cold. Ere long the rain stops and suddenly it is hot. These are natural phenomena from our point of view, but they are supernatural mysteries in the vision of the Upanishads. Events first take place in the highest heaven, then their presence is felt gradually as they come down to our level of grossness, visibly and tangibly as in the case of a disease. The illness does not manifest itself suddenly in the physical body. It happens deep inside first. The seed is sown within, so to say. The external symptoms are the last stage as it were. There appears to be a transcendental secret behind every event that occurs, whether in the world at large or within each one of us.

Continuing the earlier example, contrary to our belief, the birth of a human child in this world does not take place in this world alone, exclusively. The birth takes place in the highest region first, and the impact of this birth is felt in the lower levels until it gets visible to the physical eyes in the mortal world. This child has not come suddenly from above. There has been a complicated preceding interior process which is invisible to our ordinary vision. This is so of not only human beings, but it is so with the coming of every event in this world. Panchagni-Vidya deals with all such events and not merely birth of a human child alone. The Vidya postulates that there is a total activity, in a subtle form, taking place prior to the apparently individual expression of it in the form of expression and perception. In the Upanishad, the king, Pravahana Jaivali, in his mode of instruction, speaks to Gautama, the sage who is now the king's disciple awaiting initiation into the secrets of Panchagni-Vidya.

असौ वाव लोको गौतमाग्निस्तस्यादित्य एव समिद्रश्मयो

धूमोऽहऽरर्चिश्चन्द्रमा अङ्गारा नक्षत्राणि विस्फुलिङ्गाः ॥१ ॥

तस्मिन्नेतस्मिन्नग्नौ देवाः श्रद्धां जुह्वति

तस्या आहुतेः सोमो रजा सम्भवति ॥२ ॥

Meaning: "The Yonder World, O Gautama, is, indeed, the fire. Here the Sun is the fuel; the Light-rays are the smoke; the day is the flame; the moon is the coals; the stars are the sparks. In this Fire, the gods (luminaries) offer faith. From this oblation arises King Soma (Love)."

If we reflect a little, we shall realize that all creative processes in nature are outcome of sacrifice or Yajna. Look at the limbs of the human anatomy. No organ of the body works for its own sake but works for the overall intention of the organic body. Similarly, look at the working of a machine. The different component parts do not have their own agenda. They work for the production performance of the machine as a whole. So also in the case of a sacrifice, every part of the sacrifice is as important as any other part, and every part of the sacrifice sub-serves a purpose transcendent to it. This principle operates in every type of creative activity, whether physical, social, and aesthetic or for that matter any other aspect of life. Everything is interconnected, interlinked in an organic manner, so that everything becomes as important as other. Perhaps, this is what late J. Krishnamurti frequently alluded to when he said that we should develop non-fragmentary perception of things in life. If this inter-relatedness of the parts of the sacrifice is lost sight of, it ceases to be a meditation.

Meditation is the gathering by the mind all the parts of the psychic organ into a focused organic action. Panchagni-Vidya is such a meditation. It is contemplation by the mind in perceiving the reality that is transcendent to the visible parts of the inner sacrifice. The Upanishad now tells us that the initial vibration propelling any kind of activity or event in this world takes place first, in a higher realm. There is a hierarchy of causes cascading downward each effect becoming the cause not as a single factor but a chain of factors leading downward to the level of finite space/time reality. The immediate transcendent cause is the effect of a still higher cause and so on till the initial cause. Thus, the first cause is the true cause. The expressed form in space and time alone is known, seen, felt and experienced by us. We mistake this visible effect alone for everything and we feel the pleasure or pain thereof. In this connection likes and dislikes are only reactions of our personalities. The impersonal causes of the phenomena have nothing to do with our personal likes and dislikes or pleasure and pain.

The phrase "Yonder World" used by King Pravahana Jaivali refers to an invisible region which we may say is the highest heaven. It could be heaven or any other name, the label does not matter. The primal cause for an event in the lowest finite atmospheric world we live can be traced to these celestial regions, regions which are super-physical, beyond even the astral realm, which are the causes of what we observe in the atmospheric region. By and large, every phenomenon in our world is, controlled by the Sun. It would not be an exaggeration to say that our very existence in this world is regulated by the Sun. But, who is the cause of the Sun? The Sun is also effect of some factors; which are precedent to the formation of the Sun. Astronomers tell us that Stars, of which the Sun is supposed to be one, are formed out of the condensation of nebular dust, forming what is known as Milky Way, which form themselves into rotating and flaming masses. While we have no knowledge as to the cause of such formation, there should naturally, be some vibration behind them. The vibration is anterior and precedent to what we call the manifestation of even the causal condition of this world. Prior to all this, something else must be there, and prior to that again, another thing, and so on, so that even our insignificant life in this world, in this physical body, can be said to be completely controlled by factors which are transcendent, beyond the Sun and Moon and the Stars, and where we go in this manner of tracing our cause back, we do not know. We shall reach levels that are imperceptible to the eyes and beyond thought. This is the point implanted into the mind of Gautama the disciple by King Pravahana Jaivali explaining the Panchagni-Vidya.

The theme of sacrifice is very important in the contemplation or meditation on the descent of the celestial realm of the cosmos. We have already noted what a traditional sacrifice involves. We also noted that the sacrifice have parts or limbs. The world which is called the celestial realm is itself the sacrificial Fire into which oblations are offered. Elsewhere we have referred to this world as Tapo Loka or to take the help of Astronomy the region of Novae and Supernovae which are subject to gigantic explosions and generating conflagrations of unimaginable magnitude. The fuel, which ignites the Fire (invariably Hydrogen or silicon) and causes the flames to rise up in this sacrifice, is the Sun (which is, no doubt, Hydrogen powered). Just like the smoke arises from the Fire in a sacrifice, we contemplate the emanation of the rays of the Sun, symbolically. As the flames shine, so is the shining of the Day-time due to the Fire of the Sun in the sacrifice. We may compare the embers, remaining after the flames subside in a sacrifice, to the Moon who is something like the subsidence of the flames of the light of the Sun, or we may say, the comparison is made because moonlight arises generally when the Sun's flame subside in the horizon. Compare the Stars to the sparks which are ejected from the flames of the Fire, because they are scattered, as it were, in the sky.

What is our connection with these higher regions of the world? The shining of the sun or the moon, the twinkling of the stars, or the blowing of the winds,—all these phenomena are vitally connected with our own life here. Our life is related to every phenomenon outside, and vice versa. While our way of living has something to do with the activity of the world outside, our life is also dependent on that activity. There is a mutual dependence between the outer world and the inner life of the individual. Our thoughts influence the atmosphere. Thoughts and modes of living are vibrations that we set up around us. It is not some isolated activity taking place within our heads. When we think, we do not privately think inside our skulls; it is a vibration that we create in us. And the vibration of a person is not merely in the physical body; it emanates like an aura to a certain distance from the body of the person. The distance to which the aura goes depends upon the intensity of the aura, or the intensity of the thoughts, or the force of the vibration. This is the principle behind the advice that we must have the company of good people and avoid bad company, because the vibrations interact. Thus, we can be influenced by the atmosphere around us. There is a vibration that is generated within every person whenever a thought occurs. Whenever we think something, whenever we feel something deeply, even when we speak something, there is a vibration generated because we do not speak without thinking. There is a thought behind every action or speech. Naturally, if we take into consideration the cumulative effect of the vibrations, produced by all the individuals in the world, we can well imagine the effect of the vibrations they produce. They disturb the whole atmosphere; they create a magnetic field in the atmospheric realm. And the total effect of the psychic influences set up by the individuals in the world obviously influences the conditions of the manifestation of natural forces. Our thoughts in the form of vibration therefore obstruct the movement of the natural forces; can impede their activity; in short, we can interfere with their natural way of working.

Based on this concept of the relationship of our life with the activity of the nature outside, the Upanishad tells us that our actions are like an oblation offered in the sacrifice. Our activities are not mere impotent movements of the physical body or limbs; they are effective interferences in the way of Nature. When we pour *ghee or charu* (oblation) into the flaming fire in a sacrifice, we are naturally modifying the nature of the burning of the fire. Much depends on what we pour into it. If we throw mud into it, well, the fire is put out. If we pour *ghee* into it the fire glows bright and rising. Likewise, is the activity of the human being or, for that matter, any other being. The interference by a human activity in the working of Nature is an important point to consider in the performance of the sacrifice. If we coordinate and cooperate with the activity of the Nature, it becomes a Yajna, but if we interfere with it and adversely affect its normal function, it will also set up a reaction of a similar character. Invariably, we would be the losers. Whether we like it or not, we offer our actions as oblations in this sacrifice of natural phenomena. Every one of our actions produces an effect called *Apurva* (not before), that occurs in the process of the thought that underlies it. Every action is preceded by a thought and thought is a vibration as we have already observed. Every vibration impinges upon its atmosphere. It has an effect produced in the environment, and this subtle effect that the action produces, invisible to the eye though, is called *Apurva.* As we are the causes of this *Apurva,* or the effects of the actions, we would be the reapers of the fruits of these actions. The whole point of the foregoing description in the context of the Panchagni-Vidya is to tell us that the higher realms are activated by the consequences produced by our action here, and those very consequences of action become the cause of our descent, later, in the reverse order. Earlier, we tried to understand the meaning of *Manma,* in this context the teaching is not to be taken literally in a purely grammatical sense. It is a highly esoteric technique needing deep contemplation.

पर्जन्यो वाव गौतमग्निस्तस्य वायुरेव समिदभ्रं

धुमो विद्युदर्चिरशनिरङ्गारा ह्लादनयो विस्फुलिङ्गाः ॥

तस्मिन्नतस्मिन्नग्नो देवाः सोमं राजानं जुह्वति तस्या

आहुतेर्वर्षꣳ सम्भवति ॥

Meaning: Parjanya (the deity of rain) is indeed the fire, O Gautama. Of that, the air is the fuel, the cloud is the smoke, the lightning is the flame, the thunderbolt is the embers and the rumbling of the thunder are the sparks. Into this fire the deities offer the oblation of King Soma. Out of that oblation rain arises.

In the previous section the king made a mention of 'Yonder World'. Now he says the rain deity represents a region below. Rain deity is *Parjanya here.* When rain falls, it is not merely some isolated event that takes place, somewhere. Rainfall is not an unconnected activity; it is also a universal phenomenon. Many factors go to play their roles in the production of rain. There is a vibration in the higher realms first, and as mentioned, these vibrations are, to some extent, influenced by our own deeds here. So, whether there is a good rainfall or not has something to do with how we live in this world. The lower realms, which are concerned with the production of rain, are to be contemplated as a sacrifice. Every stage of development is a sacrifice; it is a meditation. The principle of rainfall, we may call it the rain deity or *Parjanya*, is the Fire in the sacrifice. The fire is stirred into action by *Vayu,* the wind that blows. We consider the Wind as the fuel which ignites the Fire of this sacrifice. When there is such a stimulation taking place in the atmosphere, Clouds are formed. Similar to a smoke that arises from the fire of a sacrifice, as the flaming force of the Fire, *Abhram,* the Clouds, forming themselves into a thick layer are the effects of this internal activity of the atmosphere by the action of the wind etc. in a particular direction. The Clouds are the smoke of this sacrifice. The brilliance of the Flames in this sacrifice is the flashing forth of the lightning, *Vidyut,* through the clouds. We know how bright the flames are in a Sacrificial Alter. We have to contemplate here, in the context of rainfall, the flashing of the lightning as the blazing, brilliant flames of the fire. The clap of the thunders may be considered to be the embers remaining after the subsidence of the flames in a sacrifice. The rumbling of the clouds after a heavy rainfall, which we hear from all quarters are the sparks, as it were of this Fire. This is a meditation because the region of rainfall is stirred into action by the vibrations that take place earlier in a higher plane. Rain is the cause of all food stuffs.

प्रिथिवी वाव गौतमाग्निस्तस्याः सम्वत्सर एव समिदकाशो धूमो

रात्रिरर्चिर्दिशोऽङ्गारा अवान्तरादिशो विस्पुलिङ्गाः ॥

तस्मिन्नेतस्मिन्नग्नौ देवा वर्षं जुह्वति तस्या आहुतेरन्नꣳ सम्भवति ॥

Meaning: The Earth is, indeed, the Fire, O Gautama. Of that, the Year is the fuel, the Sky is the smoke, the Night is the flame, the Quarters are the embers, the intermediary Quarters are the sparks. "Into this Fire, the Deities offer the oblation of rain. Out of that oblation, arises food."

The Earth as the Fire is an object of meditation. We contemplate the whole Earth as the Fire in the third stage of the cosmic sacrifice recommended by Panchagni Vidya for meditation. The Earth is a sacrificial Fire. The productive capacity of the Earth depends upon another factor, viz., the cyclic changes produced by the process of time. The Time factor has an important part to play here. What we call time is, in fact, the effect produced by the rotation of the earth on its axis and its revolution round the sun, and the effect that the sun produces, consequently, upon this earth. This is called the *Samvatsara,* or the year. The Year is the time factor involved in the capacity of the Earth to produce food-stuff. Because the Year is the inciting factor in the production of food-stuff in the world, it is called *Samit,* or Fuel, for it is what causes the blazing of the

117

Fire of the sacrifice. Just as smoke rises up from the Fire, we contemplate the whole sky as if it is a dome that is rising from the Fire of the Earth. Just as flames rise from the Fire in a sacrifice, the Fire from the Earth is cause of the rise of the flame, the particular phenomenon called night (We may include the day also because it is the reverse of the coin, so to say). We know that day and night are the result of the rotation of Earth on its axis. Inasmuch as Earth is the cause of day and night, even as the Fire is the cause of rising Flame, in this meditation we are to regard the night and day as the Flame in the sacrifice. The Quarters are the embers, because they are calm and quiet, looking apparently undisturbed by the movements that take place in the world. When we look at the horizon, we feel a sense of calmness, as though it is the subsidence of activity, like the embers after the flame subsides. Like sparks from the Fire, which moves in different directions, we have the Intermediary Quarters of the heavens which are in different directions, which are to be contemplated as if they are Sparks in the sacrifice.

In the previous vidya we were informed how rains arise as gift of the deities. In the present vidya, we are informed how the same deities bless us by production of food stuff. The same deities are the presiding deities of the senses. Therefore there is an intimate connection between our sense activity and the deities in heaven. Unless there is a harmonious give-and-take understanding between us and Nature, Nature will not give anything to us. Nature gives us what we give to it in the form of our own deeds in this world. We do not get what we do not deserve, and we cannot get what we have not given actually. It requires little imagination to realize the involvement of Atom of science in all these activities, known by the nomenclature Indra in the Vedas.

पुरुषो वाव गौतमाग्निस्तस्य वागेव समित्प्राणो

धुमो जिह्वार्चिर्श्चक्षुरङ्गारा श्रोत्रं विस्पुलिङ्गाः ॥

तस्मिन्नेतस्मिन्नग्नौ देवा अन्नं जुह्वति तस्या आहुते रेतः सम्भवति ॥

Meaning: Man indeed is the fire, O Gautama. Of that speech is the fuel, Prana is the smoke, the tongue is the flame, the eye is the embers and the ear is the sparks. Into this fire the deities offer the oblation of food. Out of that oblation seed arises.

It is fairly simple to understand that it is by speech man shines among his fellow beings. As fuel brightens the fire in a sacrifice, so speech brightens man. Prana goes out of the mouth just as smoke goes out of the fire in a sacrifice. Not only the tongue and flame are red, they both feel the heat. The eyes are the embers because they both contain light. As the sparks are scattered about, the ears also turn around to all sides to receive sounds.

योषा वाव गौतमाग्निस्तस्या उपस्थ एव समिद्धुपमन्त्रयते स

धुमो योनिरर्चिर्यदन्तःकरोति तेऽङ्गारा अभिनन्दा विस्फुलिङ्गाः ॥

तस्मिन्नेतस्मिन्नग्नो देवा रतो जुह्वति तस्या आहुतेर्गर्भः सम्भवति ॥

Meaning: Woman indeed is the Fire, O Gautama. Into this fire the deities offer the oblation of the seed. Out of that oblation the foetus arises.,

इति तु पञ्चम्यामाहुतावापः पुरुषवचसो भवन्तीति स उल्बावृतो

गर्भो दश वा नव वा मासानन्तः शयित्वा यावद्धाथ जायते ॥

Meaning: At the fifth oblation, (the oblation called water) comes to be designated as man. That foetus, covered with membrane, lies within (the mother's womb), more or less, for nine or ten months, and is then born.

From water, through gradual development the foetus arises and in this development water (two parts of Hydrogen and one part of Oxygen—H_2O) is the predominating element. At the fifth oblation this water turns in to a child.

स जातो यावदायुषं जीवति तं प्रेतं दिष्टमितोऽग्रय

एव हरन्ति यत एवेतो यतः सम्भूतो भवति ॥

Meaning: Having born, man lives whatever the length of his life span. When he is dead, as ordained, they carry him from here (for cremation) to fire itself from which alone he came, arose.

So, one who knows these five Fires, is free. It is difficult to know these Fires unless we live a life of meditation. One's whole life should be one of meditation. Our meditation should not mean merely a little act of half-an-hour's closing of the eyes and thinking something ethereal. It is a way of living throughout. When you see a thing, you see only in this way; when you speak, you speak from this point of view; when you think, this is at the background of the thought. Thus, you cease to be an ordinary human being when you live a life of this Upanishad. You are conditioned by this great knowledge, and it becomes, therefore a liberator of your soul. Even if you are in the midst of atmospheres which are not conducive, you shall be free from contamination, because no such thing as undesirable exists for such a person. The knower becomes co-extensive with the way in which Nature works in all its ways. And everything is nature working some way, desirable as well as undesirable, as we may call it. We become commensurate with the way in which Nature works in everyway because of the constant meditation conducted by us in this manner. Accordingly, we cannot be harmed by any atmosphere, by anyone or by anything that is around us. Perhaps, on the other hand, we may be able to influence positively the atmosphere in which we are living. When late J. Krishnamurti used to be frequently asked why he continues his lectures, since he has no motive to do so, and his reply used to be mostly on these lines. He was very dedicated to Nature.

Now it is the turn of another great king Asvapati to explain another vidya known as 'Prana-Agnihotra'. Six great scholars of the time approached him and sought his help in understanding the secret knowledge regarding the self as the universal whole. The king acknowledges that all of them are sincere in their respective meditations and honest in their pursuit. But they are not aware of the pitfalls in their meditations. In the beginning, everything looks all right even in an erroneous meditation, but afterwards some difficulty arises, which cannot be rectified even by the best of medicines. They have considered some parts of the whole as the whole. They have mistaken the finite for infinite. As mind and thinking are wedded to a finite outlook, they cannot conceive of the infinite whole. The scholars' objects of meditation like Sun, Earth, Water, Space etc. are all finite. Furthermore, the scholars were conceiving these objects as Atman, as though Atman is an external object. How can Atman be outside one? Atman is your own self, within you. It amounts to an outlook where your own self is a non-self, a contradiction. In this context it is well to remember the axiom which late J.Krishnamurti was fond of quoting: "Many parts cannot make the whole". Perhaps the scholars were planning to understand the Great Being, little by little, part by part, gradually. Gradually we hope to realize the Truth. This gradual process inducts time element which is a finite activity as late J. Krishnamurti used to say. Truth is always in the present and hence it does not permit of a gradual process. One cannot realize the Great Being gradually.

Through these discrete forms of meditation that the scholars were pursuing, they may obtain different benefits, but by a process of total meditation all the benefits accrue in one stroke, which is the meditation of Vaishvanara Atman. A man who contemplates in the mind the true Vaishvanara as that which extends from the earth to the heavens, and from heavens to the earth; from the topmost level to the lowest level, missing no link whatsoever, visualizes the whole. That man who so contemplates becomes the self of every being all at once. One becomes the Self of all the worlds; he becomes the Self of anything that can be anywhere; and becomes the possessor of the glory of anything that exists anywhere, in any realm, in any form, and in any circumstance. All the parts that the scholars were meditating upon are various limbs of the cosmic body. All these limbs have to be brought together and conceived as a whole, at once in the consciousness, without missing anyone limb whatsoever, by feeling oneness with Earth, Water, Sun, Air, Space and Heavens.

One who so meditates cannot stand outside this Great Object of meditation. Due to metamorphosis of his personality, he becomes the Great Object himself. Whatever action he does becomes the action of Vaishvanara Atman. Then such a man's action becomes a Cosmic Sacrifice, just as the deities thought Creation as a Universal Sacrifice in the Purusha-Sukta of Rig-Veda Mandala 10, Hymn 90. Thus the daily activity proceeding from an individual who meditates as mentioned above, would be a Cosmic Sacrifice. This sacrifice is called the Prana-Agnihotra, the sacred oblation at the Universal Alter of the Fire of the Absolute. The fact of the organic connection of the individual with the Vaishvanara implies that there are cosmic aspects operating even in the individual, just as everything that is in the Ocean is also in the wave, notwithstanding the difference between the crest called the wave and the body which is the ocean. Thus, the meditation by the individual on the cosmic, or the Vaishvanara, means the establishment of an inner coordination and the effectuation of non-difference between the meditating principle and the object that is meditated upon. If every function that is going on in the individual is ultimately inseparable from the Universal, meditation is just awareness of this fact. The simple acts such as eating, drinking, breathing and working becomes universally significant. They are not private deeds or individual affairs, as they are usually taken to be. The Upanishad points out that, ultimately, there are no such things as individuals. To keep focused, we are asked to recapitulate a universal invocation even during the performance of an individual action.

In the Prana-Agnihotra, or the sacrificial offering to the Universal Fire, the food that we take daily is a holy oblation to the All-pervading Vital Fire. Ritualistically, the Agnihotra means the daily performance of a Yajna, by a householder. The Upanishad points out that this Agnihotra is perpetually taking place in our own bodies, of which we have to be conscious in our meditation, and there is no such thing as external anymore to the person who meditates on Vaishvanara. There is no such thing as external action, because everything we regard as external is internal to Vaishvanara. Even late J. Krishnamurti used to say that there are no two worlds as external and internal. External is internal and internal is external, like the waves that come to the shores and then go back to the ocean.

The three ritual fires which the householders exoterically worship in their houses are called *Garhapatya, Anvaharyapachana and Ahavaniya*. These three sacrifices are internally constituted in the individual, in the act of this meditation. These fires are within the body of Virat, the Vaishvanara Himself. As we are inseparable from Vaishvanara, these fires are inside our own Self. Thus, when we offer food into the mouth, it is not an animal act that we are performing for the satisfaction of the bodily organism, but an ultimate impulse that is arising out from the Universal Reality. Hunger is not merely a function of the stomach. It is something wider than what we are, indicating that we are related to something vaster than what we seem to be from our points of view. The food we take is digested with the help of Vaishvanara Fire. It is not the physical body alone that is working in digestion, because the physical body is visible even in a corpse, but there is no such heat there. What has happened to the heat? That heat is not the heat of any physical fire; it is not the heat of any chemical compounds in action in the body. The Upanishad identifies this heat, which is the living force in us, with the Ultimate Reality, called Vaishvanara here, or the Universal Fire, is what consumes everything. The Vaishvanara operates with five Pranas: Prana, Apana, Vyana, Samana and Udana. The food we eat is digested by the action of Pranas. The process of Prana Agnihotra mentioned here, is the act of introducing a universal significance into what are apparently individual functions. There is an invisible link identified between the five Pranas and the natural phenomena in the meditation which one should be conscious of.

When we sit to eat our food, we are expected to take only five morsels in the beginning, and with the intake of each morsel we have to say, Pranaya Swaha, Apanaya Swaha, Vyanaya Swaha, Samanaya Swaha and with the last morsel Udanaya Swaha, to commence the meditation. Thus, through the Prana, we touch the cosmic border and invoke the Universal being. In this meditation, there is an attempt at universal satisfaction and not merely some individual's pleasure, in the act of eating, drinking, etc. When the Prana is satisfied, the Upanishad says, due to an inward connection, the eyes are satisfied. When we eat food and have a square meal, we feel a satisfaction opening up from the eyes. When the eyes are satisfied, the Sun is satisfied, because he is the presiding deity of the eyes. When the Sun is satisfied, the whole atmosphere is satisfied, because Sun is also the presiding deity of entire atmosphere. If the atmosphere is satisfied, whatever is the support of both the atmosphere and Sun is satisfied and ultimately Vaishvanara is satisfied.

So is the case with every other morsel that we eat. We then take the second morsel for the satisfaction of Vyana, the other aspect of Energy, the all-pervading force within. Vyana is responsible for the movement of the blood streams in the canals of the body. This is the meditation with this second morsel of food. There are some internal mystical connections, such that when Vyana is satisfied the Ears are satisfied. Everything that is around us in the form of the directions is satisfied from which sounds come and impinge upon the ears. Then the causes behind this phenomenon are also satisfied. Thus Vaishvanara is satisfied.

Then the third morsel should be taken for the satisfaction of Apana. When the Apana is satisfied Speech is satisfied. With satisfaction of Speech, fire is satisfied, which is the superintending principle over Speech. With the satisfaction of fire, the very Earth is satisfied and so Vaishvanara is satisfied.

The fourth offering, or the morsel we take, should be for the satisfaction of Samana. When the Samana is satisfied, the mind is satisfied. Samana is the central acting force that immediately acts on the mind. When the mind is satisfied, everything that is connected with the mind, the rain deity and the heavens are satisfied. Vaishvanara is satisfied.

Then the fifth and last offering is for the satisfaction of Udana. When Udana is satisfied, the tactile sense is satisfied. Thereby its deity Air is satisfied. When Air is satisfied, its abode, Sky (space) is satisfied. The cause behind this phenomenon is satisfied. Vaishvanara is satisfied.

Thus, the Upanishad point of view is that a rightly conducted human activity, such as the intake of food, with a meditation on the universal implication of one's existence, will touch the corners of creation. The satisfaction of performer of this kind of meditation, the performer of the Vaishvanara-Agnihotra Vidya, shall be for the blessedness of all mankind, nay, in the whole creation. He will be blessed with plenty and glory.

Let us see, the influence of Vaishvanara Vidya on modern science. The scientists constantly meditate with the help of their mathematical tools, on all the natural forces such as Protons; Gravitational force; Fire; Dimensions other than space and time; Atoms; Oxygen and other constituents of the air, and Water, which are the true cause of this universe, even like the six scholars of King Asvapati's times. Accordingly, the scientists enjoy prosperity and glory but invariably reach a watershed in their quest. Only in the recent years the quest for a Unified Force has gathered momentum. This Unified Forced was labeled, the Vaishvanara Agni or the Universal Consciousness with which Angirasa Rishis were constantly associated. Vaishvanara is Agni in the individual self is confirmed both by Saunaka (Brhadevata 2, 18) and endorsed by the great authority of Yaska in 8000 BCE. We have already seen earlier that this Agni is the individual consciousness as per Mantrartha Manjari.

Chapter 7

Indra—The Maker of Illusion

Matter and Spirit are two sides of the same coin. One may look at the universe from the spiritual point of view or look at it from the material point of view, what we see will be essentially the same phenomena. The difference is only in the label. This is nowhere more eloquent than when we consider Deity Indra of Veda or Atom of modern science. Read on . . .

Indra is a very familiar Devata (luminary) in the Rig Veda. Out of the 10552 Mantras in the Veda, nearly 2500 of them are devoted to Indra. That is nearly 25%. It is further stated that hymns that do not carry a mention of a specific Devata (luminary) should be considered as addressed to Indra. In fact, all devatas other than Agni and Surya may be regarded as Indra alone. In science we know it as atom and its particles. Indra is inseparable from his Vajra Astra (electron). What does the Indra label indicate that it is so important in the Veda?

Rishi Jeta Madhuchchhandasah has the following vision of Indra (Atom) in Rig Veda Mandala 1 Sukta 11 Mantra 4:

पुरां भिन्दुर्युवा कविरमितौजा अजायत ।

इन्द्रो विश्वस्य कर्मणो धर्ता वज्री पुरुष्टुतः ॥४ ॥

Meaning: O Indra, you are born in the seeker, in the first place as a Seer who is unlimited in strength. You are also the sustainer of all actions in the universe. You are armed with Vajra.

126

Even modern science informs us that Atom (Indra) is responsible for creation of all forms and structures in this universe, including man. In our body it is in great strength, literally billions of them. Atom (Indra) wields great power due to Electrons (Vajra) which is an inseparable part of Atom (Indra). Primarily, these negatively charged electrons (Vajra) keep positively charged protons and neutrons (Ashwin Twins) with neutral charge apart in the nucleus of an Atom (Indra), so that a nuclear reaction does not take place. Electromagnetic force (Mahavishnu) operates through the electron (Vajra) in the structure of an Atom (Indra) and deposits Photons (Ray Cows from Swar world).

In an earlier Mantra, at Mandala 1, Sukta 6, Mantra3, Rishi Madhuchchhandah Vaishvamitrah had the following vision:

केतुं कृण्वन्नकेतवे पेशो मर्या अपेशसे ।

समुषद्भिरजायथाः ॥३॥

Meaning: O Indra (Atom), besides giving a form you also generate cognition in man. You have an inborn knowledge.

In science we learn that photons (ray-cows of swar world) are deposited in the structure of Atoms (Indra). These photons (ray-cows) awaken Consciousness in us. The awakening is the dawn of knowledge.

Rudradyaya occurs in Krishna Yajurveda Taittiriya-Samhita, Kanda 4, Prapathaka 5. In 1-11 Anuvakas, Rudra-Shiva is praised in beautiful poetry. Anuvakas 1. 10 and 11 are riks and the rest are Yajus Mantras. Strictly speakiing Rudra is a Homa or sacrifice performed in fire in honour of God Rudra, the minutiae of which are mentioned in the Brahmanas. While most of the rituals related to other luminaries stop, limited to the particular purpose intended in the Karma Kanda, it was felt that the Rudram could not and should not be so confined, but put to further varied uses. Hence we find the Namakam (arising in anuvakas) along with Chamakam used invariably for the Vedic and Agamic worship of Shiva in all the households and temples. Chamaka appears in Krishna Yajurveda Taittiriya-Samhita, Kanda 4 Prapathaka 7. A long list of desiderata is prayed for in it—347 to be precise in 11 Anuvakas. We are concerned here only with the 6th Anuvakas known as Ardhendram in which the names of 20 Vedic divinities to whom sacrifices are usually offered, are coupled with that of Indra. The Brahmana explains the prominence given to Indra (Atom) as due to a king of the divinities. Modern science says, as a phenomena Atom is profuse in the universe as well as within a being. He is the driving force behind man. All other forces in nature are constituted in him. It is natural that Atom should share the honour accorded to other luminaries. Thus,

अग्निश्च म इन्द्रश्च मे

सोमश्च म इन्द्रश्च मे

सविताच म इन्द्रश्च मे

सरस्वतिच म इन्द्रश्च मे

पूषाच म इन्द्रश्च मे

ब्रिहस्पतिस्च म इन्द्रश्च मे

मित्रश्च म इन्द्रश्च म

वरुणश्च म इन्द्रश्च मे

त्वष्टा च म इन्द्रश्च मे

धाता च म इन्द्रश्च मे

विष्णुश्च म इन्द्रश्च मे

अश्विनौ च म इन्द्रश्च मे

मरूतश्च म इन्द्रश्च मे

विश्वे च मे देवा इन्द्रश्च मे

प्रिथिवी च म इन्द्रश्च मे

अन्तरिक्षं च म इन्द्रश्च मे

द्यौश्च म इन्द्रस्व्हूच मे

दीशाश्च म इन्द्रश्च मे

मूर्धा च म इन्द्रश्च मे

प्रजापतिश्च म इन्द्रश्च मे

All the phenomena in the universe are shown to be associated with Indra (Atom) and present in us. What is in the Brahmanda (universal egg) is also in the Pindanda (The lumpy egg that is you and me!) What is not in the Pindanda is nowhere in the Universe. This is a Vedic statement.

Thus, Agni (Individual Consciousness) is associated with Indra (Atom); Soma (Cells in the human body) is associated with Indra (Atoms); Savita (Sun) is associated with Indra (Atoms); Saraswathi (divinity of inspiration) is associated with Indra (Atoms); Pushan (growing Consciousness) is associated with Indra (Atoms); Brihaspati (Mantras) is associated with Indra (Atoms); Mitra and Varuna (Hydrogen) is associated with Indra (Atoms); Thvashta (Carbon) is associated with Indra; Dhatu (Proteins represented by vital fluids in the body, blood, flesh, fat, bones, marrow, and semen) is associated with Indra (Atoms); Vishnu (Electro-magnetic force) is associated with Indra (Atom); Ashwin Twins (Proton and Neutron in the nucleus of the atom) is associated with Indra (Atom); Maruts (Tachyons) are associated with Indra (Atoms); Visve Devas (Other Particles in the sub-atomic world dependant on light source); Earth (The layer of universe limited by Space and Time and thought); is associated with Indra (Atoms); The vast intervening Space between Earth and Heaven) is associated with Indra (Atoms); Heaven (Where dimensions other than Space

and Time operate) is associated with Indra (Atoms); Earthly
Dimensions (Four in all made up of length, breath, and height
collectively known as Space and Time) are associated with Indra
(Atoms); Other Dimensions (six more that are unimaginable by
ordinary humans) are associated with Indra and lastly Prajapati
(Controller of Mortality-Shiva) is associated with Indra (Atoms).
For a moden science student it will be quite evident that all the
phenomena that science investigates or hopes to investgate in
future were already well known to the Rishis of yore.

In the Rig Veda, in Mandala 6, Hymn 47, Mantra 18 Rishi Gargah
Bharadvajah offers a definition of Indra. Thus,

रूपम् रूपम् प्रतिरूपो बभुव तदस्य रूपम् प्रतिक्षणाय

इन्द्रो मयाभिः पुरूरूप ईयते युक्ता ह्यस्य हरयः शता दश ॥

Meaning: Every form that we see in the universe there is an
image as a counter form of Indra (Atom). With all these forms
he is constantly in movement giving an illusion as though riding
thousand horses.

This aspect of Indra has been taken for elaboration in
Brhadaranyaka Upanishad at Mandala 2, Fifth Brahmana. The
whole of fifth brahmana is called Madhu-vidya (the honey
doctrine). A story is narrated. Rishi Dadhyan Atharvana imparted
this secret knowledge (Madhu-Vidya) to Indra (Atom in science).
Indra realized that this knowledge pertains to his very existence.
He was apprehensive. Understandably, Indra did not want others
to have this knowledge. He had therefore told his Guru—'If you
tell this to anybody else, I will cut off your head.' Indra was a very
strange disciple, and the Guru said nothing. Instead of showing
his gratitude, Indra threatened his Guru. Then two other devatas
(luminaries), Ashwin twins (Proton & Neutron in science) wanted
to have this knowledge. That these two luminaries approached
the Guru is very relevant in view of the fact that they form a
constituent part of atom, as per science. When they approached
Dadhyan Rishi he expressed his inability in view of Indra's threat.

The Rishi told Ashwin twins: 'If I tell you the secret vidya my head will go.' 'Oh, you do not bother about it.' The twins said, 'We shall look to it.' 'We will cut off your head, then we shall bring the head of a horse and place it on the trunk of your body, and you speak through the horse's mouth. Then Indra will get angry and cut off your head. But what he will cut off will be horse's head. Afterwards we will replace your real head and join it so that you become alright. Thereby you would have not lost anything.' That was a very good idea. Then Sage Dadhyan began to speak and the Ashwins cut off his head and kept it somewhere in secret. Then they brought the head of a horse from somewhere, fixed it on the Sage's trunk and gave it life. Immediately the horse started speaking the Madhu-Vidya, and through the mouth of the horse it is that this wisdom has come. Indra got enraged on seeing that the sage had started imparting the Madhu-vidya. He went and cut off that head he found on the sage's neck-the horse head. Then the Ashwins came and put back the original head on the sage and made him whole again. But whatever the story is behind this enunciation of the Vidya, it is a magnificent statement of the Upanishad, where it tells us that everything is originally related to everything else.

Madhu-Vidya tells us that when you touch anything, you are touching everything. When I see anything, I see the Sun, when I hear anything, I hear everything in all directions, when I smell something, I smell everything in the universe, when I speak to someone, I speak to everybody and when I touch a thing, I touch everything including distant planets and stars. When I know one thing, I know everything. Nobody can understand the mystery behind this phenomenon. Everything is vitally connected, not merely artificially related. This point is a magnificent theme in the Brihadaranyaka Upanishad. No wonder, Indra was very fond of it and did not want others to know it. This earth is the honey of all beings. It is the essence of all beings. People suck this earth as if they suck honey which has such a beautiful taste; and earth sucks everybody and everything as if they are honey to it. The earth is the honey of all, and everyone is the honey of the earth. The earth is absorbed into the 'being' of everything, and everything is absorbed into the 'being' of the earth.

Apart from earth and the being that are correlated in this manner, there is another superior principle present in the earth and in all beings. That superior is Luminous Consciousness. It acts as the animating being behind this physical entity called earth, and an animating principle behind what you call all the creatures, and individuals in the world. That which is cosmically animating all creation and that which is individually animating every little creature, that also has to be brought into consideration in the correlation ship of the subjective and objective aspect of creation. The earth that is mentioned here is not merely this small isolated planet on which we are standing. It is the entire physical creation. Just as the objective world and the subjective individual are organically connected, so is this animating consciousness in the objective world correlated with the individual consciousness. One is hanging on the other, as it were; one is incapable of being without the other. That being which animates the cosmic and individual aspects of creation is called the Luminous Immortal Being (Unifying Force). This Immortal Being is called the *Purusha* because the *Purusha* is etymologically that which exists in anybody, or that which animates anybody. It may be *Purusha* in the individual; otherwise it is known as *Purushottama* in the universe. There is no distinction between the two. The individual is not constitutionally separate from the substance of the whole, and the whole is not in any way different from the structure of the part. They are essentially same. This is also known as Atman. This is also known as Brahman, the absolute. It is filling all space, existing everywhere, and filling all things. It is a plenum; it is fullness; and therefore it is called Brahman. The word Brahman comes from the root brahm, to fill everything, complete everything, and to be self-sufficient in every respect. Brahman is that which is overwhelming and complete by itself, and that is the *Atman* or the Self of all beings.

Just as the earth element is of this nature, so are all other elements capable of being correlated in this manner. The objective phenomenon is present in the individual bodies in some form. The physical body is an individual projection of the cosmic physical substance. Our physical solidity is actually and substantially the earth element. It is the earth that appears solid, and there is nothing in this body of ours which is not of the earth. Even so, the water principle is present in us; fire-principle is present in us; the air-principle and all other principles are present in us.

The water-principle is the honey of all beings, and all beings are the honey of the water-principle as the cause thereof, and the cause which is the water principle is not independent of the part which proceeds from the whole. That which is animating the water principle and that which is animating the parts thereof, is the immortal Being. The seed in the individual; the vital force in the individual is the representation of the water-principle in the cosmos. Both these are correlated to each other, and they are animated by a single Being, the immortal Atman, the self of all which is, veritably, everything, the Absolute Brahman.

The fire-principle is the honey of all beings, and everything that is a part thereof is naturally included in the whole. We need not mention it once again. This fire-principle is manifest in the speech of the individual. The speech is an action, an activity which is superintended by the fire-principle. If there is no fire in the system, you cannot speak. So, these are correlated with each other as part and whole, cause and effect. But this causal relationship between the fire and the speech-principle is made possible by the presence of the immanence of the Cosmic Being who is the Purusha Supreme.

This air is also of the same nature. The air that we breath, is the vital energy in us, the correlate in the individual aspects, of the Cosmic Hiranyagarbha (golden womb), the source of all phenomena including wind. Prana (individual breath) and Vayu (wind) are correlated, so that when the part is conceived, the whole is automatically conceived. The Upanishad will take pains to make clear the point that this correlation is not mechanical or artificial, but vital, living and organic. It is to bring out this point that the Purusha is brought in as the connecting principle. Consciousness is equally present in the cause as well as the effect. It is in the outside world and also in the inner individual. So, when any particular task of the individual is taken into consideration for the purpose of effecting or producing anything, the cause has to be taken into consideration at the same time. If the cause is forgotten and the individual alone is emphasized in a particular action, it would become a basis of bondage. The bondage we experience as individuals is due to the emphasis on our individuality rather than the task, and independently of the cause which is organically connected by the very same Atman that is present in both. So, the essence of the Madhu-Vidya is the cosmic contemplation of the reality of Prana within and Vayu outside, and the correlation with the Universal Consciousness.

Now, the sun is connected with the eye due to photon emission. We are able to see things on account of the principle of the sun that is present in our eyes and the connecting link between the sun and the eyes is again the same Purusha. Wherever you see the connecting link between the macrocosmic and microcosmic you find the same Purusha. So, the one Being is the active, energizing Reality of any aspect of the cosmos as well as the corresponding aspect of the individual. So, here the sun and eye are correlated.

Likewise, the quarters of the heavens and the ear are correlated. The mind and the moon are correlated, and the Upanishad goes on to correlate the light that is flashed forth by the lightening above and the light that is projected by the body by its own energy. The sounds that are made outside in the world are also causally connected with the effect as the sounds made in our own bodies. It is the same space that is operating inside also. The space in the heart within is the space that is outside. Both are internally connected.

The law that operates outside is the law of the cosmos. There are no two laws—Natural law and man's law; universal law and individual law. There is only one law operating everywhere, in all creation, visible or invisible, in all realms of the being. The same law is there for the luminaries, the humans and sub-human creatures. This is called Dharma. This Dharma becomes the integrating principle because of the presence of Atman that is behind it.

What we call Truth is one. There cannot be two truths. The truth that always succeeds (Jaya) is that correlative, integrating principle, Satya, which is, again, a manifestation of Atman. So the Sanskrit phrase:

सत्यमेव जयते ॥

Meaning: Only truth prevails. The humanity that we speak of is also of the same nature. There are two types of humanity which we learn in psychology. Mankind, as a species, is connected with spatially construed humanity. The psychological mankind and the physical mankind—*the Jiva Sristi and Iswara Sristi*—are also interconnected, correlated vitally, and this correlation is possible on account of the *Self*, the Atman.

The Cosmic Being is feeding upon the individual and the individual is feeding upon the Cosmic. They are inter-related like the mother and the child and much more correlated with each other in an organic unity which is inscrutable. This Atman is not your Atman or my Atman. The Atman we are speaking of is the Atman of all beings. Rather it is not the Atman of all beings; but it is the Atman, which is all beings, ultimately. It is the Lord of all beings. Everything is controlled by the very existence and presence of the Atman, without any movement on its part. As spokes are connected to the wheel, everything visible or invisible is connected to this Atman. All beings, whatever can be conceived of or not conceived of, all luminaries, all gods, all the worlds that can be conceived of in any level of manifestation, everything that is vital and real, in any form are located in the Atman, in the same way as every spoke is located in the hub of the wheel.

This is the Madhu-Vidya which the Dadhyan Rishi, the Sage Atharvana imparted to the Ashwins, the two celestials, who wanted to learn this Vidya, by placing a horse head on his trunk. This Being which is responsible for the inter connectedness of things has become, what you call, the living and the non-living; the visible and the invisible; the creatures that are two footed and those that are four footed.

At this concluding stage, the Rishi explains to Ashwins the Rig Vedic Mantra above. "In every form He appears in a corresponding form. He casts into the mould of every creature and becomes formulated into the structure of that particular creature. When he casts Himself into the mould of a bird's body, it looks as if he is the bird. When he casts Himself in a human body, it looks as if He is a human being. When He shines as a celestial, it looks as if He is an angel. He is, then, what you visualize with your eyes. These forms, these bodies, these visible individualities of things, are really intended for the recognition of His presence in all things. He has not created this world merely for nothing, as if he has no other work to do. It is intended to give an indication of His presence; an indication of the variety which He can comprise within Himself; an indication of the contradictions that can be reconciled in His Being; an indication of the majesty that is within His own stature; an indication of the inscrutability of His nature. All these forms are visualized by us directly with our own eyes as a contradictory world where nothing is clear; everything is enigmatic, if considered in isolation. However, everything is reconcilable if it is connected in its proper perspective in the manner which we have just described in the Madhu-Vidya. So there is no contradiction in the world; everything is harmonious. We unfortunately find it impossible to see the harmony as we are not in a position to harmonize ourselves with the harmony that is His. His intention is to make it possible for us to visualize the harmony and the inter-connectedness through every finite form.

Due to the magnificence of His nature and the variety of His manifestation we are unable to see the truth of things. We visualize only one particular form and are not able to connect this form with other forms. So we are not able to see things as they ought to be seen. We are not supposed to see one thing only, or a few things only, or a hundred things only. We are supposed to see anything in its connection with other things. If this connection is lost it is as if we see nothing and know nothing, and one day we will be full of sorrow. "So, let it be understood," says the great Rishi, "that the Master magician who can be called the great Mayavi (illusionist), the Supreme Being who is labeled here as Indra—the Lord of all beings (Atom), appears in such manifold forms that it is impossible for the physical eyes to connect the forms with the circumstances in which they are really placed."

He alone is all our sense-organs. He is especially the ruler of our thought and mind. They are not outside Him. It is he that appears as sense organs; He appears as the forms and He appears as the perception of the objects. He is Hari. Hari means the Lord Supreme (one who takes away), in one way, it may mean the senses which drag you away to the objects, *Harayah Hari.* He may take away the ignorance of an individual, and then He will be called Hari; or He may take away your consciousness from the objects outside; that is also another function of His, and so He is called Hari.

The essence of Madhu Vidya has been expressed in a different way in latter years. Thus, the appellation, Indra's Jeweled Net was attributed to Indra (atom) by a Buddhist in 557-640 B.C.E. He asks us to envision a vast net, which has at each juncture a jewel; each jewel reflects all other jewels in this cosmic matrix; every jewel represents an individual life form, atom, cell or unit of consciousness; each jewel, in turn, is intrinsically connected to all the others; thus, a change in one gem is reflected in all the others. This is reflected in the words of Sir Charles Elliot: "In the Heaven of Indra, there is said to be a network of pearls, so arranged that if you look at one you see all the others reflected in it. In the same way each object in the world is not merely itself but involves every other object and in fact is everything else. In every particle of dust, there are buddhas without number." The similarity of this image to the Hadrons Bootstrap is indeed striking. The metaphor of Indra's net may justly be called the first bootstrap model, created by Eastern sages some 2500 years before the beginning of particle physics. It establishes the principle of inter-relatedness of everything in this universe.

In this connection, there is an important mantra prescribed for Japa, meditative repetition in the mind (only the portion related to Indra is quoted):

यरछन्दसाम्रृषभो विश्वरूपश्चन्दोभ्यष्छन्दाᳵ स्याविवेशं ।

सताᳵशिक्यः प्रोवाचोपनिषदिन्द्रो जेष्ठ इन्द्रियाय ऋषिभ्यो ॥

Meaning: Indra (Atoms) who manifests in the whole universe, who also represents the most excellent Pranava taught in the Vedas is the embodiment of the universe, who as (Pranava) leads the Vedic utterances in Gayatri and other matters standing in their beginning. He is the foremost causal link that enables contemplative sages to learn the sacred Vedas and Upanishads, because he also pervades their inner subjective world and therefore enlightens them with the power of (illuminating) knowledge.

In the context of modern physics, this Indra is the label for Atom. It is everywhere in the cosmos in abundance. Indra is one of the first three manifestations of God as per Rig Veda. The three manifestations are the Surya (Sun), Indra/Varuna (Atom/Hydrogen) and Agni (Individual Consciousness). Varuna is Hydrogen. Hydrogen is basically an atom composed of one proton and one neutron in its nucleus. Like Atom, hydrogen is also present everywhere and active in this cosmos. Therefore it is often clubbed with Indra in the Rig Veda. Om (Pranava) represents all the forces in the universe collectively, of which atom is a vital part. If OM (Pranava) is the embodiment of the universe, Indra (atom) is responsible for giving structure and form to the constituents of this earth, especially man. With the help of Photons (ray-cows of Swar world), Indra also imparts enlightening knowledge to man.

We are all familiar with a cinema theatre operation. When we enter the hall, we encounter a big screen in front from where we sit. Opposite the big screen and behind us on the big wall above us, we find some square apertures. When the show starts, the lights are put off and the theatre is in darkness. From one of the apertures a light beam hits the screen and we see pictures thereon. We can also see the light traveling from the aperture to the screen and in that beam of light we see many particles dancing. Here is a great Scientific or Vedic Truth. Three fundamental principles are involved in the theatrical experience. An atmosphere of darkness and space (Shiva); bright light that travels and impinges on the screen (Vishnu) and the millions of Atom particles flow dancing in that light beam and impact on the screen creating the moving images that unfolds the movie world for our experience. Besides, these three principles, there is also the sound principle which enables us to understand the meaning of the experience. We will also not consider the other paraphernalia like equipment, film reels, electricity etc., which are also important for the experience. Here, we are concerned only with the Atom particles that go dancing towards the screen and draw images on the screen—The Image Makers.

It has become a tradition to believe that science originated in the Greek confederation. Not only this, scientists have taken Dalton as the pioneer in rediscovering Atom in its modern avatar. The great Indian sages working scientifically and logically, not only propounded the philosophy about the Consciousness, but also undertook to prescribe the proper technology to achieve the desired aim. In this pursuit they did not ignore the study of phenomenal world outside, but their enquiries were confined to the fields which helped them to understand Consciousness.

Around 600 BCE, the Vaisesika system (One of the Shat Darshans of Indian Philosophy) came into being. It was essentially a school of Atomic Theory. In fact, in a period still earlier, Charaka postulated that atom is the smallest particle of matter and air and action (energy) are responsible for the combination and separation of atoms, in his Charaka Samhita, (7.17). However, sage Kanada (The name itself means atom eater!) the founder of Vaisesika school is credited with atomic theory. The smallest state of matter is *paramanu* (atom) and the largest state is called 'mahat (the vast).' So he considered atom to be indivisible, a point source, without magnitude, a concept nearer to Boyles' concept. It has potentialities which come into play when it is combined with others. Before becoming manifest in the form of matter, atoms make primary combinations (e.g. water molecules) to make dyads and triads. Astanga Sarira believes that active air is responsible for the combination and separation of Atoms, 5/01. On breaking the matter it goes on breaking into smaller particles until we reach a point where further sub-division is not possible. Such state is known as the atomic state. Nyaya system as per Nyaya Vartika believes that atom of earth, water, fire, and air are different from one another. They are spherical in nature, (4-2-45). Since they have a shape, they can combine with other atoms around them, (4-2-25).

In 1808, John Dalton, a Quaker formulated the atomic theory that matter consists ultimately of individual, discrete particles (atoms) and the atoms of the same element are identical. Chemical action takes place as a result of attraction between these atoms, which combine in simple proportions. But Vaisesikas had considered atom as a cause. Further, Vyasa in his Vyasa Sankya (5/87-88) considers atoms to be action and as such believes that they can be further sub-divided, a concept which is much nearer the modern concept of atom.

Some Buddhists thinkers conceive of atom as the minutest particle capable of occupying space (Van der Waal's concept). According to them it also remains for the minutest duration of time, coming into being and vanishing almost in an instant only to be succeeded by another atom caused by the first. This concept resembles Plank's quantum theory. Buddhists and Ajivikas believed that in normal condition, no atom exits by itself; rather they exist in a variety of combinations (samghata or kalapa). Every unit of combination contains one atom of all the four types of elements (they do not consider akasa as an element even as modern science has discarded ether as an element) and obtain its character from the predominance of an elemental character. This accounts for the fact that matter shows characteristics of more than one element.

Thus, wax may melt and also burn, because it is a samghata by virtue of the atoms of water acting as adhesive.

According to Jain concept of *pudgal* (matter) many atoms combine together to make a *skanda* (compound) which is matter joined together. The attributes of each atom when combined together go to make the attributes of the compound. These *pudgal (atoms) are called skanda (compounds)* as long as they are held together by their binding power(Mitra in the Rigveda). These compositions and the distribution of these *skandas* are dependent on their binding power and power of differentiation (*bheda shakti*) which are of six types. These atoms are perennial, but they can be created and consumed. The six are:

Very gross (ati sthula): Those substances that do not combine by themselves after separation, e.g. wood, stone.

Gross (sthula): Those substances that recombine after separation, e.g. water, milk, oil, etc.

Gross-subtle (sthula-suksma): Those that appear to be gross but cannot be held, e.g. shadow, darkness.

Subtle-subtle (suksma-suksma): Those which are subtle but appear to be gross e.g. taste, smell, touch, etc.

Subtle (suksma): Those that cannot be felt by the body, e.g. karma.

Very Subtle (ati-suksma): Those that is smaller than karma (dasmuk skanda) very minute aggregate.

Actually, in 430 BCE, the Greek philosopher Democritus invented the word *atom*, Greek for "unable to be cut". He developed a concept of atom which was later revised by Dalton in 1803 to account for the observation that elements combine in certain definite proportions by weight. The Dalton atom was very much different from the version of Democritus, but essentially the same as that developed by Kanada in India in 600 BCE.

Writing in the Journal of Chemistry (1976 Edition), J. S. Witten says: "The science never got any final answer for what matter is but proceeds through a tension of empirical facts and theoretical concepts to progressively more powerful and general ways of explaining its behavior." An answer to all these questions was given by Veda long back. The Vedic seers tried to symbolize the various attributes of matter in terms of individuals, e.g. heat energy and radiation represented by *Agni*; light by Surya; lightning by *Apsara;* electricity by *Indra,* etc. (Satapatha Brahmana-13/2.12.3), (Susruta Sutrasthana-1.21.3) and (Taittiraya Samhita—2, 6.2.1.2). The attributes of *Asvins* (Nirukta-12/1) which pervades everything are given as *rasa* and *jyoti.* They are described as *citra* (possessing different and opposite characters) *Sakhya* (friends of having attraction for each other). This fits the description of protons and neutrons forming the nucleolus of the atom. Indra himself is atom and his weapon, Vajrayuda is Electron. In the nucleus of the atom, Proton exhibits a positive electric charge, neutron being neutral and electron has a negative charge

Rig Veda in mandala 10, hymn 106, mantra 3, uses the word *parijman* Indra which means going round or spin. In Atomic science, it is stated that elementary particles possess an intrinsic quantum mechanical property known as spin. This is analogous to the angular momentum of an object that is spinning around its center or mass or nucleus. Thus all elementary particles inside an atom electrons, protons and neutrons spin.

Modern science has discovered that this entire universe is pervaded by Atoms. Naturally maximum attention has been given to the study of this phenomenon. For a long time till the end of Newtonian era, it was believed that the Atom was an irreducible matter, but with new breathtaking discoveries it was found that Atom itself contains particles and sub-particles. Moreover, water, and air are made up of molecules and particles of Atom. While undertaking scientific investigation into a particle, the study is still considered as Atomic science. At the nucleus of an Atom there is a very important particle called electron which challenges our normal scientific observations in a very fundamental way.

The great Rishi Veda Vyasa wanted to spread the knowledge of physics to the people at large in a manner which was exciting and at the same time easy to assimilate. So Maha Bhagawat Purana came into being. We shall consider only two episodes from the purana to make our point. This purana considered the manifestation of almighty as Krishna. Krishna is in fact the electromagnetic force of science which sustains human existence. Krishna himself declared that he manifests in human form from time to time to protect humanity and prevent the destruction of human kind by elements inimical to its existence. While he was growing up as a child, he observed that human kind was inclined to worship Indra the atomic force as all powerful in the world (even like science considered the Atom as all powerful up to Newtonian era). Indra realized that his status was threatened by child Krishna who became the living God in the eyes of the residents of Gokul. Indra wanted to teach a lesson to the residents of Gokul, so he unleashed his might in the form of forceful winds, terrible thunder rains and scorching heat. Houses were uprooted, animals and men died in large numbers. They prayed to Krishna who led them to Govardhan hill, he raised the hill on his little finger well above the earth such that all the residents of Gokul and their cattle could get shelter under it. Indra's might did not work here. Indra realized that he was combating a superior force than himself and he surrendered. Krishna became a household deity thereafter. Krishna then became popular as Giridhar (upholder of hill). This episode supports the 'string theory' in new physics. It is the electromagnetic force that makes the atoms dance in the cosmos as we saw in the cinema theatre experience.

The Mahabharata narrates another episode. After Draupadi's swayamvara the survival of pancha Pandavas from the great fire at their palace stood confirmed. They wanted to pay respects to their king Dirtharashtra. The Pandavas sent Krishna as their emissary in advance. When king Dirtharashtra heard the news that the Pandavas not only survived the devastating fire but won the hand of princess Draupadi, he was very happy and wanted to offer a gift. Sakuni, the brother in law of the king suggested that Pandavas should be offered Kanda Presta as the said gift. Krishna said that Pandavas were willing to accept any gift, big or small and undertook to convince the Pandavas that it is a worthy gift. Evidently, this Kandapresta was an abandoned piece of land in a corner of the kingdom with ruins of an ancient palace in it. When Krishna takes this news to Pandavas, their mother Kunti was very upset and considered the act of Dirtharashtra as an insult. Krishna pacified Kunti and took Arjuna along with him to have a first hand assessment of the property. While there at the site of Kandapresta, the electro-magnetic force that Krishna is in reality, he orders Viswakarma to manifest. Viswakarma is the architect of devatas (luminaries). He himself is therefore a luminary whose business like any other architect, is converting a dream, a concept, an idea into reality. Krishna (electro-magnetic force) the lord of devatas (luminaries) orders Viswakarma to resurrect the ruins to its pristine glory. In due course Krishna is informed that there is a treasure trove hidden somewhere in the ruins and that it was protected by a poisonous snake. They locate the treasure trove but are unable to access it. Krishna and Arjuna were informed that they have to seek the help of Indra (Atom) to retrieve the treasure chest. Krishna therefore asks Indra to manifest and lead them to the treasure chest (consisting atomic particles?)*. Indra (Atom) is only too happy to oblige as Arjuna is, in fact, his own son. Thereafter the place was renamed Indrapresta. The ruins were converted into a beautiful and miraculous palace. All the land surrounding the place once again became a green land.

*It has been an established knowledge in India that various precious stones have individual chemical properties. This has also been acknowledged by science. The stones are thus atoms since they have chemical properties. Chemical variation is identified by corresponding variation of proton numbers in the nucleus of the atom. Ruby (manikya), Pearl (moti), Coral (Moonga), Emerald (Panna), Diamond (Heera), Sapphire (Neel) and Topaz (Pukraj) are all thus atomic particles.

Chapter 8

Surya—The Diffuser of Light

Big Bang is the prevailing cosmological theory of the early development of universe in modern science. Before the Big Bang nothing is known to science either. Big Bang refers to the idea that the Universe was originally extremely hot and dense, around 13 to14 billion years ago. Since then started cooling and expanding rapidly. Big Bang involved an explosion of a primordial fireball into Space and thereafter a cooling and expansion everywhere. Within the first second of the event, quark-gluon plasma came into being, but by first second, nuclear processes, light elements and the heavier elements appeared. Hydrogen, and then Atoms formed some 3, 79,000 years after the event. Then nuclear gas clouds formed paving the way for stars, galaxies and our own Sun. In all this theoretical knowledge, where is the place for the Unified Force that is eluding science thus far? Whereas the ancient Rig Vedic Rishis began their discovery with the Unifying Force and proceeded to unfold the many facets of reality. Read on . . .

The Rig Veda is the oldest literature known to the world. A study of this time-honored scripture reveals the fact that the ancients of India eulogized or prayed (and not worshipped) to Nature as the manifest Deity (Luminary). These eulogies or prayers addressed to Nature are called Riks, in the phrase Rig Veda. It is interesting to note that what was prayed during the Rig Vedic time got subsequently corrupted into worship for a section of Hindus, during the time of other Vedas, Brahmanas and Puranas. This section of Hindus became predominant in later centuries. Naturally, for the early Christian Missionary to India the practice of worship of Nature looked barbaric and irreligious and they declared the Hindus as Nature worshipping tribes. But for the original Rig Vedic rishis that the phenomenon permeates with life was patent to them, even like it is so to the modern scientists. If you look at the matter carefully, in every respect science is predominantly concerned with discovery of Nature! No wonder, in the West, science divorced from their established religion especially after Einstein's discovery at the beginning of twentieth century and thereafter. The divide is increasing day by day and the chasm has become unbridgeable. The fear has been expressed that the Christian religion is decadent. As we noted, establishing a reverential relationship with the manifest world was the religion of rishis of Rig Veda. To them earth, wind, rivers etc. beamed with luminosity and a source of enlightenment. Amongst the aspects of nature the Sun assumed a foremost status. Now as well as then the adoration of this luminary is a part of the practice of religion by the Hindus. This sacred relationship with the phenomenon aided their pious probe into the transcendental. The ancient rishis observed that Consciousness and Thought are very different things. Thought entangled man in the web of space-time constraint and Consciousness released the same man from the clutches of the space-time constraint and enabled him to probe the transcendental life. Their vision was then proclaimed in unmistakable terms, that Reality is one. When experienced through the ordinary intellect and senses (thought) that Reality presents itself as phenomenon. The same senses when divinized (illumined) function transcendentally on the sense-objects. By this devout attitude, they realized that the senses and intellect gets uplifted. Transcendental senses and the intellect are an inviolable prerequisite for the development of intuition. Such are the people who are alone known as Vipras in Rig Veda. After the Vipras gain transcendence the conclusions arrived at by the rishis are all-embracing. What is visualized by them and what is ordinarily sensed are not two different things. The same reality is Nature when contacted through the ordinary senses and the intellect, and it is God (Universal Consciousness) when contacted with *divya chakshus (extraordinary vision) by Vipras,* as Bhagawad Gita points out in chapter 11.8. Thus, Sri Krishna tells Arjuna in the middle of the battlefield:

146

न तु मां शक्यसे द्रष्टुमनेनैव स्वचक्षुषा ।

दिव्यं ददामि ते चक्षुः पश्य मे योगमैश्वरम् ॥

Meaning: Arjuna, you cannot see my true form with these ordinary human eyes; therefore, I will provide you with an extraordinary vision (*divya chakshus),* so that you can behold my divine power of Yoga.

What is this extraordinary vision? Normally we are used to four dimensional vision limited by space and time. At best it is a partial vision with great limitation. It is therefore an erroneous vision. This needs to be corrected with an extraordinary vision that brings into play all the dimensions in Nature, which are, ten in number. Even modern science agrees with the existence of these ten dimensions in the speculations under 'String Theory'. Then we are said to be properly focused to see the Truth.

In the Rig Veda, the deity Surya (Sun) is frequently linked with the luminary Savitr or Savitri so that in many places the epithet Surya-Savitri is used to denote them together. Further, in Mandala 1, Hymn 22, Mantra 5 Rishi Medhatithih Kanvah declares:

हिरण्यपाणिमूतये सवितारमुपह्वये ।

स चेत्ता देवता पदम् ॥

Meaning: I call Savitr, the golden armed, for progress. He is the enlightened, the Light and the goal.

Rishi Shyavashva Atreyah explains his vision of Sun in no uncertain terms, in Rig Veda, Mandala 5, Hymn 81, Mantras 1-5. Thus:

युञ्जते मन उत युञ्जते धियो विप्रा

विप्रस्य बृहतो विपश्चितः ।

वि होत्रा दधे वयुनाविदेक

इन्मही देवस्य सवितुः परिष्टुतिः ॥१ ॥

Meaning: The wise conjoin their mind and their thoughts to the illumined godhead, to the vast luminous consciousness. Knowing that all phenomenon he (Savitr) orders, are the energies of the sacrifice. Great is the praise of Savitr, the creating Godhead.

Atom (Indra) with his shining hosts; the enlightened thoughts (Maruts-Tachyons); Agni, the (individual consciousness) or divine force, are the most important deities of the Vedic system. Agni (Consciousness) is the beginning and the end. Perhaps, this prompted late J.Krishnamurti to title one of his books 'First and Last Freedom'. This Individual Consciousness in us that is transcendental knowledge is the initiator of the upward effort or journey of the mortal towards Immortality or Universal Consciousness; Indra (Atom), lord of Swar (Photon), are our chief helpers, in converting our material mentality into the luminous intelligence, in order to make us eligible for the divine consciousness. The Maruts (Enlightened thoughts) take our animal consciousness made up of the impulses of the nervous mentality (neurons), possess these impulses with their illuminations and drive them up the hill towards the world of Swar (Photons) and the truths of Indra (Atom). Our mental evolution begins with these animal troops, or these *pasus*; become, as we progress in the ascension, the brilliant herds of the Sun, *gavah*, or rays, the divine cows of the Veda.

विश्वा रूपाणि प्रति मुञ्चते कविः

प्रासावीद् भद्रं द्विपदे चतुष्पदे ।

वि नाकमख्यत्सविता वरेण्योऽनु

प्रयाणमुषसो वि राजति ॥२ ॥

Meaning: The Seer (Surya) takes unto himself all forms, and he creates from them good (bhadra), for the twofold and fourfold existence. The Creator, the supreme Good, manifests heaven wholly, and his light pervades all as he follows the march of Dawn (Usha, the first rays of the Sun).

Who is Surya, the Sun, from whom these rays proceed? He is the Master of Truth, Surya the Illuminator, Savitr the Creator, Pushan the Increaser. Suns rays in their own nature are transcendental activities of revelation, inspiration, intuition, luminous discernment, and they constitute the action of that transcendent principle which the Vedanta calls Vijnana (higher physics), the perfect knowledge, the Veda Ritam, the Truth. But these rays descend also into the human mentality and form at its summit, the world of enlightened intelligence, Swar (photon enlightenment), of which Indra (Atom) is the lord.

Now the forces and processes of our inner physical world repeat, by simulation, the truths of the transcendental action which produced the phenomenon in Nature. Since it is by the same forces and the same processes, one in the inner physical nature and the other transcendental, that our inner life and its development are governed, the Rishis adopted the phenomena of physical Nature for simulation for those functioning in our inner life. The solar energy is the physical form of Surya, Lord of Light and Truth; it is through the Truth that we arrive at Immortality, final aim of the Vedic discipline. It is therefore under the images of the Sun and its rays, of Dawn, day and night and the life of man between the two poles of light and darkness that the Rishis represent the progressive illumination of the human soul.

यस्य प्रयाणमन्वन्य इद्ययुर्देवा

देवस्य महिमानमोजसा ।

यः पार्थिवानि विममे स एतशो

रजांसि देवः सविता महित्वना ॥३ ॥

Meaning: In the wake of Savitr's (Individual Consciousness) march, his force, the other luminaries (Atom and other particles) reach the greatness of God, the creator (Universal Consciousness). Creator Savitr has also charted out the realms of earthly light, by his might (through photons).

All the other gods (Atoms and particles, labelled Indra) follow in this march of Surya and they attain to his vastness by the force of his illumination. That is to say, all the other divine faculties or potentialities in man expand with the expansion of the Truth and Light in him. The Truth in its largeness casts all into the terms of the infinite and universal Life, replaces with it the limited individual existence. This also is in us a creation, although in reality it only manifests what already exists but was concealed by the darkness of our ignorance.

उत यासि सवितस्त्रीणि रोचनोत

सूर्यस्य रश्मिभिः समुच्यसि ।

उत रात्रीमुभयतः परीयस

उत मित्रो भवसि देव धर्मभिः ॥४॥

Meaning: O Savitr, you reach the three luminous heavens; expressed by the Surya's (Sun's) rays; encompass the night upon either side by the law of your action of bonding (Mitra).

We can see that the realms of the physical earth are concealed from our eyes by the darkness, but reveal themselves as the sun in his march follows the Dawn and measures them out one by one to the vision.

It is not only the full capacity of our physical or earthly consciousness that this divine Truth illuminates and forms for a perfect action. It pervades the three luminous realms of the pure mind (*trini rocana*); it puts us in contact with all the divine possibilities, a) of the sensations and emotions, b) of the intellect, c) of the intuitive reason, and liberating the superior faculties from their limitation and constant reference to the material world.

We have in this figure of various psychological levels, each considered as a world in itself, a key to the conceptions of the Vedic Rishis. The human individual is an organized unit of existence which reflects the constitution of the universe. So it is said:

यथा पिन्डे तथा ब्रह्मान्डे ।

Meaning: What is in the Lumpy Egg known as man is the very stuff that is in the Universal Egg?

Surya enlightens the mind and the thoughts with the illuminations of the Truth. He is *vipra*, the illumined. In scientific terms, solar energy divinizes Indra (the Atoms, billions of them in us). It is he who delivers the individual human mind from the space-time constrained two dimensional world perceptions and releases it to enlarge the limited perception which is imposed on the mind by its preoccupation with its own individuality. Therefore he is *brhat*, the Large. Sun holds in himself a clear discernment of things in their totality (Vaishvanara Surya mentioned in the chapter on Agni), their parts and their relations. Therefore he is *vipascit*, the clear in perception. Men, as soon as they begin to receive something of this solar illumination, strive to conjoin their whole mentality and its thought-contents to the conscious existence of the divine Surya within them. This yoking (*yunjate*) becomes their Yoga.

उतेशिषे प्रसवस्य त्वमेक इदुत

पूशा भवसि देव यामभिः ।

उतेदं विश्वं भुवनं वि राजसि

श्यावाश्वस्ते सवितः स्तोममानशे ॥५॥

Meaning: O God (Individual Consciousness) by marching in the secret path towards the (Universal Consciousness), you illumine the path as you alone are the creator.

The human being contains in himself the same arrangement of states and play of forces in Nature. Man, subjectively, contains in himself all the worlds in which, objectively, he is contained. Thus, the Rishis speak of the individual consciousness as the physical world, Earth, Bhu, or Prithivi. They describe the mind liberated from the limitation of space-time consciousness as heaven or Dyau, of which Swar (photon—enlightened), the luminous mind, is the summit. To the intermediate dynamic, vital or nervous consciousness, entangled in space-time, they give the name either of Antariksha, the intermediate vision, or Bhuvar.

In the vision of the Rishis a world is primarily a formation of consciousness and only secondarily a physical formation of things, whether of phenomenal nature around us or the inward being of an individual personality. A world is a *loka*, a way in which consciousness projects itself. It is the causal Truth, Surya Savitr (Consciousness manifesting through Surya) that is the creator of all its forms. It is the causal Idea in the Infinite Being that originates the law, the energies, the formations of things and the working out of their potentialities in specified forms and processes. Therefore it is called *Satyam,* because the causal Idea is the Truth in being; because it is the determining truth of all activity and formation, so it is called *rtam, the* right order, it is broad and infinite in its reach and in its operation, it is therefore labelled *brhat*, the Large or Vast. For this reason alone, we have to perceive everything, whether phenomenal or individual in relation to the Truth.

The Truth of the divine existence becomes eventually the sole Lord of all creation in us; and our continual journey with the Consciousness becomes the Increaser, Savitr becomes Pushan. Even as Shyavashwa, the son of Atri, succeeded in affirming Savitr in his own being as the illuminative Truth.

Frequently, conquest and recovery of Sun and Dawn is mentioned in the hymns of Rig-Veda. Sometimes it is the finding of Surya (sun), at other times the finding or conquest of Swar (photons), the world of Surya. Swar (world of photons) is the name of a world or supreme Heaven above the ordinary heaven and earth.

Sometimes the term Swar (photon light) is used for that solar light provided to both Surya (Sun) and to the world which is formed by Surya's illumination. We also learn that the waters (Apah) which descend from heaven or conquered and enjoyed by Indra (Atoms) and the mortals who are befriended by him, are explained as *Swarvatih apah,* the water of *Swar* (photon world). The thunderbolt of Indra (Electron) is called the heavenly stone, *Swaryam asmanam;* its light is the light from this world of *Swar* (photons). Indra himself is the *Swarpati,* the master of Swar, of the luminous world (of Photons). Thus, we find that Swar (Photon) and Surya (Sun) are two different concepts in the minds of the Vedic Rishis, but always intimately connected. So we see Rishi Baradwaja proclaim (Rig-Veda 6.72.1):

इन्द्रासोमा महि तद् वां महित्वं युवं महानि प्रथमानि चक्रथुः ।

युवं सूर्यं विविदथुः युवं स्वः विश्वा तमांसि अहतं निदश्च ॥

Meaning: O Indra (Atom) and Soma (bliss), you are great because of your might, you have created (brought into being in me) great beings in the beginning. You found the Sun, and you found the Svar (Photon); you slew all darkness and limitations (in me).

Then, Satchidananda the higher kingdom of the Immortality becomes imminent. There is an integration of the higher and lower being in the exposure. The dark ignorance, the Night, is illumined upon both sides of the complete being. This higher kingdom manifests for us the principle of Love and Light. He then appears as the Lord of Bliss. The law of his being, the principle regulating his activities is seen to be Love.

Darkness needs to be understood in its full perspective. If you look at the cosmos it is enveloped by darkness and dark energy to the extent of 95% of the total contents of the universe including light sources and the light thereof. Naturally, there are occasions when the light source is engulfed by this darkness, only to be rescued by the Swar world of Aditi or action of Photons. The Rishis had proclaimed the ancient axiom, what is in the universe is also in man, and therefore, what is not in man is nowhere in the universe. Hence, there is this darkness in every nook and corner of our own personality. Left to itself, our thoughts and mind are also enveloped by this darkness. It is well known that all our personality including the physical being in operation is prevailed by our thoughts and mind, which are tainted by darkness. At the level of thought and mind the darkness takes the form of ignorance, and it is this darkness that is required to be banished. We can only influence and deal with only our inner darkness. We have no control over the natural phenomenon of darkness in the universe. This slaughter of darkness is clarified in another hymn by Rishi Vamadeva, when he proclaims in Rig-Veda 4.16.4 while praising Indra, thus:

स्वः यद् वेदि सुद्रशीकम् अर्कैः महि ज्योती रुरुचुः यत् ह वस्तोः ।

अन्धा तमांसि दुधिता विचक्षे नुभ्यः चकार नुतमो अभिष्टौ ॥

Meaning: When by the hymns of Angiras Rishis, Swar (Photons) were found and made visible and shined out of the night, Indra (Atoms, charged with Photons) made the darkness become weak.

In another passage, Rishi Vasishthah Maitravarunih (Rig Veda 7-75-1) says:

वि उषा आवो दिविजा ऋतेन आविः-क्रिण्वाना महिमानम् आगात् ।

अप द्रुहः तम आवः आजुष्टम् अङ्गिरस्तमा पथ्या अजीगः ॥

Meaning: Usha (Dawn), born of the Light (Swar or Photon world born) has unveiled the darkness, by the True Light. She reveals the vastness. She has drawn away the veil of afflicting darkness and all that is unloved. Most full of Angirasaahood, she manifests the path for the great journey. Obviously, we have to penetrate the universal darkness to reach the Universal Consciousness which is the controller of both darkness and light.

One of the most intriguing words in the Rig-Veda is the Cow, or *'Go'*. This word *Go* in Sanskrit has seven different meanings besides the four footed animal called cow. Credit should go to Sri Aurobindo for rightly pointing out, that in most instances, the context demands that the word should be assigned the alternative meaning, ray of light. For most part, Rig-Veda deals with natural phenomenon and the biological meaning of the four footed animal for cow is out of context. However, in the thinking of ancient Rishis, being and consciousness are intimately related. The infinite, universal consciousness is referred to as mother Aditi in many places of the Veda, with her seven names and seven seats *(dhamani)* and she is also conceived as the Cow, the primal Light manifest in seven Radiances, *Sapta Gavah and Saptagu*, that which has seven rays. In another perception, the sevenfold principle of existence is imagined as the Rivers that arise from the ocean, *Sapta Dhenavah (seven cows)*, and in one more perception, Rays of all-creating Surya Savitri, as *Sapta Gavah*. *Surya-Savitri* can also imply the ordinary solar rays and other light rays, essentially charged with photons that belong to *Swar* world (world of Photons). Incidentally, in the ongoing scientific research in the west, the effect of solar rays on the four-footed animal cow is under study. Preliminary results show that, by its physical constitution, it is the most suitable being to absorb all solar rays. Moreover, it has been observed in scientific studies that cow always tends to align with the earth's magnetic field notwithstanding the position of Sun and Moon.

The image of Cow is constantly associated in Veda with the Dawn and Sun. It also recurs in the symbolic legend of the recovery of the lost cows from the cave of the Panis by Indra (Atoms) and Brihaspati (Brahma, the repository of all energies) with the aid of hound Sarama and the Angirasa Rishis. That the word *Go, the cow* stands only for Rays of eternal Light and not the four footed animal is evident in the early part of the very first mandala of Rig Veda. Thus, Rishi Madhuchchhandah, son of Rishi Vishwamitra in the mantra 1-7-3 has this to proclaim:

इन्द्रो दीर्घय चक्षस आ सूर्यं रोह्यद्दिवि ।

वि गोभिरद्रिमैरयत् ॥

Meaning: Indra (Atoms) made the Sun ascend in heaven for the eternal Light. By the rays of this Light he burst the hill of ignorance. Obviously, a four-footed cow cannot do the job, if we assign the meaning cow to *Go,* in this context. There are many more explicit passages to draw a conclusion that Rig-Vedic Rishis did not have cow in their mind, but only rays of the Sun, unless the context specifically warranted the meaning of four footed animal.

Usha, dawn is frequently extolled as the mother of Cows in Rig-Veda. Therefore if cow is the symbol for the physical light or for illumination, the word must either bear this sense that she is the mother or source of the physical rays of the daylight or else that she creates the radiances of the supreme Day (source of the light of Photon). It is already evident in the Veda that Aditi, the Mother of deities, is described both as the cow and as the general Mother; she is the supreme Light and all radiances proceed from her. Aditi, in the Veda refers to Infinite Universal Consciousness in opposition to Diti, the divided consciousness, mother of Vritra and other Dhanavas of Rig-Veda; dark forces as opposed to luminaries for man in his transcendental life. Usha, the dawn, as the mother of the cows, can only be a form of Aditi. This perception is explicitly brought out by Rishi Kutsah Angirasah in Mandala 1 Hymn 113 Mantas 18 & 19 as follows:

या गोमतीरूषसः सर्ववीरा व्युच्छन्ति दाशुषे मर्त्याय ।

वायोरिव सूत्रतानामुदर्के ता अश्वदा अश्ववत्सोमसुत्वा ॥

Meaning: Usha, associated with the all-powerful rays (Photon Rays), manifest in the aspirant. Even like the wind, Usha forms the hymns of the auspicious Truths sung towards the end of Yajna. May Usha give momentum to the emotionally charged aspirant towards the Truth.

माता देवानामदितेरनीकं यज्ञस्य केतुर्बृहती वि भाहि ।

प्रशस्तिकृद् ब्रह्मणे नो व्युश्च्छा नो जने जनय विश्ववारे ॥

Meaning: Aditi, you are the Mother of all the luminaries. You remind us as the great spirit of Yagna. Considering us fit for the sacred Word, induct us in the company of realized souls.

Aditi (an aspect of infinity) who is the source of all light is envisaged as the mother of Adityas (sons) by Rishi Kurma Garthsamadah, son of Rishi Grtsamadah in Rig Veda Mandala 2 Hymn 27, Mantra 1. Thus:

इमा गिर आदित्येभ्यो धृतक्नूः सनात् राजभ्यो ।

जुह्वा जुहोमि श्रुणोतु मित्रो अर्यमा भगो नः तुविजातो वरुणो दक्षो अंशः ॥

Meaning: The Rishi here is addressing the sons of Aditi. O ancient kings Adityas, do hear my prayer expressed with my enlightened tongue, Mitra, Aryaman, Bhaga (of multiple births), and Varuna, Daksha and Amsha.

In the following mantra Rishi Kashyapah Marichah states that the Adityas are not six but seven. In the Puranas, Rishi Kashyapah is the spouse of Aditi. Thus in Rig Veda Mandala 9 Sukta 114 Mantra 3:

सप्त दिशो नानासूर्याः सप्त होतार ऋत्विजः ।

देवा आदित्या ये सप्त तेभिः सोमाभि रक्ष न इन्द्रायेन्दो परि स्रव ॥

Meaning: There are many Suns in the seven direction (this is fundamental to modern cosmology); seven are the invokers and ritviks in an Yajna; seven are the Adityas; O Soma (Love), you protect us along with all of them; O Indu flow for Indra.

In another Mantra it is stated that there are, in fact eight Adityas born to mother Aditi. How she disposed off the eighth son is stated here by Rishis, Brhaspatih Laukyah, Brhaspati Angirasa and Aditih Dakshayani. The last is a female Rishi. This mantra occurs in Rig Veda Mandala 10 Sukta 72 Mantra 8, thus:

अष्टौ पुत्रासो अदितेः ये जातास्तन्वस्परि ।

देवाँ उप प्रैत् सप्तभिः परा मार्ताण्डमास्यत् ॥

Meaning: Aditi had eight sons who were born from her body. With seven she approached the luminaries and the eighth Marthanda was sent away. The next mantra explains that this Marthanda was consigned to repeated births and deaths, that is our world earth. In fact he is the one who acts as a total cover around the earth and protects it from the bombardments from rest of universe outside. We have already learnt the names of the six Adityas. According to Taittiriya Aranyaka (1.13.3) the seventh Aditya is Vivasvan.

The Sookta 164 of Mandala 1 of Rig Veda is considered a very important one from Indian philosophical development. Rishi Dirghatamah Auchatayah states in mantra 2:

सप्त युञ्जन्ति रथमेकचक्रम् एको अश्वो वहति सप्तनामा ।

त्रिनाभि चक्रमजरमनवं यत्र इमा विश्वा भुवनाधि तस्थुः ॥

Meaning: Here Sun is addressed as number seven. He deposits the seven rays in his one-wheeled chariot. A single horse with seven names draws it along. The three axle chariot is undecaying and immovable. The entire world is supported in this car.

The seven rays of the Sun energize man in seven different ways. Each ray is an Aditya and therefore a source of energy. Hence the rays are labeled as Mitra, Aryaman, Bhaga, Varuna, Daksha, Amsha and Vivasvan. In the later Vedas such as Yajur and Atharva, the original concept of Gayatri mantra was expanded to include the seven *Vyahrties* or *lokas* in our body as a replica of cosmic reality. These Vyahrties are: Bhu, Bhuvaha, Svahahaa, Mahaha, Genaha, Tapaha and Satyam. In that era, *Yoga Shastra* (then known as Hiranyagarba Shastra) *was developed by Kapila muni.* It is a long and parallel tradition to Vedas. An offshoot known as Tantra Shastra was developed with many innovations. One of the great contributions of Tantra shastra was discovery of the existence of seven *Chakras* (Energy Centers) in our body: Muladhara, Swadishtana, Manipura, Anahata, Visuddha, Ajna and Sahasrahara. The Vyahrties or Chakras are not two different units but only labeled differently, draw solar energy from the seven solar rays. Obviously, each Vyahrti or Chakra draws energy from a specific solar ray to fortify itself constantly.

Rishi Madhuchchhandah, son of Vishvamitra has declared in Rig Veda Mandala 1 Hymn 2 Mantras 7-9:

मित्रं हुवे पूतदक्षं वरूणं च रिशादसम् ।

धियं घ्रुताचीं साधन्ता ॥ ७ ॥

Meaning: I call Mitra of clarity and Varuna the banisher of hunters. Together they enlighten our intelligence.

ऋतेन मित्रावरुणाद्बुताद्बुधाद्बुतस्पृशा ।

क्रतुं ब्रुहन्तमाशाथे ॥८ ॥

Meaning: Mitra and Varuna who are in touch with Truth constantly, increase its manifestation. This proximity with Truth gives them a vast will-power.

कवी नो मित्रावरुणा तुविजाता उरुक्षया ।

दक्षं दधाते अपसम् ॥९ ॥

Meaning: Mitra and Varuna are Seers. While they are residents of vast space, they manifest in humans and other friends in many ways. They encourage discriminating intelligence.

Out of the seven solar rays, Mitra (Bonding) and Varuna (Hydrogen) are vitally important. Rig Veda makes a repeated reference to them, both independently and in conjunction with other luminaries like Agni, Indra, Brahmanaspati and Soma to name some. A root meaning of Varuna is to cover or pervade. It is appropriately so because the Sun that we see in the yonder sky is wholly made up, for all practical purposes, of Hydrogen which gets converted into Helium at its core, the Photosphere, according to modern science. Accordingly, the ancient Rishis saw it as a concrete representative of the Infinite. Metaphorically speaking, this spread of Varuna over the sky is conceived as an intermediate ocean, above our earth, which as Sun, rises out of the inconscient cave, retrieved by Indra and Angirasa Rishis. The inconscient caves are the black holes and dark regions of modern science. The kingdom of Varuna is above all these. There the shining Dawns arise, the rivers travel and the Sun unyokes the horses of his chariot. Varuna contains, sees and governs all these in his vast being and by his illimitable knowledge. Even the inconscient darkness is his to govern. Varuna is the oceanic surge of the hidden Divine Truth as He rises, manifesting to his own infinite wideness and a cause of ecstasy for the enlightened seers.

A root meaning of the word Mitra is to contain with compression. Here, it is very interesting to see the close involvement of modern science in understanding this concept. In science, hydrogen is an amorphous substance, a shapeless and non-crystalline matter. It requires a perpetual bonding for separate identification. This bonding function is performed by Mitra. For this reason, perhaps, in the Rig-Veda, in most of the Riks where their reference occur, we find Mitra and Varuna are addressed together. In the Vedic imagery, Mitra the luminary, who effects the right unity of which Varuna is the substance and the infinitely self-enlarging periphery. These two kings are complementary to each other in their nature and their divine works.

Chapter 9

Apas—The Water of Life

Have you ever wondered why scientists looking for other intelligent beings in the vast universe first look for signs of water in different planets they target for exploration? There is no possibility of biological life, without existence of water in some form. This fact was not unknown to ancient Rishis. Even today, the search is on to find some sign of water now or in the distant past in the planet Mars which is the nearest planet to us. In September 2009, Chandrayan-I was able to locate water in moon with help from NASA. A few days later, NASA sent two unmanned rockets to moon that crashed on the surface, with the objective of tracing signs of water there. Read on . . . .

It has been discovered in the universe there is only one place, earth a small speck in the milkyway that sustains humans an organism in very intimidating circumstances. From the deepest part of the ocean to the highest peak, the area that encompasses all life forms is only about 20 kilometers (about 8 miles). Even out of these 20 kilometers or so, we as humans have restricted our life as land based as we have to breathe oxygen. Consequently, about 99.5% of the world's habitable space is unsuitable for human life, because it is made up of water bodies. If we look at it from chemical point of view, we are thriving in a world predominantly made up of H_2O—Dihydrogenoxide a compound which has no smell or taste. While it is usually benign, many times it could be so lethal that it can strike with fury that no manmade edifice can withstand destruction. Yet we long to be beside it. It has no taste and yet we love the taste of it. Water is everywhere. All fruits, vegetables and grains contain water from 10%-95%. For example,

161

water melon or tomato at 95% is little else but water. Even human beings are composed of 65% water. This is a recently discovered fact in science. The ancient rishis of Rigveda are well aware of it.

We saw that water's chemical formula is H2O, which means that it consists of one big oxygen atom with two smaller hydrogen atoms attached to it. The hydrogen atoms cling fiercely to their oxygen host, but also make casual bonds with other water molecules. Hydrogen is known as Varuna in Sanskrit and it bonds with Prana (Oxygen) to form water molecules (Apas).

Narayana Upanishad states:

आपो वा इद॰ सार्वम् विश्वा भुतान्यापः प्राणा वा आपः

पशव आपोऽन्नमापोऽमृतमापः सम्राडापो विराडापः

स्वराडापश्छन्दा॰ स्यापो ज्योती॰ ष्यपो यजू॰ष्यापः

सत्यमापः सर्वा देवता आपो भुर्भुवः सुवराप ॐ ॥

Meaning: Verily all this is water. All the created beings are water. The vital breaths in the body are water. Samrat (perpetually shining) is water. Virat (manifoldly shining) is water. Svarat (self-luminous) is water. The matters are water. The luminaries are water. Vedic formulas are water. Truth is water. All deities are water. The three worlds denoted by *Bhuh, Bhuvah and Suvah* are waters. The source of all these is the Supreme, denoted by the syllable 'Om".

It is very important to bear in mind a vital fact. Whereas Western enquiry is based on material substance *(Padartha)*, which was believed to have independent life of its own, till the time of Isaac Newton, Indian enquiry was always spiritual based. While matter and spirit are two sides of the same coin, there is a great difference. In material enquiry there is the observer different from the object or matter that is under observation. Even though materialists had achieved much in their research into matter till the time of Newton, they had never felt the need to discipline the observer, so that he does not interfere with the observation. By this neglect they have missed the sacred relationship between the object and observer. This sacredness is of great primacy in Indian religion. Whether western society felt the need to discipline the observer or not, a revolution took place in the beginning of 20th Century, initiated by Albert Einstein. He proved that matter has no independent existence and that in the ultimate analysis matter was energy. This revolution, in many ways irrevocably aligned western science to eastern philosophy. The ancient Indian religion also says, after all, the observer is the object of observation in the ultimate analysis. You may call it Light of lights or Universal Consciousness or Infinite which is being searched by the finite Individual Consciousness. The sacred relationship is based on love and sacrifice the fundamental cause of existence.

Sacredness has been a subject of considerable study in India for ages. They arrived at the conclusion that one of the important components for sacredness is cleanliness, besides others, cleanliness, physically, mentally and intellectually. By entertaining uplifting thoughts and working for the good of other beings, mind and intellect develop the right attitude to create an internal sacred atmosphere. Physical cleanliness necessitated taking bath daily, preferably early in the morning. Biology teaches us that our body is composed of billions (14^{10} i.e., 140,000,000,000) of cells. To keep us healthy, the cells have to wage a constant war within our body. The war being waged with inimical forces (injuries and diseases) which are determined to undermine our well being and survival at all times, just like the war Mother Durga wages with Rakshasas in Devi Mahatmya or Sat-Chandi in Markandaya Purana. In the war, literally billions of cells are destroyed and pushed out of the body. They cling to the different layers of the skin. They are called exfoliation. These are the minute particles, not visible to the naked eye, that need to be washed off in a bath. Your body remains clean. In the rest of the world including west this concept was totally unknown even a hundred years back. Taking bath was a rear event, if at all. It is even rumored that Queen Elizabeth-I took bath only once in her life! In Indian Culture, it is almost a daily religious rite. Thus, in the next Mantra of the text mentioned above, while taking bath, a dwija (twice born-Brahmin) is supposed to do *Achamana* (sipping water) uttering the following Mantra:

आपः पुनन्तु प्रुथिवीम् प्रुथिवी पूता पुनातु मम् ।

पुनन्तु ब्रह्मणस्पतिब्रह्मपूता पुनातु मम् ॥१ ॥

यदुन्छिष्टमभोज्यम् यद्वा दुश्चरितम् मम ।

सर्वम् पुनन्तु मामापोऽसताम् च प्रतिग्रह॰ स्वहा ॥२ ॥

Meaning: 1) May this water cleanse my physical body that is made of earthly substances. Thus purified, may the earthly body purify me, and the Soul with in! May the Supreme purify me! May the water purified by the Supreme purify me!

2) My defilement, repast on the prohibited food and misconduct if any, and the sin accruing from the acceptance of gifts from persons disapproved by the scriptures—from all these may I be absolved. May the waters purify me! Hail!

In the Rig Veda, Rishi Medhatithih Kanvah introduces the deity Water in Mandala 1, 23rd Hymn, Mantras 16-23. He takes up the central theme of the Veda that of Individual and Universal Consciousness. The Rishis never seem to lose thread of this theme, because it is like the unifying force in modern science. He says the Universal Consciousness is like a mother. From it arise, as if from the womb, the Individual Consciousness (Agni) the sibling of the Atoms that are showered on earth that bear in its embryo Hydrogen (Varuna) that forms the water molecules called Apas. These Atoms are generators of life in all forms. Agni of course makes your journey (Yajna) towards the Universal Consciousness.

Thus:

अम्बयो यन्ति अध्वभिर् जामयो अध्वरीयताम् ।

प्रन्चतीर् मधुना पयः ॥१६॥

Meaning: The motherly waters go on the sacrificial paths to those desiring the sacrifice and so do the sisters. The waters mix the honey of Delight with the milk of knowledge.

The streams of hydrogen atoms (Varuna) that pour into the world we live in is the motherly waters. The sisters are Prana (Oxygen), together they form water as we see it on earth. They are motivated by a spirit of sacrifice to the universal consciousness. This water is a source of delight and knowledge for man.

अमूर् य उप सूर्यें याभिर् व सूर्यः सह ।

ता नो हिन्वन्तु अध्वरम् ॥१७॥

Meaning: The waters that are near the Sun or together with the Sun, may they increase our spirit of sacrifice.

This mantra clarifies our explanation of first mantra. Water in the form we see on the earth cannot exist near the sun even for a moment. However, the Sun is filled with Varuna (Hydrogen) the mother of water. This Varuna (Hydrogen) infuses the spirit of sacrifice in us.

अपो देवीर् उप ह्वये यत्र गावः पिबन्ति नः ।

सिन्धुभ्यः कर्त्वं हविः ॥१८॥

Meaning: I call the Waters and Luminaries in whom our enlightenment is nourished. From the streams (of energies) the offering is to be made.

The Rig Vedic Rishis were absolutely clear about their goal in life. Therefore all those luminaries in nature that are dedicated to the universal consciousness were their well wishers. Naturally the energy these luminaries provide help in the journey.

अप्स्वन्तरऽमृतमप्सु भेषजमपामुत प्रशस्तये ।

देवा भवत वाजिनः ॥२९॥

Meaning: Nectar is the essence of Waters; the healing powers are in the Waters. O Luminaries, become full of plenitude so that Waters are praiseworthy.

The eternal spirit of consciousness is the essence of waters and so all the healing powers are in waters. The healing powers are those that clear the path for achieving the goal of life. Dark forces can obscure the path hence appeal to luminaries.

अप्सु मे सोमो अब्रवित् अन्तर् विश्वानि भेशजा ।

अग्निम् च विश्व शम्भुवम् अपः च विश्वभेषजीः ॥२०॥

Soma has said to me; all medicines are in the Waters. Agni is the bestower of happiness for all; Waters are medicine for all.

The Rishi is pursuing the goal of life, that of merging individual consciousness with universal consciousness. A principle aspect of consciousness is Soma or spirit of love. This Soma is responsible for our well being as per Mandala 9 of Rig Veda. When this Soma makes a statement to the Rishi, it is from a position of authority that it does so.

Soma says all medicines are in the waters. We may recall that we are clear 65% water or 2/3rds of our body is filled with water in one form or other. Lack of water or inadequate amount of water in our body will lead to dehydration and death. Water can generate antidotes to any poison or disease that may contaminate us in the course of our life. However it is consciousness alone that can bestow happiness in us.

अपः प्रणीत भेषजम् वरूथम् तन्वे मम ।

ज्योक् च सूर्यम् द्रुशे ॥२१॥

Meaning: O Waters—fill my body with self healing powers such that they act like armor for the continuous vision of the eternal light.

If our body suffers with diseases and disorders we would not be able to give undivided attention to our goal in life. So the Rishi appeals to the luminous waters to act as armor around him such that no disease or disorder thwarts him from realizing his goal.

इदम् आपः प्र वहत यत्किम् च दुरितम् मयि ।

यध् व अहम् अभिदुद्रोह यध् व शेप उतान्वृतम् ॥२२॥

Meaning: O Waters, carry away purge me of the bad effects of whatever inappropriate deeds done by me, or any betrayal by me or cursing or falsehood done by me.

The Rishis were well aware that such negative actions generate different kinds of poison in our body, that can obscure our focus. It is water alone that can counteract these poisons.

आपो अद्या अनु अचारिषम् रसेन समगस्महि ।

पयस्वान् अग्न आगहि तम् मा सम्स्रुज वर्चसा ॥२३॥

Meaning: O Agni, as we have united with the essence of water, I can now claim that I have completely attained the Waters; do come and submerge me with your splendor.

Here Agni is consciousness. Since the Rishi had the vision of this consciousness as the essence of water, he becomes one with the water. He appeals to individual consciousness to lead him towards the universal consciousness.

All medicines are in the water, needs some elaboration. Earlier we were told that *Bhu* (Soil) is water, the air we breathe is also water. Apart from humans, the animal kingdom; the aquatic species; the birds; flies and bacteria; flora and green vegetation are all born in water; live by water and are the basic source for different medicines. For example, there is a news report that horse urine could be a cure for cancer.

In Rig Veda Mandala 7 Sukta 49 Mantras 1-4, Rishi Vasishtah Maitravarunih continues the colloquy on water thus:

समुद्रज्येष्ठाः सलिलस्य मध्यात् पुनाना यन्ति अनिविशमानाः ।

इन्द्रो या वज्री वृषभो रराद ता अपो देवीः इह माम् अवन्तु ॥१ ॥

Meaning: May those luminary water foster me in my body, the waters that were released by Indra (Atoms) with Vajra (Electrons). These are the same waters that are greatest oceans that are constantly on the move and purify all.

Waters are made luminary because of the presence of Varuna (Hydrogen) molecules in them. Hydrogen is an atom with one proton and one neutron and electron. Thus, Indra (Atom) is the power which release water in the form of great oceans as well as 65% contents of our body.

य आपो दिव्या उत वा स्रवन्ति खनित्रिम् आ उत वा याः स्वयंजाः ।

समुद्रार्था याः शुचयः पावकाः ता आपो देवीः इह मामवन्तु ॥२ ॥

Meaning: Rivers flowing into the ocean; man made channels that direct water to the seas are the substance of the ocean. The luminary waters are pure and purifying. May the lustrous waters foster me in the body.

यासां राजा वरुणो याति मध्ये सत्य अनृते अवपश्यन् जनानाम् ।

मधुश्रुतः शुचयो याः पावकाः ता आपो देवीरिह मामवन्तु ॥३ ॥

Meaning: Waters are pure and purifying because of the presence of King Varuna (Hydrogen) in them. King Varuna moves among the waters and looks on the truth and falsehood in creatures. May the lustrous waters foster me in the body.

यासु राजा वरुणो यासु सोमो विश्वे देवा यासु ऊर्जं मदन्ति ।

वैश्वानरो यास्वग्निः प्रविष्ट स्ता आपो देवीरिह मामवन्तु ॥४॥

Meaning: In the waters, besides King Varuna there is Soma and all other luminaries in their full force. Then Vishwanara as Agni Consciousness makes the entry. May the lustrous waters foster me in the body.

All the phenomena in nature is present in water. Besides Hydrogen, there is bliss (Soma). Atoms, Electromagnetic force, Gravitational force, Nuclear Force, Photons are all present. Finally the unifying force consciousness (addressed as Vishwanara-Agni here) makes entry. The picture is now clear why water is important for our survival.

In Mandala 10 Sukta 9 Mantras 1-9 the Rishis Trishira Tvashtra, and Ambarisha take us a further step in making us understand the importance of water. These mantras are part of Sandhya (at three conjunctions in a day—dawn, mid-day, and dusk) prayers of a Brahmin (one who aspires to merge with universal consciousness), thus:

आपो हि ष्ठा मयोभुवः ता न ऊर्जे दधातन महे रणाय चक्षसे ॥१॥

Meaning: O Waters, you are the bestower of happiness. Give us that strength which will enable us to have the vision of the supreme consciousness.

As ordinary human beings, we are provided with the strength that is sufficient to live in this four dimensional world. This strength is inadequate when we attempt to transcend other dimensions of the universe. It is more so to a Brahmin whose avowed purpose of living is merging with the universal consciousness. Consider a similar example in science. An astronaut is expected to undergo a rigorous training along with regulated diet, so that he will be able to adjust to 0 gravity condition in his planetary mission.

169

यो वः शिवतमो रसः तस्य भजयतेह नः उशतीरिव मातरः ॥२॥

Meaning: O Waters, give us your beneficent essence like a loving mother.

The essence becomes potent when delivered with best love and affection. What could be better than a mother's love? After all water is a mother to us.

तस्मा अरं गमाम वो यस्य क्षयाय जिन्वथ आपो जनयथा च नः ॥३॥

Meaning: O Waters bestow us with those powers (of Maruts) that enable us to create forms and we are only too glad to accompany you to the source.

Maruts are tachyons in nature. They are mass less but travel at speeds beyond that of light. In fact, it was association of Maruts with Indra (Atoms) that enabled Indra to secure the sobriquet form maker. In the present mantra, the Rishis envisage two form making activity to man with the help of Maruts (Tachyons) also found in water: 1) creation of progeny and 2) creation of such progeny suitable to preserve this transcendental knowledge.

शं नो देवीरभिष्टय आपो भवन्तु पीतये शं योरभि स्रवन्तु नः ॥४॥

Meaning: O luminous waters be gracious to us (by protecting us from disease and ill-health). Be potable so that we may drink water for health. Thus they would render us blissful and happy.

How waters provide us with health and happiness is explained in the ensuing mantras.

ईशाना वार्याणां क्षयन्तीश्चर्षणीनाम् अपो याचामि भेषजम् ॥५॥

Meaning: O waters, you are sovereigns presiding over precious things; the strength to possess the vision of consciousness, please bestow that power on us.

अप्सु मे सोमो अब्रवीत् अन्तर्विश्वानि भेषजा अग्निं च विश्वशंभुवम् ॥६ ॥

Meaning: I have learnt from Soma (Sap) that water contains all things that heal. It is Agni (Consciousness) that confers bliss.

With their penetrating vision of Soma, the Rishis have learnt that it is indeed water that contains all healing substances, whether it is a tree or plant or it is man and other beings. Consider, if we lob a pill in our mouth to cure an ailment, for sure the medicine in that pill can be sourced to water through plant, animal or other sources that are bases of pharmacopoeia. It is one thing taking medicine and another thing returning to normal health and 'be at peace with the world,' which is attributed to Agni (Consciousness), the warmth in our system. Remember, human being is also a kind of complicated vegetation.

आपः प्रुणीत भेषजं वरूथं तन्वे मम ज्योक् च सूर्यं द्रिशे ॥७ ॥

Meaning: O Waters, equip my body with healing powers so that I may feel safeguarded, in order that I may have uninterrupted view of that Sun (Consciousness).

इदमापः प्र वहत यत् किं च दुरितं मयि यद्वाहमभिदुद्रोह यद्वा शेप उतान्रुतम् ॥८ ॥

Meaning: O Waters—carry away the ill effects in me arising out of a) any wrong done by me; b) any cursing done by me; and c) any falsehood spoken by me.

The three acts mentioned are detrimental to natural law. They generate some kind of poison in the internal system of man. Only water with its curative powers can wash away these poisons.

आपो अद्यान्वचारिषं रसेन समगस्महि पयस्वानग्न आ गहि तं मा सं स्रुज वर्चसा ॥९ ॥

Meaning: Having penetrated the essence of water, I now seek benediction of Soma (Love) and Agni (Consciousness) for vision of the Supreme Splendor.

Chapter 10

Vayu—The Vital Breath

* Taittiriya Upanishad sets the proper tune for introducing Vayu with the famous Shantipaathah (Peace invocation) at its beginning. Before commencing the process of Brahma Yajna, the sacrificial spirit of learning the knowledge of Brahman (Universal Consciousness), both the teacher and the taught invoke Mitra-Varuna (Hydrogen); the solar ray Aryaman connected with the eye; Indra (Atoms); Brihaspathi (Individual Consciousness); and Vishnu (the all pervading electro-magnetic force) to help them in understanding the mighty Brahma (repository of all energies in nature) like God Vayu (Wind), who is the visible Godhead. Read on . . . .

As the invocation above indicates, all the luminaries are eternally associated with Truth or Universal Consciousness. They are the limbs of the Godhead, so to say. In the grand sacrifice that is existence, these luminaries perform their allotted duty towards the Godhead. Man is also no exception to this relationship, except that he is lost in the darkness within and forgotten his relationship. He has forgotten the majesty of the Godhead. He flounders in the darkness of his being, and wrongly attaches great importance to thought and thought based action, rather than Consciousness which is the Godhead in him. He is so engrossed in his misdirected activities that he fails to even recognize the existence and beneficial influence the luminaries can bestow on him, just by recalling them affectionately. Indra (atom) and Vayu

---

* ॐ शं नो मित्रः शं वरूणः । शं नो भवत्वर्यमा । शम् नो इन्द्रो बृहस्पतिः । शम् नो विश्णुरूरूक्रमः । नमो ब्रह्मणे । नमस्ते वयो । त्वमेव प्रत्यक्षं ब्रह्मासि ॥

172

(wind) are ever ready to play the key role in enlightening his mind and thought, provided man gives his total attention to them.

Thus, Rishi Medhatithih Kanvah says in Rig Veda Mandala 1 Sookta 23 Mantra 3:

इन्द्रवायू मनोजुवा विप्रा हवन्त ऊतये ।

सहस्राक्षा धियस्पती ॥

Meaning: Indra and Vayu are very active like our mind and are great visionaries who can protect our intelligence (from the prevailing darkness).

Turning to science, we can say, atoms are already present in our body in billions. So also wind is present in our body at every nook and corner. They come from Sun and other planets in our solar system through space. Indra (Atoms) and Vayu (Wind) make the life of man. The rishis add that, left to himself, man gets lost in a gloom and plods in his life time without a sustainable goal. So he needs enlightenment by the very elements that keep him alive, because the origin of Indra and Vayu is the enlightened solar world. This is hinted by Rishi Paruchchhepah Daivodasih in Rig Veda Mandala 1 Sookta 135 Mantra 9. Thus:

इमे ये ते सु वायो बाह्वोजसो अन्तः नदी ते पतयन्ति उक्षणो महि व्राधन्त उक्षणः ।

धन्वश्चिद् ये अनाशवो जीराः चित् अगिराओकसः सुर्यस्येव रश्मयो दुर्नियन्तवो हस्तयोः दुर्नियन्तवः ॥

Meaning: O Vayu, as a limb (of the Godhead) you carry great force that traverses the mid-space between the Sun and Earth. They are not lost in (the solar) upper regions. Just like the Suns rays which cannot be stopped (from reaching the Earth).

Rig Veda Mandala 4 Sookta 48 Mantra 1 reads:

विहि होत्रा अवीता विपो न रायो अर्यः ।

वायवा चन्द्रेण रथेन याहि सुतस्य पीतये ॥

Meaning: In his vision, Vamadevah Gautamah calls Vayu (Wind) and Indra (Atom) as his charioteer, to come in the car of light, and manifest the sacrificial energies of man (buried in the darkness) in the delightful and congenial atmosphere of the Soma (cells).

When Vayu (wind) accepts the hospitality of man, he manifests in the body of the appellant and makes his body fit for receiving the energies of other luminaries. The joint work of Indra (Atom) and Vayu (Wind) results in the fullest mental potential of man being channelized towards the enlightenment. Indra is the master of mental force and Vayu is the master of nervous force. The union of Indra and Vayu will modulate thought and action in man. Further, Vayu is the repository of the multitude of desires that gathers in man; and he tastes all the food that man partakes. He builds a home for the man. Rishi Isha Atreyah said so in Rig Veda Mandala 5 Sookta 7 Mantra 6. Thus:

यं मर्त्यः पुरूस्पृहं विदद्विश्वस्य धायसे ।

प्र स्वादनं पितूनामस्ततातिं चिदायवे ॥

This home for the man is no ordinary brick and mortar house. In the microcosm it is called *Pranamaya Kosha* of man. *Pranamaya Kosha* is the compartment of our body predominated by *Prana,* another name for Wind. In the macrocosm, in the vast space, it is identified as midregion or *Antariksha or Matari.* In this *Antariksha,* Vayu breathes so he is called Matarishvan. It is interesting to note that all the battles between Indra and the titans like Vrtra happens in this mid region.

The Brhadaranyaka Upanishad takes the *Prana* mentioned above for elaborate explanation in Chapter 1 Brahmana 3. We have often heard that there are divine forces (Devatas) and nondivine forces (Asuras) that are constantly at battle in the Indian Puranas and Mythology. It would be better understood if we restate it as actually, integrating and disintegrating forces that vie for dominance over our mind. That is the constant battle. This is allegorically explained in Brhadaranyaka Upanishad in the first eight mantras. The Devas wanted to overcome Asuras. The Devas are always smaller in number compared to Asuras. Whereas the Asuras strongly depend on their physical strength, the Devas do not entirely depend on the strength of their powerful arms but also take the help of a superior power. That power, in this instance, is the chant of an efficacious Mantra; we can even say a weapon which they wanted to use to overpower Asuras.

Now, the question arose as to who will chant the mantra? These Devatas or Luminaries are the presiding deities of our senses. We have luminaries in the cosmos and the same luminaries preside over our sense organs. The microcosm and macrocosm are organically correlated. The luminary of the eyes is Surya (Sun); of speech (Agni); of the nose Ashvini Kumaras (Proton-Neutron, the atom nucleus); of the ears the Dig-Devatas (the Dimensions); of the taste principle Varuna (Hydrogen), of the touch principle is Vayu (Wind); and there are Agni (Fire), Indra (Atom), Vishnu (Electromagnetic Force), Prajapati (Genetics), Mrtyu (Mortality) presiding over Mouth, two hands and legs, the Genital organ and the Anus. The Moon presides over the mind; Brahma (the repository of all energies) presides over the intellect; Rudra (Gravitational Force) over the ego; and Vishnu over the Psyche. The Mantra is an incantation which attunes the microcosm to the macrocosm. Therefore it should be correctly recited otherwise the Mantra will not work. All the luminaries in man conferred and decided that Speech should do the chant.

When Speech began to chant, the Asuras (disintegrating forces) got wind of the plan and they attacked the speech, afflicted the speech with evil. The speech faltered, wrong utterances, blabbering, floundering and use of improper words entered the speech so that it failed in its mission. We can do some good, but also do great harm through our speech. Why is the capacity of speech afflicted with this propensity to do harm? It is under the influence of Asuras. Then the presiding deities asked eyes to do the chanting. When the eyes started chanting, the Asuras attacked the eyes with evil. The eyes began to see good things as well bad things. We can see objects in a good manner so that it is conducive to proper judgment, as well as see them in a manner that clouds our judgment and misleads us. The eyes also failed in their mission. It was the turn of the ears. It was also attacked by the Asuras and it started hearing both good and bad things. Ears are an open door. Anything can enter at any time into it. It also failed. Every organ was, thus, affected. We can taste good and bad, we can smell good and bad and we can touch good and bad. The Luminaries then asked the mind to do the chanting. It also was influenced by Asuras and started thinking what is improper. Lastly, the presiding deities requested internal unifying *Prana Shakti* to chant. This *Prana* does not belong to any sense-organ. It is a single force that operates through out the human system. Without this *Prana*, the eye cannot see, the ear cannot hear and so on. It is an impersonal unifying force. The Asuras failed in their attack. They were thrown back and broken into pieces when they tried to obstruct *Prana*. This is the cosmic phenomenon taking place all the time, not at some historical or mythological time.

The Devas and Asuras are two different tendencies in us and not any substances. Whereas the Luminaries (Devas) tend to unify, the Dark forces (Asuras) urge diversification. The sense organs are incapable of action one way or other and they are easily susceptible to the forces that influence them. Now, an epistemological issue arises, that of origin of this universe. In the beginning there was only the Universal Being alone. It had no need to seek anything because it was itself everything. The question is, why then this self contained Universal Being manifested the complicated universe that we see today? One classical approach as explained in Aitareya Upanishad is the introduction of the concept of *Pralaya,* or catastrophe. There is a *Maha Pralaya*, say a big bang at the end of the expansion phase of the universe. This big bang (contraction phase) is a reverse process (the after effect of big bang we are at present subjected to, is a process of expansion), in that everything is withdrawn into the Universal Being such that only the Universal Being is. What is withdrawn is contained in the Universal being in some form called *Vasanas*, impressions in the Universal Being.

At the next big bang, these Vasana or Impressions once again surface where they left off. In this re-manifestation, first to evolve is *Vaishvanara or Virat Purusha,* universal man. Then each one of his organs manifested, like eyes, nose, ears, mouth and the body. They in turn manifested Sun, Wind, Space, Fire, Water and Earth etc. They are the last evolutes in the process of the Divine manifestation. They are therefore part of the Universal Being, the subject of creation. However, there is a reversal of the roles seen when the individual came into being. Take for example Fire. Fire is the effect of Cosmic Principle, of Speech, identified with *Virat,* whereas the Fire Principle becomes an object for individuals, so that human speech is controlled by Fire Principle, as it is not the case in *Virat* where Speech is the controller of Fire. Similar role reversal happens with all other organs. The Organs which are attributed to *Virat a*re causes, rather than effects. And in individual case, they become effects, like a mirror reflections. The evils of Asuras or demons we are speaking of here, are the tendencies to regard the Universal Subject as an object, and the desire of the individualized subject to run after the object, for 'contact' with it. Under the influence of Asuras, the sense organs run after every object they come in contact. There is a constant tendency to diversify instead of unification. But the *Prana* is a unifying force. This *Prana* in the individual is *Hiranyagarbha* in the cosmos. To establish the inter-connection between *Prana* and *Hiranyagarbha,* our senses have to be redirected to their own source, so that they do not run after objects. This is known as *Prana-Vidya* or meditation on the *Cosmic-Prana.* The *Prana-Shakti* mentioned here is not merely the breathing principle. We normally tend to translate the word *Prana* as breath, but it is much more than that as we have seen. It is the energy, the subtle force (In Homoeopathy they call it Dynamis), a vitality, that which keeps the whole body well coordinated and in unison. When we feel a sensation of unity in the whole body, we know that it is a harmonious movement of *Prana* in our whole system. Alas, we are so eager to run after the external objects that we have no time to notice our own well being! Anyone can observe that our body is not one whole. It is made up of parts. That is why the body is considered a system, or as per homoeopathy, it is considered an economy, even like the national economy. It is made of parts, billions of them and with a vast and an unimaginable range. Every cell is different from every other cell; every limb is different from every other limb. But in spite of this diversification we are a whole. We are a whole, an indivisible completeness. This is due to *Prana* which is the manifestation of the Individual Consciousness within us. This Individual Consciousness is indivisible and everything which represents this indivisibility is an aspect of it. *Prana* is regarded as an immediate expression of this Consciousness within us, and correspondingly in the cosmos, we may say, *Hiranyagarbha* is the reflection of Universal Consciousness.

The Chhandogya Upanishad also explains the mighty *Prana* in chapter IV, sections 1-3 under the title of *Samvarga-Vidya*. This Samvarga-Vidya was taught by sage Raikva to a king by the name of Janasruti. He was not any king in the past history of India. He was one of those jewels that out shines others by the strength of his knowledge and virtue. He has even been compared to King Janaka, the great philosopher king. The word Samvarga refers to the process of absorption. Thus the title means the knowledge of the all-absorbing one. We are introduced into that which is all-absorbing. There is a great 'wind' that blows everything into itself. This is not the ordinary wind that blows here. It is also not an ill wind that does well to no one. It is a wind that absorbs everything into it, everything rises from it, everything is maintained in it and everything goes back into it. It is on this great *Vayu* that I am meditating says Sage Raikva. It is not an ordinary wind is clear from the fact that it is an absorbent of even the sun. It is this cosmic wind that makes the sun rise and set in the proper direction. It even makes the planets and stars to rotate and to direct their courses in given manner. All the planets therefore revolve in a symmetrical manner around the sun, and in its turn the sun is rushing away towards the Milky Way. The fire burns due to it; and the rain falls due to it. Even death comes under its influence. When water dries up it goes there. From the objective universal side, this is how the great deity, the cosmic air which blows everything into itself is explained.

Now, from the internal microcosmic angle it is being explained. In the universe this air is the absorbent of everything into itself. In the individual level also it works in a similar way and it is called *Prana*. When we go to sleep the mind is withdrawn by the action of the *Prana*. The *Prana* draws the mind into itself. Even so, the speech and other senses are drawn into it. All these are governed by this Universal Principle which works as *Prana* within us. It is thus in the *Brahmanda* and *Pindanda*, macrocosm and microcosm. These two, the *Hiranyagarba* in the cosmos and *Prana* in the microcosm are to be brought together (Yoga) in this meditation and envisaged as one single Reality.

An application of this Samvarga Vidya is now explained to highlight a nicer point. Full time practitioners have no time to even earn their livelihood by working. For food they used to wander from house to house for alms. If they get it they ate it otherwise they went without food. Their only purpose in life was this meditation. Such was a *Brahmacharin*, a bachelor by modern reckoning. Such was this gentleman who followed the Samvarga Vidya for a long time and felt that he had completely identified with the deity. One day he went for begging for food as usual. He happened to go to the residence of two well known scholars Saunaka and Abhipratarin. These scholars were about to eat their meals when the Brahmacharin arrived asking for food. They were indifferent to the appeal for food outside. Even at that time there was this great tradition that a guest cannot be turned away before one takes one's food. It is one of the five tenets a brahmana had to follow as per the scriptural injunction. The scholars should be aware of it. Yet they were indifferent. This indifference on the part of the scholars, lead to the motive of the scholars, whether they were testing the beggar for his sincerity? No food was given. On his part, the brahmacharin pointed out to the scholars that there is but one great God who swallows up four others. Who is this God? He is the protector of all the worlds. No one can behold his presence. O Saunaka and Abhipratarin, you two great beings do not realize that all the food of this world belongs to this God, and it is to this God that you have refused food. Since the brahmacharin was quite advanced in the Samvarga Vidya, he had in him the power of the deity. The deity is the Universal Being. Therefore it is as though the deity himself is asking for alms. All the food in the entire creation is by right belonging to the Universal Being. So, by denying the food and not acknowledging his presence, the scholars have committed a great offence, he said. They must therefore be prepared to face the dangerous consequences of their act, said the brahmacharin.

The first scholar retorted to the brahmacharin. You are saying that the food has been refused to the great Deity, the all-pervading one. You are presuming that you know to meditate on Samvarga Vidya and we do not know about it. You had remarked that we are ignorant of the presence of this great god to whom all the food belongs. We are meditating on that great Soul, the Self of all beings, the source and essence of all luminaries, the creator and the progenitor of all things. He is the one who eats through the mouth of knowledge itself. It is the essence of knowledge which is the essence of his Being, and He swallows all things. There is nothing in creation which He cannot devour. Everything is food for Him and He consumes it through his own being and not with the help of any external instrument. He cannot be eaten by anybody or not even affected by anyone, or contacted and contaminated in any manner whatsoever. The eaters themselves are eaten up by him. This is what we are meditating upon. It is implied here that the scholars possess a superior knowledge as compared to the brahmacharin. Presumably, Saunaka approved the boy for his knowledge and ordered the servants to serve him food. What is the point of difference in the two approaches of that brahmacharin and the scholars?

Samvarga is both cosmic and individual. It is *Vayu* as cosmic counterpart and *Prana* in the individual. So it is *Prana-Vayu (Atoms of oxygen)*. [Remember in Rig Veda Indra (Atoms) and Vayu are close associates]. As the brahmacharin said, the four great luminaries that were swallowed up by the God are the Fire, the Sun, the Moon and Water that are all comprehended in *Vayu of the Hiranyagarba*. *Prana* is the devourer of four things in the individual that are dependant on it. The four things are eyes, ears, speech and mind. The brahmacharin seems to have a mistaken notion that the cosmic is different in some way from the individual, or at least, there is a line of demarcation between the universal and the particular, *Vayu and Prana*. Both are atoms of oxygen. But in the superior form of meditation that Saunaka and his friend Abhipratarin pursued this differentiation seems to have been obliterated completely.

The subject of *Prana* has been extensively dealt with in Tantra and Yoga Shastras and is very popular in the world today. All the postulates have been accepted as correct by modern science. *Prana* as we saw earlier relates to the inward working of man. As we all know breathing is a sign of life. Man cannot live without breathing air. It has been found that man cannot do without breathing for more than three minutes. However, when we talk of breathing called *Swara* here, we are talking about something more than the air which we take in through the two nostrils; we are also talking about the flow of prana (oxygen atoms), a very subtle and vital aspect of the breath. Man is born with his breath, which continues to accompany him to the very end of his life. But when he ultimately dies, the subtle prana (Oxygen), which is the essence of his breath departs with him. This prana, the Individual Consciousness, merges with the Universal Consciousness. By practice of Swara Yoga, the breathing process is streamlined to facilitate a rhythmic movement of Individual Consciousness into the Universal Consciousness.

We think we breathe with both the nostrils simultaneously. It is an incorrect notion. If we take a little time to observe, we will notice that most of the time respiration takes place through only one of the nostrils. Actually, we do respiration and expiration with one nostril for some time till that nostril closes, only to be taken over by the other nostril which opens. Every hour or so, there is this nostril change for respiration and expiration. This is the steady state. If this Swara or rhythm is irregular, we have an indication that something is not properly functioning in our body. It also implies that it must have a particular effect on our nervous system. Furthermore, it has a specific influence on our brain which requires absolute orderliness. We only considered the flow of breath through the two nostrils, the left and right nostrils. There is also a third flow of breath through both the nostrils, which is infrequent. When the left nostril flows, it indicates that the mental energy is predominant, by this we mean that the sensory nerves of eyes, nose, ears, tongue, and skin are being vitalized. When the right nostril flows, prana controls the organs of action: speech, hands, feet, reproductive, and urinary/excretory organs. When on rare occasions, both the nostrils flow simultaneously we have an indication that the Individual Consciousness is in power.

The prana circulates through the different sections and organs of the body, through the medium of the breath. Prana produces special energy waves through out the body. Prana adjusts to the requirements of each organ and section. Depending on this modification or adjustment of prana to the functional requirements of different sections of the body, the *prana vayu* has been classified and given different names. Thus, there are ten prana vayus of which, five have greater influence on our body. They are the *Pancha-Pranas*, five pranas, known as prana, apana, samana, udana and vyana. The remaining five are *Upapranas* or subordinate pranas. The body, as well as all the faculties of the mind with senses is directly connected with prana.

Each prana is located in different sections of the body according to its particular direction of flow. The most powerful vayus are prana and apana, the upward and downward movements. Prana functions in the thoracic region to stimulate the respiratory system and the absorption of prana from outside the body. When the muscle known as the diaphragm contracts, a vacuum is created in the lungs sucking in air and prana, hence it is known as 'in breath'. Working in opposition to this function is apana, the 'out breath' which is located below the navel in the pelvic region. It is the energy of expulsion which is stimulated in the lower intestines and urinary/excretory complex. The downward action of apana eliminates wind and excreta from the body. Our whole body is ruled by these two movements of prana and apana. During the day time, the action of prana predominates and at night it becomes subordinate to apana.

However, the gateway to liberation depends on samana, the third vayu, which equalizes prana and apana. Samana is the middle breath, located in between the heart and navel, and its important function is assimilating prana. In the process of breathing, samana is the time gap between inhalation and exhalation. It provides vitality to the liver, pancreas, stomach and digestive tract. Samana links prana and apana so that they are complimentary to each other. The principle goal of raising the Individual Consciousness is accomplished when the normal movement of prana and apana are reversed such that apana moves up and the prana moves down meeting at navel centre. When they are thus united, an incredible force is created, which pushes prana through sushumna nadi, which in turn awakes the entire pranic capacity and that raises the Individual Consciousness.

The fourth vayu is Udana. It is located in the throat and face enabling swallowing, facial expression and speech. It is also responsible for maintaining strength in the muscles. According to Patanjali's Yoga Sutras, when prana and apana are united with samana as mentioned above, it is udana that finally leads Individual Consciousness to Universal Consciousness. Normally however, udana carries prana from samana to the fifth vayu, vyana. Vyana spreads prana throughout the body; regulating and circulating nutrients, fluids and energy. Vyana holds all the parts of our body together and resists disintegration of the body. The action of the five main pranas give rise to the five Upa-pranas or subordinate ones that give finishing touch, as it were, to the body mechanism. Thus, the eyes are lubricated and kept clean by the blinking power of kurma. Krikala stimulates hunger, thirst sneezing and cough. Devadatta induces sleep and yawning. Naga induces hiccup and belching. Finally, after death, dananjaya lingers with the remnants of the body.

The Kaushitaki Brahmana Upanishad in third part states, "It is prana alone as the conscious self that breathes life into this body. Therefore, prana is the essence of the life breath. And what is life breath? It is pure consciousness."

Chapter 11

Mahavishnu—
The Sustainer of Universe

James Clerk Maxwell is credited with the discovery of the fact that both electricity and magnetism are truly one force field and reducing it to four simple formulae. This electromagnetic force is one of the four only fundamental forces of nature. Integral part of this fundamental force is the fields consisting of space with north and south poles. Light (Jyoti) is a prerequisite for propagating this energy. Electromagnetic waves travel at the same speed of light. Electromagnetic force plays a vital role in holding in place, nuclear reacting proton and neutron in the nucleus of an atom, and mediates by exchange of photons. Electromagnetic Force is crucial in chemistry (Rasayana). Read on . . . .

Modern science states that there are only four fundamental forces in nature. These are gravitational, electromagnetic, strong and weak nuclear force. In the Vedas by clubbing together the strong and weak nuclear force, the ancient Rishis add a fourth fundamental force as vibration/sound. The labels given to these forces in Veda are Rudra/Siva for gravitational force, all pervading Vishnu for electromagnetic force, goddess Shakti for vibration/ sound and Ashwin Kumars (twins) for strong and weak nuclear force. For all intents and purposes, Indra (atoms) takes the place of Ashwin twins (strong and weak nuclear force) because these sources of strong and weak nuclear forces are constitutional part of Indra (atoms). In science, the composition of an atom shows that the nucleus of the atom is made up of protons (positive charged) and neutrons (neutral charged) (the Ashwin twins) that are capable of producing nuclear energy.

In this chapter, however, we are concerned with Vishnu as electromagnetic force in nature. This identification is strongly brought out in the very first mandala (chapter) of Rig Veda by Rishi Medhatitihih Kanvah in six verses. Mandala 1 Sookta 22 verses 16-21. These six mantras are called *shad-vaishnavyah*. Thus:

अतो देवा अवन्तु नो यतो विष्णुर्विचक्रमे ।

प्रिथिव्याः सप्त धामभिः ॥१६॥

Meaning: The luminaries, who dwell in the seven fold realms or the seven rays of the Sun, protect us because of the all pervading Vishnu (Electromagnetic Force).

There is a famous mantra which a brahmana has to utter, in his daily prayers, invoking the Sun, facing east, north or west depending on the time of the day, like morning, noon and evening respectively. It is a meditation. It is a description of Mahavishnu, only the first line is quoted:

ध्येयः सदा सवित्रमन्डल मध्यवर्ति ।

I meditate on the Lord who resides in the centre of the solar orb.

Mahavishnu (Electromagnetic energy) is foremost among all luminaries according to *Satapatha-brahmana* and according to *Aitaraya-brahmana* he is the guardian and protector of all luminaries. Thus the other luminaries, Indra (Atoms) and others (other particles in the nature), derive their power, pervasion and position directly from Vishnu (Electromagnetic force). The luminaries in turn protect and preserve human beings according to the mantra in Rig Veda Mandala 1 Sookta 3 Verse 7.

इदं विष्णुर्वि चक्रमे त्रेधा नि दधे पदम् ।

समूळ्हमस्य पांसुरे ॥१७॥

Meaning: Mahavishnu (Electromagnetic energy) strides three realms in three steps. The first realm is the solar region, the second region is the intervening space and the third is the earth. In the dust of his feet (Atoms and particles) were all established.

It is the origin of the universe that is concealed in the dust-laden feet of Vishnu, the electromagnetic force. Ananda-Tirtha a great authority on Rig Veda has said that these dust particles are luminaries that delight in Vishnu's feet. It is not surprising, since, modern science now relates creation to big bang. The forward stride of expansion after big bang naturally involves electromagnetic force, atom and other particles.

This dust of the feet has also a science parallel in the very popular string theory. After nearly 40 years the theory is still in a fluid state. It has been an excellent formula but nothing has been proved by observation. Hopefully, the experiments with Large Hadrons Collider at Franco-Swiss border address many of the enigmas related to this theory. The scientists say that each mass or energy quantum is a harmonic tone of the vibration of a tiny string, such that particles can be thought of as vibrating strips or loops of the string. Further these string traverse ten dimensions. We know only three dimensions of space (length, breath and height) and of time. It is in the other dimensions that the particles vibrate. So, all the variety in fundamental particles arises just because of the pattern of vibration of the string, its harmonics, but not the string itself.

In the famous composition of Vishnu Sahasranama, thousand names of Vishnu, at number 784 we have the name sutantuh. The name means well expanded. Just as the thread is drawn out in different counts from cotton which is later used as material for infinite varieties of cloth, so too, from the Vishnu Consciousness, the endless variety of beings and things gets projected to constitute the enchanting tapestry of His mighty universe. As the thread is the substratum for all the various fabrics, Vishnu is the beautiful string, the substratum for this entire wonderful universe.

This subject is also elaborated in Bhagavadgeeta, Chapter 7 Verse 7. Thus:

मत्त परतरं नान्यत्किंचिदस्ति धनंजय ।

मयि सर्वमिदं प्रोतं सूत्रे मणिगणा इव ॥

Meaning: Lord Krishna, the incarnation of Vishnu tells Arjuna in the battle field of Kurukshetra, "There is nothing whatsoever higher than Me, O Dhananjaya (Arjuna). All this is strung in me, as clusters of gems on a string".

It is being stated here that Vishnu (electromagnetic force) is the common factor in all forms (atoms and particles) in the universe. He holds them all intact as the string holds all the pearls in a necklace. The pearls in the necklace are uniform and homogeneous, and its thread, which is generally unseen, passes through the central core of every pearl, and holds them all into a harmonious ornament of beauty. The substance of which the pearls are made is totally different from the constituents that go to make the thread.

त्रीणि पदा वि चक्रमे विष्णुर्गोपा अदाभ्यः ।

अतो धर्माणि धारयन् ॥१८ ॥

Meaning: Vishnu placed the three steps for establishing the inexorable natural law of the phenomena and upholds the law.

The natural law that is being upheld has been clarified by Ananda Tirtha. Events like sun shining, wind-blowing, fire burning and so on. They are, in fact the laws that support the structure and functioning of the universe.

Jayatirtha another authority on Rig Veda and a disciple of Ananda Tirtha mentioned earlier says that the three realms, in fact, consist of a few threefold division's observable in nature. These are: a) time principle as past, present and future; b) the constituent qualities of the elements of existence known as gunas like sattva, rajas and tamas; c) the realms like bhuh, bhuvaha and svaha; d) the souls like luminaries, humans and dark forces and e) things living, non-living and mixed like the body with soul.

विष्णोः कर्माणि पश्यत यतो व्रतानि पस्पशे ।

इन्द्रस्य युज्यः सखा ॥१९॥

With the help of his close friend Indra (Atoms) Vishnu (Electromagnetic force) establishes the cosmic order in motion.

This verse is addressed to all human being to behold the marvel at first hand. Friendship is all about bondage, an intimate relationship between Vishnu and Indra. For a modern student of science this is common knowledge. Atoms (Indra) are everywhere, in the solar regions; in the intermediary space and on earth. Even in our human body there are billions of atoms. Each cell in our body contains 100,000,000,000,000 atoms and there are no less than 100,000,000,000,000 cells in our body. Our thoughts and the process of thinking is driven by these atoms in the form of neurons.

By definition, electromagnetic force is one of the fundamental interactions in nature. It is this force that causes the interaction between electrically charged particles and the areas in which this happens are called electromagnetic fields. The nucleus of the atom has proton which is positively charged and it is the negatively charged electron that keeps, the proton and neutron with no charge from colliding into each other. There is an exchange of photons in the process.

तद्विष्णोः परमं पदम् सदा पश्यन्ति सूरयः ।

दिवीव चक्षुराततम् ॥२०॥

Meaning: That transcendental, the third of the three steps cannot be perceived by ordinary mortals, but is a constant vision for the enlightened ones.

The effects of the electromagnetic force, as conditioned by space and time are only visible for the ordinary mortals. Space and time constitute only four dimensions, three for space—length breath and height and the other for time. To witness the third step of Vishnu, the sages penetrated all the ten dimensions in nature, so that they became visionaries and constantly witnessed Mahavishnu in the form of nature's full glory. This aspect is dealt with in the next stanza. Such were the Angirasa Rishis of Rig Veda. This ability is not shared by modern science.

तद्विप्रासो विपन्यवो जागृवांसः समिन्धते ।

विष्णोर्यत्परमं पदम् ॥२१॥

Meaning: Those wise men, who are geniuses, being constantly aware, light up their heart to witness the supreme foothold.

Such wise men are called *Viprah*. A *Vipra* is a sage who is inspired by intuitive vision, one who is ecstatic and also excited (Rig Veda 8-6-7). He is also equipped with vibrant speech (Rig Veda 5-68-1) and he is the leader of all wise and far-seeing sages (Rig Veda 3-5-1). A vipra is truly an offspring of Agni (Individual Consciousness) and it is Agni that bestows light and inspiration to the vipra (Rig Veda 3-10-5). Medhatithi, the seer of this sukta, is often cited as a vipra.

It is heartening to know that late J.Krishnamurti laid great emphasis on the subject of consciousness and total awareness in the 20th century. Those who attended his lectures would no doubt consider him a vipra in the pristine sense. He was solely responsible to highlight and explain this aspect of existence which benefitted millions of his admirers. He generally does not quote examples to buttress his point of view in his lectures. But in a rare instance, he did quote two examples in the above connection. The first example is straight forward. If you are in a closed room where there is also a snake, imagine, you are all the time aware of only that snake and nothing else. That is awareness. While in India, it appears, he was once travelling with two other gentlemen in a car. He was in the front seat while they were in the rear seat. They were hotly discussing as to what is awareness? Unfortunately, the driver ran over a goat on the way. The gentlemen behind were deep into their argument and were oblivious of the accident. He pointed out that this lack of attention on the part of the gentlemen will not help them in anyway to be aware!

The point he raises is, is it possible to be totally aware of the whole field of consciousness and not merely a part, or fragment of it? Thoughts, feeling and action are fragments. if you are able to be aware of the totality, then you are totally attentive too. This is important because, with total awareness of the whole field of consciousness there will not be friction. Friction arises due to fragmentation.

Rishi Dirghatamah Auchatyah also enjoyed a similar vision of Vishnu as Rishi Medhatithi as per Rig Veda Mandla 1 Sookta 154 Mantras 1-6. Thus:

विष्णोर्नु कं वीर्याणि प्र वोचम् यः पार्थिवानि विममे रजांसि ।

यो अस्कभायदुत्तरम् सधस्थम् विचक्रमाणस्त्रेधोरूगायः ॥१॥

Meaning: Vishnu (Electromagnetic force), whose very name indicates expansiveness and pervasiveness, is well acclaimed for his three strides through which he covered the whole universe, be praised.

In the three steps that he has taken are the three worlds; the earth the world of matter; the mid-world the vital realm of Vayu, the lord of the dynamic life principle; the triple heaven and its three luminous summits (Trini Rochana). We could say, on the basis of Vyahrities, the lokas of Janah, Tapaha and Satya. Looking at astronomy we can say, a) vast region of planets and stars; b) beyond that the region where nova and super nova are frequent; and c) even beyond that the region of dark matter and energy.

प्र तद्विष्णुः स्तवते वीर्येण मृगो न भिमः कुचरो गिरिष्ठाः ॥

यस्योरूषु त्रिषु विक्रमणेष्वधि क्षियन्ति भ्वनानि विश्वा ॥२ ॥

Meaning: That Vishnu, the creator of three realms with his three strides, is vigorously praised, who like a ferocious lion resides in the mountains, moving in difficult tracts.

According to Sri Aurobindo, by comparing to a mountain lion, the Rishi reveals the rare violent aspect of Mahavishnu (Electromagnetic force) to highlight that he has close but covert connection with Rudra (gravitational force) who is a fierce and violent godhead in nature. It is very pertinent to note here that Vishnu or electromagnetic force is light dependent, whereas Rudra or gravitational force can operate in darkness. In fact, gravitational force is at its full vigor in dark matter and black holes according to science. After all our universe is made up of 95% dark matter of which we know very little.

प्र विष्णवे शूषमेतु मन्म गिरिक्षित उरूगायाय व्रुष्णे ।

य इदं दीर्घं प्रयतं सधस्थमेको विममे त्रिभिरित्पदेभिः ॥

Meaning: The Rishi once again offers his deep praise to Mahavishnu. This deep praise (Manma) has a special connotation in Rig Veda. The word with its meaning has altogether vanished in the modern Sanskrit. According to Yaska the oldest known commentator, the meaning of the word merits deep reflection, or something worthy of contemplation and it is often related to Vipra who are qualified to understand the meanings of the passages in Rig Veda, in the true spirit. The praise is related to his celebrated three strides of Mahavishnu. The three worlds that came into existence are immense in time and space, but they exist all together in Vishnu's exalted steps. The Rishi prays that his praise may reach Vishnu.

Vishnu stands at the goal, on the peak of the mountain. He makes the universally wide movement, he being the Bull of the world, who enjoys and fertilizes all the energies of force and all the herds of thoughts. The force and thought of man, the force that proceed from Rudra the Mighty and the thought that proceeds from Brahma, have to go forward in the great journey towards Vishnu.

Electromagnetic force is the source for generation of light. All other phenomena in nature are dependant on this light, including living creatures like man and beast. We may therefore say, that the existence in the three worlds, earth, intermediate space and upper solar regions (all the areas where light reaches, not necessarily our planet sun) have come about because of electromagnetic force.

यस्य त्री पूर्णा मधुना पदान्यक्षीयमाणा स्वधया मदन्ति ।

य उ त्रिधातु पृथिवीमुत द्यामेको दाधार भुवनानि विश्वा ॥४॥

Meaning: Continuing the previous theme, the Rishi states that the three strides of Vishnu are the three realms inhabited by all creatures. They are laced with the invigorating mead (*Purna-Madhuna*—mixture of sweet honey and water) and therefore are imperishable (*akshiyamana*). Vishnu not only supports and maintains the three worlds but also lives in them.

There is a delight in existence. All the three realms created by Vishnu are full of the mead of this delight of existence. In other words it is called *Ananda* (bliss). This *Ananda* is part of the triple principle of *Sat-Chid-Ananda* which is total and complete by itself. He holds this *Sat-Chid-Ananda* in his being.

तदस्य प्रियमभि पाथो अश्याम् नरो यत्र देवयवो मदन्ति ॥

उरूक्रमस्य स हि बन्धुरित्था विष्णोः पदे परमे मध्व उत्सः ॥५॥

Meaning: The Rishi appeals to Vishnu for permission to enter the pathway (Vishnu's paramam padam) which abounds in nectarine springs and where devotees of Vishnu rejoice, for Vishnu is a dear friend of the mortals. This is the pathway that leads to the abode of Vishnu in the solar region or within oneself.

As we saw in the earlier stanza, it is Ananda all the way for the ascending man towards Vishnu. In the ascent, he tastes the divine delight, possesses the energy of divine consciousness and realizes his infinite existence. He finds the fellow travelers who live in utter ecstasy.

This Vishnu being dear friend of mortals is well articulated in Indian mythology of a much later period. Even today this bonhomie is evident in the Indian psyche. If you chance to travel the length and breadth of India, many people greet each other not by 'good morning or evening' but refer to each other as 'Jai Ramjiji or Radhe-Radhe or Hari Om'. These appellations are intended to remind us, that we are not the apparent mortal being in front but the immortal electromagnetic force that drives the body! We are here referring to the two great epics Ramayana and Krishna Avatar (incarnation) or Maha Bhagavatam. It is a great marvel to realize that electromagnetic force can play such a leading role in shaping human conduct and behavior. In Ramayana, Rama leads his royal life by an exemplary high moral behavior. In Krishna Leela (saga), Krishna is a darling of the people in his younger days, performing incredible feats, a feast to the eye of his devotees, and as he grows into maturity, demonstrating to the people how to conduct oneself in the various situations in life, culminating in his counsel to Arjuna in the middle of the battlefield Kurukshetra (symbolic of battle field of the life of man), his great and detailed magnum opus *Bhagwat Geeta*. Significantly, in the epic, Arjuna is son of Indra (Atom) being one of the Pandava brothers who are all born to different luminaries like Sun; Wind; and Moral code etc. Krishna (electromagnetic force) is very friendly with Arjuna (Atom) who is close to his heart! It is interesting to note that these two epics are in no way sectarian and they are eternal. They are not relevant only for a few eras and thereafter become ineffectual. Like Vishnu (electromagnetic force), as long as life exists, the prescriptions of the epics will influence man for best behavior and conduct, so that he can live a happy and fruitful life.

ता वां वास्तून्युश्मसि गमध्यै यत्र गावो भुरिश्रुङ्गा अयासः ।

अत्राह तदुरूगायस्य वृष्णः परमं पदमव भाति भूरि ॥६॥

Meaning: Our goal of journey is the abode of you two, Vishnu (electromagnetic force) and the herds of moving thoughts (Maruts). From there, the highest step of wide-moving, Vishnu shines down on us.

In Mandala 1 Sookta 156 Mantra 4 Rishi Dirghatamah Auchatyah gives further expression to his vision thus:

तमस्य राजा वरूणस्तमश्विना क्रतुं सचन्त मारूतस्य वेधसः ।

दाधर दक्षमुत्तममहर्विदं व्रजं च विष्णुः सखिवाᳬ अपोणुते ॥

Meaning: Vishnu (electro magnetic force) is closely associated with

Ashwins (Protons and Neutron), Varuna (Hydrogen), and is the creator and dispenser. Varuna and other luminaries carry out the mission of Vishnu (to protect the world). Vishnu possesses the potency (daksha), to accomplish activities which are incidental to his mission. In this he is assisted by Indra (Atom) and Maruts (Tachyons).

Creation needs two fundamental objects: matter and living beings. Universal Consciousness, called Purusha in Purusha Sukta (Rig Veda Mandala 10 Sookta 90 mantras 1-16) manifests these in the first phase. This can be called the primary creation. He also manifested out of himself as the Virat, the immense being, the totality of all objects and beings in their seed or root form. Virat Purusha entered into Consciousness again and brought the Luminaries, Sadhyas and Rishis who could carry on further or secondary creation as entrusted or directed by him. They are the various centers of power and action in the body of Virat. In fact, the luminaries are themselves Sadhyas and Rishis who take on the task of secondary and tertiary creation. This secondary act of creation by the Luminaries is called what is known as Yajna or Sacrifice. Vishnu is called Yajna Purusha, he is the Virat

Purusha. It is thus that popularly *Purusha Sukta* is associated with Mahavishnu. Only the free meaning of the 16 Mantras of *Purushasukta* as envisioned by Rishi Narayana in Rig Veda are given below:

Purusha, the Universal Consciousness; the Infinite, appears having innumerable heads, eyes and feet. He pervades the universe from all sides and is beyond the ten dimensions. We are creatures of four dimensions, the three dimensions of space, length, breath and height and the fourth time. There are six other dimensions we do not know anything about.

All that we see in the present in this universe is Purusha. He is all that has gone by in the past and all that is yet to be born in future. He is therefore also immortal. The Consciousness we mentioned above have five planes in the ascending order of subtlety: matter (Anna); life-energies (Prana); mind (Manas); scientific knowledge (Vijnana) and bliss (Ananda). Anna (matter or food) is the lowest and gross plane. Beginning with Anna He transcends all planes up to bliss.

So great is He that all the beings form a small part of him. Three parts of Him are immortal and hidden in heaven. Heaven here is the upper regions of this universe.

The Purusha ascended the three planes above, but with one part kept renewing this world again and again having pervaded all sentient and insentient beings.

From the Purusha was born Virat and from Virat was born Purusha. Born, he spread over the earth from behind and in front. Creation of this universe is considered a two phase affair. In, the primary phase of creation, Purusha brought into being Virat. He then reentered Virat and brought out the luminaries which were in the seed form in Virat Purusha, that in turn was the secondary creation, which accords well with findings of modern science. At the big bang, the first moments of present creation, the energy of the primordial fireball was so high that the four interactions (electromagnetic, gravitational, strong and weak nuclear energy) were all unified as one highly symmetrical interaction. As this fireball of swirling quarks, colored gluons, electrons and photons expanded, the universe cooled and the perfect symmetry began to break. First gravity was distinguished from the other interactions, and then the strong and weak nuclear, electromagnetic interactions became apparent and there after, as the universe kept on expanding the rest of the creation emerged.

When the luminaries performed a Yajna (sacrifice) using the (Virat) Purusha as havis (sacrificial material), for that Yajna the Vasanta (spring season) became the ajya (ghee), Grishma (summer season) its idhma (faggots of wood for fuel) and Sharat (autumn season) filled the place of havis (the edible offerings). There is a class of people who literally follow this as an injunction. But the original class of Rishis intended a symbolic representation of a universal truth. Yajna is not intended as a physical action. Yajna is simply a transformation of entities from one form into another. Yajna is properly defined as an activity of collaboration between the Virat and the luminaries. In the lower activities involving cooking etc, we know it is a collaboration between luminaries and human beings. Consider a mundane example. Every person is born as a child, who becomes a boy or girl after a few years, who subsequently becomes a youth after some more years, thereafter an adult man and finally a old person. We may say, the child is sacrificed to become a boy who in turn is sacrificed to be a youth and so on till he becomes an old person. The person is the same from the baby stage to old age but there is a perceptible change in appearance.

The (Virat) Purusha who was born in the beginning is Vishnu who is also the Yajna (Taittiriya Samhita 3-1-10), the spirit of sacrifice and he was placed on the Consciousness platform and was anointed. The luminaries performed the Yajna. The luminaries are always in a Yajna (sacrifice) mode. They work towards a common goal incessantly. The simile generally given is that of human body. Every limb of a man's body works in harmony with every other part towards the objective of the man. However, man forgets this fundamental reality and carries on his activity in contradiction of this principle of sacrifice and suffers trouble and tribulations in his life accordingly. This is an inexorable law of nature.

From that act of complete giving, a complex outpouring of light was collected. From that arose different forms of knowledge, pertaining to life-energy, the commune (grama) and that which was spread out (aranya), flora and fauna.

From that act of complete giving, Rik, Saman, Channdas and Yajus were born. Rik refers to the ability to contemplate on the phenomena in nature and their root cause Consciousness. There is a great harmony and rhythm in nature. Therefore, channelizing the same contemplations in a musical form is Saman. We noted earlier that the Rishis employed Mantra Shastra (science of Mantra) for visualizing the phenomena in nature. This mantra shastra followed rules of poetic matter that are predominant in nature which is called Chhandamsi. Lastly, the whole nature works on a principle of Yajna or sacrifice, as we noted in early stanza and that is called Yajus. In modern term we are here dealing with pure science!

From that was born the constantly moving heavenly regions. From that was also born the light sources of the universe, and waters of life (microbiology).

In what ways did the luminaries imagine the Purusha to be when they set him up for the yajna? How did they imagine the mouth, the strong arms, the productive skills and the powers of locomotion?

Man of mantras (Brahmin) was imagined as his mouth. The arms were construed as king who protects (Rajanya). The productive skill as business men, engineers, doctors etc. (Vaishya) and the man of service, foot soldier so to say (Shudra). This category usually needs to be led by the above three categories.

Man having emerged now he can turn his attention towards the phenomena in nature. Therefore it is said that from Virat Purusha's (electromagnetic force) mind was born the moon, from his eyes the sun was born, from his mouth Agni (Fire), and Indra (All the atoms and particles of nature dependant on light). And from his breath Vayu (Wind) was born. Significantly, except for gravitational force, every other phenomenon in nature is considered as born.

From the Purusha's navel was born the mid-region called Antariksha, the intervening vast space in universe; the heavens evolved from his head; the earth emerged from his feet and directions from his ears (Sound principle).

The luminaries embodied the Purusha in the Yajna (sacrifice) putting a space limitation (bound him) to the seer. Seven were the surrounding sheaths viz., Bhu, Bhuvaha, Suvaha, Mahaha, Janaha, Tapaha and Satyam and thrice seven the prepared fuels (samit).

In this last stanza of Purusha Sukta, we find the summing up of the early 15 stanzas in a nut shell. The luminaries sacrificed (Vishnu) by sacrifice (Vishnu) in the sacrifice (Vishnu). The natural laws that govern this universe came into being by this action. By this means the mighty ones reached the bliss, even to join the other ancients who cleared the path earlier.

Matsya Purana (versus 2.25-30) gives an account of initial creation. After Mahapralaya, the great dissolution of the Universe, there was darkness everywhere. Everything was in a state of sleep. There was nothing, either moving or static. Then Self-manifested Being (svayambhu) arose, which is a form beyond senses. It created the primordial waters first and established the seed of creation into it. The seed turned into Hiranyagarbha (golden womb). Then Svayambhu entered in the Brahmanda (great egg) and it is called Vishnu because of so entering. Brahmanda Purana (1.4.25) adds that it is called as Vishnu because it pervades the whole Universe. Modern science also tends to concur with this observation. Black holes, Dark energy and Dark matter are all a subject matter of ongoing research, concluding evidence is still emerging. The great scientist Stephen Hawking in his book "A brief History of Time", in the chapter "Black holes Ain't so black" says there is what is called Cerenkov Radiation a form of light emanating from black holes in the universe, so black holes are not so black after all. No body can hope to see the inside of a black hole, but they guess that there is a light source nevertheless.

There is a criticism against the Rig Veda that there are so few mantras addressed to Vishnu and Rudra. There is a reason. Vishnu the electromagnetic force plays a back stage role in all aspects of life. Vishnu is the driver, so to say. It is Surya the Sun, and Indra or atoms, and to a lesser extent other luminaries that front for him. Rudra/Shiva is altogether in the background. It is only during the time of remaining Vedas such as Yajur, Sama, Atharvana Vedas, Brahmanas and Puranas, which came much later, when the two deities Vishnu and Shiva gained ascendancy overshadowing all other deities. In any case, the mantra count is not at all an instrument to measure the might of a deity or phenomenon in nature.

Chapter 12

Rudra (Shiva)—The Transformer

If Big Bang entails expansion of the universe, we can as well imagine a Big Crunch involving a reversal process such that the universe will begin to fall back on itself. Unlike matter moving away from each other through electromagnetic force and other light dependant phenomenon in nature, matter tends to come together under gravitational force in the Big Crunch. Since this attractive and repellent forces balance, the universe continues to expand, though at a much slower rate compared to the early stage at the time of Big Bang. Our universe is just right.

In their search for a unified model, modern science is stumped by a big deterrent, the gravitational force. The standard model built to date includes all the forces in nature (that involve repulsion) except gravitational force and strong nuclear force (that involve attraction). While the expansion process involves light and light dependant phenomena, the contraction process involves anti-matter, black holes, dark energy and dark matter. Read on . . . .

व्यापयेद् भुवनं सर्वं व्यापयेत् सर्वदेहिषु ।

अवस्थितश्च सर्वत्र तेनासौ सकलः स्मितः ॥

व्योमस्थं निष्कलं तत्वं वाच्यवाचकवर्जितम् ।

निनादकलयातीतः स वै निष्कल उच्यते ॥

(Nihsvasa-Tantra, 28, 6-7 and 13)

Free meaning: From the supreme (universal consciousness), energy (para-shakti) inherent in Shiva revealed itself first, and from it sound (nada) issued forth; and from that came forth the primeval nucleus (bindu) which became Sadasiva. From Sadasiva, emerges Isvara, from Ishvara Rudra (Gravitational force), from Rudra Vishnu (Electromagnetic force), from Vishnu Brahma (Strong and weak nuclear reactions) and from Brahma all creation (Atom onwards), animate and inanimate. The Supreme God (Paramesvara-Universal Consciousness) is the cause of all the five aspects of creation: Srshti (emanation); Sthiti (preservation), Samhara (transformation), Tirobhava (concealment) and Anugraha (grace). Compare this with what modern science has discovered. If we go back to the time of big bang, in the initial moments, the energy of the primordial fireball (Agni-Consciousness) was so high that the four interactions were unified as one highly symmetrical interaction. As this rapidly spinning fireball of quarks, colored gluons, electrons, photons and anti photons expanded, the universe cooled and the perfect symmetry commenced breaking. First gravity (Rudra) was distinguished from the other interactions, then the electromagnetic interaction (Vishnu) and then the strong and weak interactions (Brahma). In 1978 Arno Penzias and Robert Wilson received Nobel Prize in Physics for discovering the sound micro waves (Nada-primordial sound) from the time of big bang thus effectively proving that a big bang did take place very long ago.

When we contemplate Rudra Shiva, we have to look at his three distinct phases that distinguishes him from other divinities. In the last chapter we have noted the reach of Lord Vishnu (electromagnetic force) into all the corners of this wide universe with his three steps and directly protecting and sustaining life everywhere. Rudra Shiva also protects and sustains life both in the macroscopic and microscopic world, but in an indirect way. We also noted in the last chapter that Mahavishnu (Electromagnetic Force) is concerned with all light dependant entities, whether humans or devatas (luminaries). He is involved in steady expansion of this universe. The expansion happens at the speed of light. He is also involved in creating more and more space. On the contrary, Rudra Shiva (Gravitational Force) is involved in contraction.

Another consequence arises from this expansion and contraction functions. While Mahavishnu's expansion entails repulsion, Rudra Shiva's contraction entails attraction. Since, electromagnetic force involves North Pole and South Pole in reality Mahavishnu has both attractive and repulsive aspects, whereas Rudra Shiva has attractive aspect alone. This attractive aspect translates into the action of unifying and bringing together things (Yoga). It also results in mending and repairing disjointed and damaged things. Thus, Rudra provides the essential balm to the diseased, weak and disabled with effective remedies, so the label Shiva the benevolent and auspicious. He is variously known as Nataraja (king of dancing), Yogeshwara (lord of Yoga) and Vaidhyanatha (the eternal medical man).

Rudradhyaya (the chapter on Rudra), a portion of Krishna Yajur Veda Taittiriya Samhita (Kanda 4, Prapathaka 5, extols Rudra in one hundred aphorisms (Satarudriya). At Anuvaka 1 Mantra 6 his name is identified as follows:

अध्यवोचदधिवक्ता प्रथमो दैव्यो भिषक् ।

अहीँश्च सर्वाञ्जम्भ-यन्सर्वाश्च यातुधन्यः ॥

Meaning: Rudra is hailed as the foremost physician, who cures all ailments, physical, mental, and spiritual; he eliminates sins, diseases, poverty and transactional bonds, and all afflictions. He suppresses known enemies like poisioning by snakes and other unknown tormentors. Rudra may cause misery for the devotee for the time being, but it will be for his own good in the long run. Therefore in later spiritual literature he gained the appellation *Vaidyanatha*, healer.

The Upa Veda (secondary Veda)—Ayurveda (science of longevity) can be traced to Vedic mantras on Rudra. There is another school of medicine in South India called Siddha Vaidya which can be directly traced to Shiva. Originally this form of medicine was an exclusive preserve of Siddhas or those who attained Siddhi (spiritual enlightenment) with competency in herbal remedies.

Moreover, the Siddhas were competent in Yoga Shastra, by the grace of Yogeshwara Shiva. The first such Siddha was Sri Dakshinamoorthy of Mahendragiri of yore. Also, there is a school of thought which states that Rudradhyaya (the chapter on Rudra), is an exhaustive treatise on medical remedies. There is a book titled "Shri Rudram—Decoded" by Mr. K. T. Shubhakaran, published in 1997 by Sagar Publications, New Delhi which states "Mystery of Vedas revealed—Mantra & Medicine for healing". Since, the healing is largely dependant on biology (plants, roots and herbs) association of Shiva with Soma is very apt. In fact, this relationship is visualized by Rishi Bharadvajah Barhaspayah in Rig Veda Mandala 6 Hymn 74 Mantras 1-4 addressed to Soma and Rudra jointly for healing power.

Practically, much of Tantra shastra (the codes of Tantra) except Pancharatra, widely known as Sakta and Shakti Tantras are the subject matter of revelations between Siva and his spouse Parvati. Tantras deal with the subject of Yoga in all its aspects such as Swara Yoga and Pranayama; Kundalini Yoga; Hatha Yoga; Raja Yoga; Mantra Shastra; Spanda Shastra; Sambhava Yoga etc. One authority states that there were no less than 10,000,000 Tantras most of which are lost forever and many of those that survived the onslaught of time are incomplete notes. Only a fraction of the Tantras are available to us in full form. Those that are available in full form demonstrate a thorough knowledge of the dynamics of life within a human being and the universe at large. The Tantras reveal a knowledge of not only the dynamic internal mechanism in a man but remedial measures to set right injuries, breakdowns, disease and malfunctioning of the mechanism physically, psychologically and spiritually (not necessarily in the religious sense). Then there are Saivagamas such as Tatpurusha, Aghora, Sadyojata, Vamadeva, and Visana. These are, further, sub-divided into 28 agamas. Besides, there are 208 Upaagamas (subsidiary texts) that also deal with well being and happiness of man.

While the above two phases of a benevolent Shiva are easily observable and stands demonstrated by their beneficent effect on the mankind over the centuries, the other dynamic phase of Nataraja is not so apparent even though the dance form is aesthetically appreciated the world over as an art form. Shiva's dance is also known as *Tandava,* the energetic activity. This reveals the insight of ancients, when they conceived *Shiva Tandava* (the dance of gravitational energy!). The esoteric significance becomes absolutely clear when we consider the scientific exploration of the subatomic world in the twentieth century.

Till the time of Isaac Newton, classical physics prevailed in the world of science where, matter, a collection of atoms (Indra) was considered a static and independent quantity in space. It was considered an indestructible material substance, of which all things were thought to be made. It was also known by that time that the mass of a body, is a measure of its weight, which is the pull of gravity on that body and that mass measures the inertia of an object, i.e. its measure of resistance to acceleration. New physics in the twentieth century exploded this belief. According to relativity theory, mass is nothing but a form of energy. We can restate it by saying that various forms of energy already known to classical physics, gets locked up as mass of an object. Gravitons induce acceleration. Accordingly, matter is not a static quantity but is intrinsically dynamic in nature like energy. It became evident that the constituents of atoms, the atomic particles, are dynamic patterns which do not exist as isolated substances, but as integral parts of an inseparable network of interactions. These interactions require a ceaseless flow of energy manifesting itself as the exchange of particles. It is a dynamic activity where particles are created and destroyed endlessly with each variation of pattern. These particle interactions constitute the stable structures of matter and the world at large, which are again not static, but oscillate in rhythmic movements. The whole universe is thus engaged in endless motion and activity; in a continual cosmic dance of energy. The ancients aptly named this universe as *Jagat* in Sanskrit, meaning that which is in constant motion. The Shiva Tandava best symbolizes not only cosmic cycles of creation and destruction, but also the daily rhythm of birth and death as the basis of all existence. All the particle interactions seem to fall into four categories: a) The strong interactions; b) The electromagnetic interactions; c)

The weak interactions and d) the gravitational interactions. The gravitational interaction acts between all particles, but is so weak it cannot be detected experimentally in the microscopic world. However, when we consider the macroscopic world, it is noticed that the huge number of particles that constitute massive bodies in universe combine their gravitational interactions (Shiva Shakti) such that the force of gravity (Rudra) is the dominating force in the universe. Suppose for some reason gravity (Rudra Shiva) ceases to exist, we would all fly off the earth; earth and other planets would also fly off from their orbit around the sun. The sun, stars and large planets would also cease to exist, because it is gravity (Rudra Shiva) that holds them together.

It is important to remember at this point that we are not talking of a remote atom or particle in the outer space or scientific laboratory or a bubble chamber alone. We are also talking about the activity of atoms (Indra) and particles which are very much an integral part of our own body. We are predominated by atoms (Indra) of which particles and sub-particles are the constituents. It is estimated that, if all the atoms in our body are somehow collected together, the resultant speck would be difficult to see except with a magnifying glass. Moreover, each atom is made up of upto 90% empty space. That leaves an absolute minuscule space for particles and sub-particles. And that is the ground where a great battle of annihilation, survival and regeneration rages incessantly. It is remarkable that the great Rishis of Rig Veda could visualize these phenomena with mantra power which modern scientists theoretically express in mathematical terms. No doubt the particles are not only powerful, they display rhythm and harmony. Their natural interactions could be easily disturbed by a mere thought crossing our mind, for, even that thought contains an atom and the related particles. The disturbed interaction can precipitate a disharmony in our being! So long as we are following the natural law, our thought, words and deeds do not disturb this internal sub-atomic world. Even what we eat, drink, see, hear, smell, and touch could cause havoc for the same reason. Sad to say, most of us do not have any knowledge of the rudiments of natural law and we don't even care. On account of this erratic sub-atomic behavior, we are subject to various ailments that are some times diagnosed or at other times undetermined and even unknown. Some of the ailments can be cured promptly with medicine, some ailments get prolonged causing misery and a few could even turnout fatal.

In chapter 1, we have seen that there are six other lokas (worlds to traverse before we arrive at the final destination with the help of Individual Consciousness. All the lokas are within our body. The sixth loka we mentioned was Satya loka. We further noted that this Satya loka is a dark region more like a black hole mentioned in science. At the entrance to this Satya loka is a region known as Brahmaloka similar to event horizon of science. If a Yogi or a sage succeeds in traversing the five earlier lokas through Sadana (practising particular skill), at the approach of Brahmaloka, he will be drawn into the Satyaloka by Shiva Shakti (gravitational force). There he is bestowed with supreme benediction. Even according to science, when a body approaches the event horizon it is sucked in by the gravitational force at the event horizon. However, what happens to that body is not yet clearly known to science.

We shall now proceed to glean Rig Veda in the light of above introduction. In Mandala 1 Hymn 114, Rishi Kutsah Angirasah narrates his vision thus:

इमा रूद्राय तवसे कपर्दिने क्षयद्वीराय प्रभरामहे मतीः ।

यथा शमसद् द्विपदे चतुष्पदे विश्वं पुष्टं ग्रामे आस्मिन्ननातुरम् ॥१ ॥

Meaning: We offer these songs of praise to the mighty Rudra with terrible countenance who destroys the inimical forces. In this way the beings of two states and those subject to four interactions in this universe be protected as a class.

Here the Rishi is having a vision of the activity in the microscopic sub-atomic world. There is a constant battle of existence. Only Rudra (Gravitational Force) knows who is friend and who is foe.

There are the particles which are also waves (two states) and they are subjected to four interactions: a) the strong Interactions; b) the electromagnetic interactions; c) The weak interaction; and d) The gravitatinal interactions. They are a community in that part of the universe, the inside of atoms.

म्रुळा नो रुद्रोत नो मयस्कृधि क्षयद्वीराय नमसा विधेम ते ।

यच्छं च योश्च मनुरायेजे पिता तदश्याम तव रुद्र प्रणीतिषु ॥२ ॥

O Rudra, the destroyer of foes, be gracious to us and grace us with the Supreme Bliss. Through sacrifice and surrender to you our divine mind has established equipoise.

Having seen the activity in the sub-atomic world within each one of us, anyone will have a deep mental disturbance as to how we can overcome the horror of this maze and come out unscathed. Only Rudra's (Gravitational Force) grace can restore the mental equipoise to attain the Supreme Bliss (Ananda).

मा नो महान्तमुत मा नो अर्भकं मा न उक्षन्तमुत मा न उक्षितम् ॥

मा नो वधिः पितरं मोत मातरं मा नः प्रियास्तन्वो रूद्र रीरिषः ॥७ ॥

Meaning: O Rudra, protect the great ones and the little ones; protect the generating and generated ones. Protect our parents and our dear ones.

The great ones are the planets, stars and many suns in the macroscopic universe. The small ones are the particles and sub-particles in the microscopic world. There are many particles which beget other particles and energy. These particles and energy are the begotten. Parents are the building block of particles that in fact create our being and sustain it. These particles are naturally dear to us.

मा नस्तोके तनये मा न आयौ मा नो गोषु मानो अश्वेषु रीरिषः ।

वीरान् मा नो रूद्र भामितो वधीर्हविष्मन्तः सदमित्त्वा हवामहे ॥८॥

Meaning: Protect our children and descendants of our life. Protect our cows and horses. Don't annihilate our heroes in your anger. We invoke you with our offerings.

Children are the emerging particles, new energy, and photons and gravitons in the sub-atomic world as a result of constant collision where gravity is ever present to ensure that life giving energies are conserved.

आरे ते गोघ्नमुत पूरूषघ्नं क्षयद्वीर सुम्नमस्मे ते अस्तु ॥

म्रुळा च नो अधि च ब्रूहि देवाधा च नः शर्म यच्छ द्विबर्हाः ॥१०॥

Meaning: Let your annihilating target be away from our cows and persons, O destroyer of heroes, be felicitous to us. Guard us and give us your blessed message so that we are happy in both stations.

In the sub-atomic world, let the annihilating process be diverted away from photons and other life giving particles. Since these particles are life giving they are heroes. The two stations in this sub-atomic world are the annihilation of particles, resulting from collision and creation resulting from emerging particles and energies.

If Rishi Kutsah Angirasah had a vision of the microscopic world as above, Rishi Grtsamadah Bhargava Shaunakah had a similar vision of the macroscopic universe which he narrates in Mandala 2 Hymn 33 of Rig Veda, thus:

स्थिरेभिः अङ्गैः पुरुरूप उग्रो बभ्रुः शुक्रेभिः पिपिशे हिरण्यैः ।

ईशानादस्य भुवनस्य भूरेः न वा उ योषत् रूद्रात् असुर्यम् ॥९॥

Meaning: The majesticness is inseparable from Rudra (gravitational force). With his firm limbs, and numerous forms, he is forceful.

He is ruddy brown, but has taken the bright golden form. He is the supreme ruler of the vast universe.

Gravitational force takes many forms in this universe. It influences a firm grip on the planet and stars that they are able to stay in position. But for its hold, the whole universe will collapse.

अहंन् बिभर्षि सायकानि धन्व अहंन् निष्कं यजतं विश्वरूपम् ।

अहंन् इदं दयसे विश्वमभ्वं न वा उ ओजीयो रूद्र त्वदस्ति ॥१०॥

Meaning: O Rudra, you are the mightiest, as you shield the bombardment of bows and arrows thus protecting all the forces. Your necklace is a worshipful force.

In the outer space, there is incessant bombardment of particles, asteroids and comets. These asteroids and comets, some times appear with long tails as if they are arrows discharged to target earth. They are diverted away from bombarding earth by gravitational force. According to quantum field theory, there is what is known as graviton quanta along the gravity field that link large masses like stars together. For example, instead of thinking of the gravity field as some kind of force field linking the earth and moon, the gravity field is quantized into countless gravitons. This is like a necklace invisible to our ordinary eyes.

स्तुहि श्रुतं गर्तसदं युवानं म्रुगं न भीमम् उपहत्नुम् उग्रम् ।

म्रुळा जरित्रे रूद्र स्तवानो अन्यं ते अस्मन्नि वपन्तु सेनाः ॥११॥

Meaning: O Rudra, be blissful to the singer of this praise, you are well known as ageless, an eternal youth, mounted on a moving vehicle, who appear as destructive and terrible. Let not your missiles annihilate us.

In the universe, the gravitational force incessantly bears responsibility of annihilating intruding forces, travelling in the gravitational wave. If misdirected, the gravitational force can equally annihilate the earth.

परि णो हेती रूद्रस्य व्रुज्याः परि त्वेष्य दुर्मतिः मही गात्।

अव स्थिरा मगवद् भ्यः तनुष्व मीढ्वः तोकाय तनयाय म्रळ ॥१४॥

Meaning: O Rudra, may your missiles pass us by; may the wrath of terrible ones go by us; destroy the hostile forces full of energy and be gracious to our children and descendants.

In the macrocosm there is an ongoing bombardment, in the upper reaches. Powerful forces fly to and fro. Not only gravitation forces should avoid earth but the oncoming hostile trajectories, full of energy should be destroyed or diverted, so the existence of planet earth is ensured.

Rishi Vasishthah Maitravarunih also had a vision of Rudra as gravitational force in Mandala 7 Hymn 46 Mantras 1-4, thus:

इमा रूद्राय स्थिरधन्वने गिरः क्षिप्रेषवे देवाय स्वधात्रे।

अषाळ्हाय सहमानाय वेधसे तिग्मायुधाय भरता श्रृणोतु नः ॥१॥

Meaning: O Rudra, hear our words of welcome. He comes with a firm bow, swift arrows of impulsion and one who upholds the natural law. He is the conquering and invincible creator.

Gravitational wave is the bow. The arrows are gravitons. Natural law is the code and Gravitational force is ever victorious.

स हि क्षयेण क्षम्यस्य जन्मनः साम्राज्येन दिव्यस्य चेतति।

अवन् अवन्तीः उप नो दुरः चर अनमीवो रूद्र जासु नो भव ॥२॥

Meaning: O Rudra, do not entertain our thoughts (that are inimical to natural law), conquer them and enlighten us by being with us and guide us towards that heavenly abode.

211

Every one of our thoughts is constituted of atoms and therefore contains the sub-atomic world. Gravitational force has a great role in maintaining rhythm and harmony there, which can be hopelessly disturbed (by our motivations which are contrary to natural law). No doubt, Gravitational force can overcome them and improve the quality of our thoughts.

या ते दिद्युत् अवस्रुष्टा दिवः परि क्ष्मया चरति परि सा वृणक्तु नः ।

सहस्रं ते स्वपिवात भेषजा मा नस्तोकेषु तनयेषु रीरिषः ॥३॥

Meaning: O Rudra, release downward your (Gravitational) force from your abode, so that it surrounds our earth, but do not disturb our own creation and extensions. You are first remembered since you have many powers of healing.

In the macrocosm, gravitation is responsible for planets and stars to be at their respective locations with reference to other stars and planets. For example, we have our solar system where each planet has its fixed location with reference to other planets in the solar system. Besides rotating in their on location, these planets go round the sun in a strict orderly manner, all on account of gravitational pull. It is the same gravitational force of earth that can ward off intruding astroids, comets and other intruding objects from outer space that can destroy man created property on earth. Man is also able to tap the universal gravitational force to divert incoming objects from outer space in a new direction so that there is no damage to property and life on earth.

मा नो वधी रूद्र मा परा दा मा ते भूम प्रसितौ हीळितस्य ।

आ नो भज बर्हिषि जीवशंसे यूयं पात स्वस्तिभिः सदा नः ॥४॥

Meaning: O Rudra, prevent us from coming into your line of annihilation and save us from having thoughts that disturbs the equilibrium of the sub-atomic activity so that we are spared from your wrath. When our thoughts are lofty, we have a full and joyous of living that is again an expression of your presence.

212

It is important to remember that the microcosm and macrocosm not only refers to external universe, but also the inner being of man. The Rishis have again and again stressed that the inner being of man is an exact replica of the external universe. Since basis of thought is atom, every thought is also influenced by the sub-atomic activity. Gravity induces momentum. Our whole body is immersed in movement. This is evident when blood flows; muscles stretch; essence of food is distributed all over the body; various organs perform their individual functions in a consorted way. Without involvement of gravitational force, there will be a ceasation of all such functions, and existence will end. Even the solid structure of our body constitutes atoms in large numbers, so subject to sub-atomic activity.

Chapter 13

Soma—The Elixir of Life

We can define a thing which has parameters in space. But the Ultimate Truth has no parameters and it is also not time bound. How do we define it then? We can only say the Truth is. It always is. It has no yesterday or tomorrow. We therefore say it is eternal. This raises the question then, what is reality which we confront both in universe and in our own self, which has change in its nature? It is Truth in Consciousness of reality. Consciousness could be nothing or everything as it is not space and time bound. Such a Consciousness is always in a state of bliss. Conflict, the opposite of bliss, limited by space and time cannot contaminate Consciousness. Thus the ancients coined the term SAT-CHIT-ANANDA, Truth-Consciousness-Bliss. This Ananda (bliss) translates into eternal delight. It inundates the reality with the joy of life. This is the reason that in every nook and corner of Rig Veda the deity Soma pops up. He is associated with every luminary. Read on . . . .

A few years back, there was a famous Hollywood movie E-Walle, in which the role of bliss or love in existence was dramatically symbolized. Down on earth, there was this mechanical compacter (mimed as a person by name E-Walle) that was working day in and day out in a junk yard near New York City, compacting daily waste that was dumped in the yard. After compacting, the billets were taken away for melting or other means of disposal. The dumping included all kinds of material. One day E-Walle comes across a green sapling in the dump. He becomes excited to see this newly arrived variety in his lot. He picked it up and preserved it in his quarters and nurtured it lovingly since he saw it growing.

The plant also responded in its own way by its sensitiveness, which excited E-Walle and he began to consider the plant as his prized possession. Then Ava a female robot enters his life. Ava belongs to a different planet wholly consisting of robots, some manufactured in that planet and some imported originally as humans but later brainwashed to be robots. The robots are all mechanical, devoid of any sensitivity or emotion. The authorities in that robotic planet decide to send Ava to make a survey of planet earth. Ava lands in the compacter's backyard. By and by a friendship develops. During one of the trips of Ava, compacter E-Walle presents the sapling to Ava. When the sapling shows the same sensitivity towards Ava she is smitten by the new love bug, a sensation it had never known before. Perhaps the director wanted to convey a scientific fact. From the love and affection conferred by E-Walle the plant acquires super conductivity, so that it is able to transfer the feelings of love and affection to Ava. When Ava returns to its own planet, Ava is greeted with alarm bells peeling away, because she has imported a new gadget that is a taboo in that planet. But the authorities are unable to locate the gadget. After some time Ava again comes back to earth for more research. But this time it is a changed robot Ava vis-à-vis E-Walle. There is now a sense of attachment also entering the friendship. E-Walle persuades Ave to take him to the robot planet, but he is not acceptable there. Finally they both return to earth and vow to love each other for eternity. The sapling in the story symbolizes Soma of Rig Veda!

More poignant is the legend in ancient Shrimad Bagavatha. The story relates to Lord Krishna (Electromagnetic force), incarnation of Vishnu. After marriage to Rukmini, the incarnation of Devi Mahalaxmi (female luminary) consort of Vishnu, Krishna gets married a second time to Satyabhama (a typical human princess). Satyabhama was a down to earth princess attached to earthly possessions such as gold, gems, and other material wealth. She was also arrogant and possessive of her husband. Without regards to claims of the former wife, she corners the attention of her spouse Krishna exclusively for herself. These are the traits of a person of narrow outlook confined to the finite world of space-time. Space-time is but two dimensions in this universe which has ten dimensions. All of us, of course, are subservient to this space-time limitation. We cannot even imagine that there are other dimensions, let alone surmounting them. We are content with our growing bank balance, extensive landed properties and other assets which tether us to this narrow two dimensional Samsara Sagara (the ocean of finite existence).

Lord Krishna and Devi Rukmini or Mahalaxmi are infinite. They can see the binding shackles of finite existence. Out of compassion and love, they plan to rescue Satyabhama from her predicament. Sage Vyasa, the author enacts a great drama in this connection. Having killed the demon Narakasura, Lord Krishna plans to visit Heaven (Swarga) the domain of Indra (atom) to return the Ear pieces of Devi Atithi (Universal Consciousness) mother of Indra (Atom), which the demon (dark force) had snatched away as a sign of his sway over the Heavenly region. Satyabhama also accompanies Lord Krishna, perhaps to draw some of the limelight to herself. The King Indra, his wife, mother and other dignitaries in heaven were overjoyed to receive Lord Krishna and his wife. Satyabhama did not fail to notice a great fragrance permeating the atmosphere. Indra's wife showed Satyabhama the Parijath tree and said that it is the only tree of its kind in the entire universe, and that it has a unique property, in that, the person sitting under it would be eternally youthful. Lord Krishna and Satyabhama return to Dwarka, their abode. While Satyabhama was busy in her quarters, Lord Krishna proceeds to Rukmini's abode and gives her a Parijath flower which he picked while at Heaven (Swarga), Indra's abode. He plants the flower in Rukmini's plait. When Satyabhama saw the flower in Rukmani's hair, she was upset. Upset because she was with Krishna and he did not place any flower in her hair, but secretly brought one flower for Rukmini. Out of jealousy, she demanded that Krishna should get her the whole plant from heaven and not just one flower.

So once again Krishna went to heaven for getting the plant from Indra. Indra pleaded that he had even refused to give the plant to *Shiva* (the gravitational force, the great healer) and it was a fixture in heaven where everyone could enjoy its beneficial spell and he could not allow it to be taken to earth. Satyabhama was adamant and insisted in having it. When Indra declared that he was ready to protect it against all odds with his life, Krishna accepted the challenge and fixed a date for a fight. Krishna wanted to teach a lesson in humility to Indra. Krishna (the electromagnetic force in the universe) prayed to Shiva (the gravitational force) being his greatest devotee, the appearance of Shiva was also prompt. Krishna explained all the events that had happened till then and sought Shiva's permission for the ensuing fight for possession of the Parijath plant. As expected, in the fight, Krishna bested Indra and took away the plant from Indra. A humbled Indra realized his folly and apologized to Krishna, for challenging his own master. Remember, atom is ever dependant on electromagnetic force. Krishna brought the plant from heaven to earth and handed over the plant to a contented Satyabhama. However, he told her that the installation of the plant needed performance of a suitable ritual at the site of installation, by a competent priest well versed in Shastras. Thus, sage Narada was engaged to do the job. Unfortunately, the conduct of ritual was marred by a lapse. Narada opined that to expiate for the lapse, Satyabhama will have to give valuables equal in weight to her spouse, otherwise she will lose her spouse. Satyabhama readily agreed, thinking that as a man, Krishna would weigh not more than a hundred pounds. Accordingly, she placed Krishna on one scale of the balance and at the other end; she ordered stacking up all her valuable belongings. Alas, to her consternation, even after placing all the valuables in her possession and in that kingdom the scale did not tip even a bit. She was at her wits end.

Out of desperation, she consulted Rukmini the elder wife of Krishna. Rukmini smilingly told Satyabhama that the entire valuables of the material four dimensional world would not equal the weight of the Creator that is Krishna. The only thing that can gain his weight is Love. To demonstrate her advice, Rukmini asks all the valuables to be removed from the scale and plants a single Tulsi (Basil) leaf on the scale when the scale rightly balanced. Tulsi plant here symbolizes Love, because Rukmini, who is infinite, placed the leaf on the scale with eternal Love for her spouse. At this point Lord Krishna is also the infinite or measureless. Weight has significance only in the four dimensional world we live. Lord Krishna transcends all dimensions that are there in the universe. He can be most weighty and at the same time weightless. Love is a spirit that can never be material or equated with anything material, the lesson that Satyabhama learnt. Love drives the existence. Love is blissful and the delight derived from love cannot be compared with any material comfort and happiness which is transitory. Love is eternal.

There are about 1200 mantras in the Rig Veda dealing with Soma and about 1085 mantras out of that find place in Mandala 9 alone. Astonishingly, some 80 Rishis had the vision of Soma. We shall consider only a few specimens to understand the mind of the mighty Rishis. Besides addressing Soma directly the Rishis associate Soma with all other devatas (luminaries), especially Indra (atom). There has been a misconception as to what is Soma so frequently mentioned in Rig Veda. Over the ages, a popular misconception has gained ground that the word refers to a particular intoxicant. This predilection has gained so much ground that distributors in today's market, supply some of their liquors with the label "Soma" as though the meaning that it is liquor is explicit in everyone's mind. This misconception has arisen because the language of some of the mantras relating to Soma, literally leads to such an interpretation. The literal meaning was a camouflage for the deeply hidden inner meaning with reference to the context of the same mantras, the subject matter being extremely complex.

In modern science, it is a subject under active on-going research, and discoveries bag Nobel Prize year after year. We are talking of the contemporary science of Biology and Microbiology. The world of Biology and Microbiology, operate on an altogether different dynamics, which we do not see in the normal world of physics, chemistry and conventional four energy forms around us. We are relatively sure of what takes place on earth. We are able to imagine what happens in the outer space above us, we can even appreciate our own inner working. But more subtle is the working of cells, and protein in this universe. By sheer numbers they would benumb us. Without their will we would not exist in the first place. Precisely for this reason, Soma (the label the Rishis gave to cells and proteins) is still an enigma in understanding Rig Veda. The 80 Rishis of yore penetrated this world, in order to give an account of their vision to posterity.

All the phenomena in nature with which we were concerned till now were dependant on the four forces in nature: electromagnetic force; gravitational force, nuclear force and vibration but cells and proteins seem to be an exception though photons play a valuable role in their existence. From what modern science has discovered till date in the world of biology, it is quite apparent all the micro-organisms that go by the labels of cells, DNA, RNA, proteins, exist for a single purpose, that of protecting our existence, well being and happiness. That is the world of Ananda (happiness and bliss). These microbes are an integral part of the micro biotic universe that makes us healthy in order that we may enjoy the delight of existence. Lest we think that this micro biotic universe is in the yonder, let it be understood that we are the habitats for these microbes, trillions upon trillions of them, most within our body and many outside on the surface of the skin of our body. The only purpose of existence of these cells, and proteins appear to be to fight our war against disease, injury and sickness and keep our metabolism in good working condition and our health in peak performance so that we may enjoy life. Literally, billions of these microbes die in the process. A greater sacrifice cannot be found! It smacks of maternal love delivered directly from heaven.

It is amazing to realize that a tiny cell, a minute fraction of a micron in size, is house to a whole world of activity, and the most active member in a cell is protein. Hence most Rishis had clear vision of cells and proteins therein and of course the other luminaries, especially Indra (Atom) being activated by proteins.

In Mandala 1 Sookta 91 Mantra 1 & 4, Rishi Gotamah Rahuganah had this vision:

त्वं सोम प्र चिकितो मनीषा त्वं रजिष्ठमनु नेषि पन्थाम् ।

तव प्रणीती पितरो न इन्दो देवेषु रत्नमभजन्त धीराः ॥१ ॥

Meaning: O Soma, we are sure you will provide us a good knowledge of the straight path (to Consciousness). We also know that our forefathers were blessed with happiness by the luminaries after being drenched (with your delight).

Soma (Proteins) drenches the luminaries such as Indra (Atom), Varuna (Hydrogen), Vayu (Wind), Maruts (Tachyons), Ray Cows (Photons), and Vishnu (Electromagnetic Force) so that they make us blissful in order that we may give total attention to the path of Consciousness. The Rishi also says that his ancestors have been blessed with benediction.

या ते धामानि दिवि या पृथिव्यां या पर्वतेष्वोषधीष्वप्सु ।

तेभिर्नो विश्वैः सुमना अहेळन् राजन्त्सोम प्रति हव्या गृभाय ॥४ ॥

Meaning: O Soma, you are unangry and auspicious, do accept our offering. You are glorious in the luminous world, on earth, mountains, and plants and in the water.

Soma (proteins) are everywhere not only in our body but also in the wide heavens, on earth, in the mountain stream or herbal plants. Soma (proteins) spreads joy and love everywhere.

In Mandala 3 Sookta 62 Mantra 13, Rishi Vishvamitrah Gathinah had this vision:

सोमो जिगाति गातुवित् देवानामेति निष्कृतम् ।

ऋतस्य योनिमासदम् ॥१३ ॥

Meaning: Soma (proteins) knows the path by which to approach the abode of luminaries, which is the origin (of Consciousness).

Here the reference is to the cells in human body. All the luminaries congregate in the cell. Proteins produced by DNA drench the luminaries. Collectively, the luminaries are Consciousness.

Whole of Mandala 9 of Rig Veda deals exclusively with Soma. Hymn 1 is attributed to Madhuchchhandas Vaishvamitrah. In Mantra 1 he visualizes thus:

स्वादिष्ठया मदिष्ठया पवस्व सोम धारया ।

इन्द्राय पातवे सुतः ॥१ ॥

Meaning: O Soma, you are a tasty elixir that flows in a continuous swarm towards Indra (Atoms). You are pressed out (by DNA).

Indra (Atom) is a luminary and not a being like you and me, in flesh and blood. So the question of his drinking the elixir does not arise. Indra (Atoms) pervades our whole body whether in thought word or deed. His abode is cells in our body. There is a steady production of proteins in the cells. Soma drenches Indra with the elixir so that Indra is galvanized into action. Here Soma is represented as proteins.

रक्षोहा विश्वचर्षणिः अभि योनिम् अयोहतम् द्रुणा ।

सधस्थम् आसदत् ॥२ ॥

Meaning: The ever vigilant, the destroyer of inimical forces has come running from her impregnable fort. She is always in session.

Here the Rishi is talking of Cells in our body. Wherever there is danger the cells come rushing to attack the enemy and destroy them. These cells live in their cocoons, well protected. They are the busiest entities, like particles in the sub-atomic world. There are billions of cells in our body. Their mortality rate is very high. Typically, many live but for a day and then they are repaired, renewed or replaced. Some cells live life long, that is, they are with us till we live, especially in the lever and brain.

वरिवो – धातमो भव मंहिष्ठो वृत्रहन्तमः ।

पर्षि राधो मघोनाम् ॥३॥

Meaning: (O Soma), you are well entrenched in our body to ensure our well being; you are profuse to destroy all types of inimical forces (Vrtra). You are plenteous.

Modern science has in recent years discovered the exciting and mind boggling world of biology within the human system. The scientists have discovered that our body contains billions upon billions of Cells. Their only apparent objective of existence is our well being and happiness. In pursuit of this objective, the cells fight incessant war with forces that cause disease, injuries and imbalance in our system. Soma is a label that not only includes Cells, as in this present mantra, it also includes proteins that are produced inside it that exhibit the very same objective as cells. As these beings do a selfless service, they are our loved ones. Can there be any better definition of Love?

अभ्यर्ष महानां देवानां वीतिमन्धसा ।

अभि वाजमुत श्रवः ॥४॥

Meaning: (O Soma), arrive with replenishments to the mighty luminaries. Bring equilibrium to us with your large numbers and keen hearing (for anything out of balance).

The cells are a unique formation in the life of a being. A cell is indeed very tiny. Yet it accommodates DNA, RNA, an apparent factory that produce proteins, and billions of atoms within it self. DNA is the Individual Consciousness and atom represents most of the other phenomena in nature, by its very constitution. So these mighty luminaries are not to arrive from somewhere else. They are already there in a typical cell. The replenishments are in the form of amino acids that make up proteins.

त्वामच्छा चरामसि तदिदर्थं दिवेदिवे ।

इन्दो त्वे न आशसः ॥५ ॥

Meaning: (O Soma), the harbinger of delight that you are, our hope converges towards you, your objective being same, this happens every day.

The cells, fight our battle for our survival and well-being all the time within our body. Thus they make our life delightful. Naturally, when something goes wrong with our physical system, we look forward with hope that Soma will bring it back to normal. This appears to be the sole objective of Soma; this recuperating activity goes on day in and day out.

We will now turn to what the next Rishi listed in Mandala 9, Rishi Medhatithih Kanvah visualizes as recorded in Mandala 9 Hymn 2, thus:

पवस्व देववीः अति पवित्रं सोम रंह्मा ।

इन्द्रम् इन्दो ब्रुषा विश ॥१ ॥

Meaning: O Soma, inundate the mind of those that turn their total attention towards luminaries, and pervade Indra (Atom) by spraying your delight.

Indra (atom) is the ruler of our thoughts and mind. He is the emissary of Consciousness in us. When we focus our undivided attention on him, our thoughts and mind are not engaged in futile and selfish activities. We get enlightened as well. Here proteins are the link between our thoughts and Indra. When Indra (Atom) is drenched by Soma (Proteins) he is galvanized into action. Turning our attention to Indra (Atom) is redirecting Soma (Proteins) in that direction.

आ वच्यस्व महि प्सरो बृषन्दो द्युम्नवत्तमः ।

आ योनिं धर्णसिः सदः ॥२॥

Meaning: O Soma you are the womb that holds Indra (atoms), you are the sprayer (of proteins) and you are the most luminous (as you also contain the DNA—individual consciousness).

Modern science has revealed that an individual cell houses billions of atoms; it is the place where proteins are generated; and it is the abode of DNA and RNA. Soma is considered as cells in our body.

अधुक्षत प्रियं मधु धारा सुतस्य वेधसः ।

अपो वसिष्ठ सुक्रतुः ॥३॥

Meaning: O Soma, you are the abode of the creator who presses out the honey.

Soma the cells house the DNA which gives specific genetic information and replicates proteins in the numbers required. DNA is the Consciousness in us. Proteins are honey because they are responsible to sweeten our life with joy of existence. Proteins are created by a meticulous sequencing of amino acid. Thereafter they have to be replicated in large number which can only be done with the help of DNA. Without DNA proteins cannot come into existence.

महान्तं त्वा मही: अनु आपो अर्षन्ति सिन्धवः ।

यत् गोभिः वासयिष्यसे ॥४॥

O Soma, when you are clad with Ray-cows (photons), what flows like water into us is the energy and strength to withstand the exposure to the mighty one.

There is a profusion of photon energy in the water that shower as rains as well as rivers that flow from the mountains. Photons come from Swar world where Consciousness is ever present. They charge the visionary with extraordinary energy and strength that is required to gain a vision of the Universal Consciousness. The Ray-cows (Photons) are present in cells in large numbers.

समुद्रो अप्सु माम्बुजे विष्टम्भो धरुणो दिवः सोमः ।

पवित्रे अस्मयुः ॥५॥

Meaning: O Soma, you are the supporter of our world of happiness. You are purified by the waters of the ocean. Desiring us (as protiens) you go through the strainer.

Here Soma refers to proteins. It is charged with photon energy. While DNA is responsible to produce proteins, RNA acts as the sieve or strainer through which the proteins pass so as to be conducive to our body system. This is also a scientific fact. The codons, the instructions of DNA cannot be deciphered by proteins. They need to be translated by some other means. This is the job of RNA, which enables the proteins to understand the strict instructions and act accordingly.

Rishis Shunahshepah Ajigartih had the following vision in Mandala 9 Sukta 3 Mantra 1:

एष देवो अमर्त्यः पर्णवीरिव दीयति ।

अभि द्रोणानि आसदम् ॥१॥

Meaning: O divine, immortal Soma, you rush to fill our body (gated house) like a winged bird.

Once the proteins are sieved by RNA they hasten to spread through out our body. Our body is considered as a house of seven gates. The seven gates are: pair of eyes; two ears; two nostrils; a mouth; the genital organ and anus.

Rishi Hiranyastupah Angirasah says in Mandala 9 Sukta 4 Mantra 4:

पवीतारः पुनीतन सोममिन्द्राय पातवे ।

अथा नो वस्यसस्कृधि ॥४॥

Meaning: O Strainer, purify the Soma (Proteins) for approaching Indra (Atom). Fill us with joy.

The strainer is RNA. The combination of (Indra) Atoms and (Soma) Proteins are the formula for joy in a being. (Soma) Proteins must approach Indra (Atoms) with the instruction received from DNA and translated by RNA for it.

In Mandala 9 Sukta 6 Mantra 2, Rishis Asitah Kashyapah and Devalah Kashyapah have this to say:

अभि त्यं मद्यं मदम् इन्दविन्द्र इति क्षर ।

अभि वाजिनो अर्वतः ॥२॥

Meaning: Like Indra (Atom), O Indu (Soma), make the essence of joy flow and also generate the momentum (to fight inimical forces in or body).

The Cells and Protein wage the battle in our body against the forces of sickness, diseases, injury, deformity or any other deficiency that deprives us of joy. Thus they make the essence of joy flow fast and unimpeded.

In Mandala 9 Sukta 10 Mantra 2, Rishis Asitah Deevalah and Kashyapah have vision as follows:

हिन्वानासो रथा इव दधन्विरे गभस्त्योः ।

भरासः कारिणामिव ॥२॥

Meaning: The Soma is brightly established to carry out the supporting actions like a hero.

In Mandala 9 Sukta 18 Mantra 2, Rishis Asitah Deevalah and Deevalah Kashyapah have vision as follows:

त्वं विप्रः त्वं कविः मधु प्र जातम् ।

अन्दसः मदेषु सर्वधा आसि ॥२॥

Meaning: O Soma, you are not only wise but also have great insight by giving us food (proteins) that makes us delighted and blissful.

In Mandala 9 Sukta 25 Mantra 4, Rishis Drdhachyutah Agastyah has vision as follows:

विश्वा रूपाणि आविशन् पुनानो याति हर्यतः ।

यत्र अमृतास आसते ॥४॥

Meaning: (O Soma), you reach the region where all the luminous, immortal phenomena converge, after being purified and then drenching different forms that you encounter.

Here, Soma is addressed as proteins. It withdraws from the different forms it enters and gets renewed in the cells where the luminaries such as Indra (Atom), Varuna (Hydrogen), Vayu (Wind), and Ray-cows (Photons) are seated.

In Mandala 9 Sukta 26 Mantra 1, Rishis Idhmavaho Dardhachyutah has vision as follows:

तम् अमृक्षन्त वाजिनम् उपस्थे अदितेः अधि ।

विप्रासो अण्व्या धिया ॥१॥

Meaning: (O Soma), you are purified by the enlightening thoughts of wise men, and repose in the lap of Aditi (Consciousness).

When a person engages in enlightening thoughts, it has a salubrious effect on his metabolism which in effect favorably influences the proteins that also bask in the light of consciousness. This has a multiplier effect on the person. After all, the proteins have been brought into being from amino acids by DNA (Consciousness). Here Aditi is DNA.

In Mandala 9 Sukta 32 Mantra 2, Rishi Shyavashya Atreyah has this vision:

आदीं त्रितस्य योषणो हरिं हिन्वन्ति अद्रिभिः ।

इन्दुम् इन्द्राय पीतये ॥२॥

Meaning: O Soma, you are released through a process of compaction by the matrons who are triple born by. By your approach, Indra (atoms) would be delighted.

As we have already seen, DNA is basically responsible for bringing into being proteins that get assembled from amino acids in a sequence by compaction. This DNA is known as Jathavedus or one who has knowledge of past, present and future. DNA controls the genes. It is as though DNA is born in the past present and future too. DNA is in a position of a matron because it carries and gives birth to proteins.

In Mandala 9 Sukta 33 Mantra 3, Rishi Trita Aptyah has this vision:

सुता इन्द्राय वायवे वरुणाय मरुभ्यः ।

सोमो अर्षन्ति विष्णवे ॥३॥

Meaning: The Soma (Protein) is pressed out for Indra (Atom), Vayu (Wind), Varuna (Hydrogen), and Maruts (Tachyons). Soma also travels to the all-pervading Vishnu (Electromagnetic Force).

In Mandala 10 Sukta 97, the Rishi Bishak Atharvana, a healer as the prefix to his name suggests has a vision of Soma as Oshadhi. The word oshadhi means 'herb'. It also means that which brings 'thoughts of love'. The word herb also broadly includes all types of vegetation such as shrubs, ferns, trees, herbal plants, cultivated crops etc. Furthermore, Yaska the ancient authority on Rig Veda says, oshadhi is a compound word which implies 'that which destroys disease'. Thus:

शतं वो अम्ब धामानि सहस्रमुत वो रुहः ।

अधा शतक्रत्वो यूयमिमं मे अगदं कृत ॥२॥

Meaning: O mother, you have a hundred centers, and thousands of growths. Therefore with your hundred powers heal the sick person here, so prays the Rishi.

The hundred centers refer to the many places where herbal plants abound and the thousands of growths refer to herbal plants from which medicines are prepared that cure disease. The Rishi is talking of the sick patients under his care. The plants are addressed as mother as maternal care involves love as well as medicament. The Rishi makes it explicit in Mantra 4, thus:

ओषधीरिति मतरस्तद्धो देवीरुप ब्रुवे ।

सनेयमश्वं गां वास आत्मानं तव पूरुष ॥४॥

Meaning: I hail you as mother O growths of earth. O purusha, I give you horses (life energies), ray-cows (photons), abode in myself as you are the Purusha (giver of proteins) to all the growths mentioned above.

Proteins enrich the plant kingdom. One notable factor in nature needs to be borne in mind. There are some twenty types of amino acids, the basic ingredients for proteins, which can all be found in plant life, but some amino acids do not find place in human and animal bodies. This makes it incumbent for humans and animals to depend on plants to provide that supplement to the protein requirements of our body.

This interesting story is narrated in the Puranas. In Kailasa, Lord Shiva is resident with his wife Parvathi and two sons Ganesha and Karthikaya or Kumara. There was an undercurrent leading to conflict between the two sons as to who is superior which the parents observed for sometime. One day Lord Shiva called the boys and told them that he has devised a competition for the two brothers to ascertain which of them is superior to the other. As we have seen earlier, Shiva is the gravitational force in this universe. What about Ganesha and Karthikaya? Ganesha is the biological entity DNA, generator of Love in us. We saw that unifying force is defined as SAT-CHIT-ANANDA. According to Ganesha Upanishad or Ganesha Atharva Sirsha (head of Atherva Veda) as per Mantra 5 Ganesha is SAT-CHIT-ANANDA. As DNA in the cells Ganesha represents Ananda (Bliss). In the earlier chapters we have also seen that the entire phenomenon world is governed by a spirit of sacrifice. That is the reason the concept of sacrifice is so important in Vedas. This spirit of sacrifice is Karthikaya or Kumara. When the father Shiva asked them to go round the world as part of the competition, Karthikaya embarked on a trip to go round the physical universe, which does take more time than Ganesha circumambulating his parents not once but thrice, which takes much less time, and claimed the prize rightfully from his father. There is also a message in the story. The yonder vast universe is not the only place that should command our admiration. The biological universe within us is also equally vast, if not greater for commanding our respect and admiration. Both are governed by the same Truth, SAT-CHIT-ANANDA.

Chapter 14

Navagwas & Dashagwas—
The Peer Reviewers

In the year 1959, a physics professor, Enrico Fermi described a paradox. Given the age and vastness of this universe with the presence of billions of stars and planets that have existed for billions of years, we have not been contacted by another alien civilization or have any such civilization responded to our signals beamed at regular intervals directed towards outer space. No concrete signs of any life, not even the simplest bacteria, have been found on the moon, Mars and asteroids, the outer solar system planets and moons. The paradox remains unresolved. It is also being wondered that life on other planets might have evolved differently to that on Earth. A special program has been initiated in the US known as SETI (Search for Extra Terrestrial Intelligence). No break through has been achieved to date. Are we doomed to failure because of a fundamental assumption? Read on . . . .

As we have seen in the earlier chapters, the mighty Rishis of Rig Veda were well aware of all the modern scientific explorations into the fundamental structure of this universe and the forces that operate to keep it fine tuned so that our existence is sustained. This is known as Anthropic Principle in science. The Anthropic principle states that the universe is as it is because if it were different we would not be here to observe it. It is an explanation for every parameter in physics, from the size of the nuclear forces to dark energy and the mass of the electrons. If any one of the values varied even slightly then the universe would be uninhabitable. For example, if the strong nuclear force was slightly different then protons and neutrons would not stick together to make nuclei and atoms could not form. If atoms don't form chemistry would not exist. Carbon would not exist and therefore biology and humans would not exist. This was first mooted by Robert Dicke and Brandon Carter in 1970.

It was Albert Einstein who first proposed the principle of equivalence, which in effect states that the laws of physics are the same everywhere. However, lately, this postulate of Einstein has been under challenge because there is already a discovery that one of the constants in Einstein's assumption appears to be different in different parts of the universe, others may follow. Is scientific observation merely tentative until it is overthrown by new observations? Is there no finality? Or is the observations obscured by our four dimensional limitation of space and time? Needless to say, our thought is a creature of this four dimensional limitation. All the scientific discoveries are outcome of thought. We should give careful consideration to the research findings of Dr. William Tiller during the last decade. He says: "In the last four hundred years, an unstated assumption of science is that human intention cannot effect what we call physical reality. Our experimental research of the past decade shows that, for today's world, and under the right conditions, this assumption is no longer correct. We humans are much more than we think we are."

The Rishis of yore took an additional step, which the modern since is not willing to take. The Rishis questioned the primacy of "Thought". The blame for not willing to do so can be traced to the religious background of the western society, at the fundamental level. Succinctly put, the issue revolves around the question, I Consciousness or Consciousness and 'I'? 'I' is a thought, like any other. In fact the first thought and hence it is the foundation. Therefore a clear answer to the question will make a world of difference. Since 'I' is a thought it is also material, a thing. Unfortunately, therefore, if we assume the phrase I consciousness, we are in-subordinating Consciousness to the thought 'I'. As you can be easily aware, your Consciousness is not a thing by any stroke of imagination. If they are fundamentally two unlike faculties, this consciousness and 'I', a further question arises as to which takes precedence over the other, whether it is 'I' thought or Consciousness. This question is also very simple to resolve. What happens when you wake up in the morning after a good night's sleep? You first become conscious then the 'I' factor comes into picture. Again, take the case of a new born. The baby is born with developing consciousness and only later, perhaps with prompting and observation of the behavior of parents and other relatives does the child develops the idea that it is an independent entity from the rest of the world (the idea 'I' and the world). In the circumstances, Consciousness needs to be given primacy over thought, which the ancient Rishis rightly did. Many consequences follow. In the first place, to be with consciousness without being contaminated by thought is itself a big challenge. If you closely observe, Consciousness is attention; undivided attention. The second challenge is to be so attentive constantly. Thirdly, our own world appears differently, especially with reference to values we lay stress on. We can go on. There was a standing example of a man who could give such an undivided attention to Consciousness till 1985. Mr. J. Krishnamurti about whom I am talking is no more to practically guide us in this area. However, many people did benefit by his speeches around the world.

In thousands of years of experience we have had living in this world, we have gathered wide information as to what thought can do. Thought can lead us to great discoveries in every conceivable field of enquiry that man can undertake. It can also lead man towards great misconceptions from which it is almost impossible to retract. This is remarkably evident in the field of physics. The classical notion regarding the structure and contents of this universe had to be fundamentally revised in the new physics which predominates the scientific thinking since the beginning of twentieth century. It has also become incumbent for scientists to consider Consciousness as a factor. How can we be sure that thought is not misleading us? Thought in fact may be creating a mirage which we are pursuing. For all our scientific explorations we are heavily dependent on mathematics. Mathematics is wholly an output of thought. Peter Woit, a mathematical physicist at Columbia University and the author of the acclaimed book 'Not Even Wrong" says "The use of sophisticated mathematical techniques can sometime obscure basic problems". Elegant and improper use of maths can screw up the world. This devastating effect was amply demonstrated by Gaussian Cupola, a mathematical formula recklessly applied in the financial sphere in US. It has been traced as a single direct cause for the ongoing recession all over the world. The ancient Rishis therefore said that to understand any phenomenon in nature including thought, we have to transcend the phenomenon and be in a position to objectively observe its activity. If we are under the influence of the phenomenon in anyway we cannot objectively observe its operation.

In the last two millenniums, we have seen many philosophers come and go who have left their foot prints for eternity. But there are very few personalities like late Jiddu Krishnamurti who laid stress on the fact that thought is merely a tool. We should therefore understand its characteristics, utility and limitation. Without so understanding if we recklessly deploy thought in all our activities, it is bound to lead us into conflicts, confusions and delusions. Thought is a creature of time. It has therefore a definite beginning and ending. Since we are totally dependant on thought this beginning and ending becomes tremendously important in our life. In the context of our existence, we say it is living and death. The 'I' thought wants to live for ever and it shuns death. To this end it tries to secure its continued existence with various props. We are not concerned here with physical death which is inevitable. Science says that atoms on which we are physically dependant will inevitably abandon us after 650,000 hours. The ancient Rishis stated the same fact by relating our existence to breath. This is an average figure. We know that this death is inevitable but we are more concerned and afraid of the death of the 'I' thought, more clearly, psychological death. Basically this fear is what made us invent and believe in the concept of after life. Our whole life is therefore shadowed by fear. However, if one transcends thought and becomes conscious of life, then one realizes that to die is to have a mind that is completely empty of its daily longings, pleasures and agonies. In this connection, it is necessary to understand that thought is always old and any new perceptions are promptly converted into old by our thought process. Death is therefore a mutation, in the sense the old is completely abandoned and thereby there is something totally new. Thought is what is 'known', death is in fact merely a release from this known. Then we are totally living. Such were the Angirasa Rishis of yore, sometimes said to be nine of them and at other times ten, *Nawagwas and Dashagwas.*

The great poet Kalidasa narrates a story in his *Raghuvamsa.* King Dasaratha's father was king Aja. His wife Indumati died mysteriously by an accident. The king was very fond of his wife. Therefore his grief was also inconsolable. He cried before his Guru (teacher) Rishi Vashishta (of Rig Veda fame) and said "What a calamity has befallen me!" Guru Vasishta replied very briefly: What is natural is death, but what is unnatural is life. That we are alive is a mystery. Even science tells us that the whole Universe is a manifestation of death. This is most evident in the sub-atomic world. Further, if we give attention to the biological world within us, as we did in previous chapter, there is death by the millions of cells, on a daily basis in our own body, in order to keep us alive. Can we call it life? Even the great Buddha says the Universe is a procession of transitions, and a perpetual transformation of constituents. The most remarkable exposition on this subject of life and death is that demonstrated in Katha Upanishad. The word Upanishad means a secret teaching of the innermost essence of existence. We are also told that the Upanishads are the quintessence of Vedas. Since Vedas are books of knowledge, an Upanishad is essence of that knowledge. This essence of knowledge is revealed to us in Katha Upanishad in the form of a dialogue between the Lord of Death and a young boy Nachiketas who seeks answer to three questions from the Lord of Death. In effect it is the Universal answering the Individual. In the detailed contents of the Upanishad, the three fasts, the three questions, and three boons may be said to be relevant to three levels of experience through which we pass as individuals in our life. The three levels being: the senses, the mind and the Spirit.

In chapter 2, we considered the example of refrigerator. It has three levels: the outer cabinet, the internal network that governs the operation and the cause for its operation in the innermost level, in this case electricity. Accordingly, the outer cabinet represents our body and senses; the inner network is represented by our mind and the innermost causal principle is the Consciousness. Always, the internal network is concerned with conversion and transformation of source energy to engine utilitarian action through the body and senses or outer cabinet in a mechanism as the case may be. The outer cabinet or sense organs and body are subject to wear and tear by constant use and wither away naturally in course of time. The channels of internal network are also prone to wear and tear but the force behind the process of conversion and transformation and the source power are not subject to wear and tear. They would abandon the present body but are available for renewal in perpetuity. The questions of Nachiketas pertain to these levels of quest of the human soul; and the answers given by Yama, are precisely the counterpart of these questions.

What is death then? We humans, tethered as we are, to the experience of the body and the senses (the outer cabinet in our example), mistakenly presume that death is annihilation of all values. That is the reason we are afraid of death. Death is a negation of all that we hold near and dear. All our pleasures are cut off. But in this Upanishad, death itself is the teacher. If death were a negation of all things, we cannot hope to learn any lesson from it. Here, life is the student and death is the teacher. That is the grand context of the Upanishad. Death becomes such a teacher, when we awaken to the fact of this procession of transitory activity in our inner network in the example. Empirically speaking, death and life have no ultimate dissimilarity between themselves. There is continuity between life and death and between death and life.

How then is this fear of death generated? We are creatures limited by the boundary of the four dimensional world. Three dimensions of space and a dimension of time. We are not aware of other dimensions. As four dimensional beings, we are governed by thought with its limitations. This thought of ours is driven by desire and security at all times. The desire seeks pleasure all the time and shuns pain. Similarly, security concerns breed fear in perpetuity. Death is an ending of the individualized thought, which fruitlessly seeks to perpetuate itself. So the thought that governs us wants to put off death as far as possible. Nevertheless, thought meets its end; the phenomena abandon it in due course! On the other hand if the thought learns to live in harmony with the phenomena, there is greater chance for thought to comprehend the ultimate reality, or Universal Consciousness.

This subject of discussion is called *Eschatology*. Life is a series of successive states of consciousness with a common thread running through them. Death is visibly a psychophysical disintegration but it cannot reduce our existence to a dead end; rather it reopens a different state of consciousness no longer circumscribed by the limitations of the body-mind complex, in other words space-time limitation. The birth of an individual into the world of space and time is the concentration of consciousness in a spatial-temporal pressure-point which becomes the individual consciousness. The process begins generally with an obliteration or screening out of the universal sense in consciousness and a simultaneous beaming out of itself through the aperture of self willed movement of thought. Scientific attention is now being focused on the working of consciousness after physical death. This subject has generated considerable interest in disciplines like neurophysiology; cardiology; and quantum physics. For example, in neurophysiology research patients have been observed with near-death experience. The patients in near-death condition are subject to expanding consciousness, while their brains register no activity at all. A majority of the patients think a hundred times faster with great clarity than is humanly possible. Anyway, even during life time, we use our brain hardly beyond 15% of its capacity. It is now empirically proved that people can think and feel when they are clinically unconscious due to acute pan cerebral ischemia. This naturally raises the question whether consciousness is dependant on our physical existence or does it continue beyond death of the body as well? The question arises as to who observes the self and surroundings while the body lies on the clinical table, inert?

How then our identities continue beyond physical death in a post mortem consciousness? In 2001 Dr. Pim Van Lommel published a paper in Lancet and confirmed that near-death experience is an undeniable reality not confined within spiritual community but spread amongst skeptics as well. Death it would appear cannot mean the end of consciousness. Consciousness is separate from the body and it survives beyond death. During our wakeful state, the consciousness is limited to psychological reality initiated by 'I' consciousness, but after death of body-mind complex, the wakeful consciousness is exposed to many more realities beyond space-time constraint.

Rishis of Rig Veda were well aware of these aspects of existence and death. In the modern times, it has been said that Ramana Maharishi also underwent near-death vision. Rishi Brhaduktha Vamadevya had just lost his son Vajin. He then articulates his vision of near death and immediate after death experience in Rig Veda Mandala 10 Sukta 56 Mantras 1-7, thus:

इदं त एकं पर ऊ त एकं त्रुतियेन ज्योतिषा सं विशस्व ।

संवेशने तन्वश्चारुरेधि प्रियो देवानां परमे जनित्रे ॥१ ॥

Meaning: The light associated with physical body merges with one universal light, similarly the light associated with the prana megres with the universal light and the third part of the light enters the Swar loka, which is the genesis of all luminaries. Your manifestation thus gets an affectionate welcome.

Immediate after-death movement thus seems to be associated with consciousness and photons. The first two lights in the Mantra are related to the movement of the consciousness and the third light refers to photons. Universal light is Universal Consciousness.

तनूष्टे वाजिन् तन्वं नयन्ती वाममस्मभ्यं धातु शर्म तुभ्यम् ।

अहुतो महो धरुणाय देवान् दिवीव ज्योतिः स्वमा मिमेयाः ॥२ ॥

Meaning: O Vajin, may this earth that bears your physical manifestation support us with riches and beauty and may it give peace to you when you become one with it, on disintegration. Then you enter your own form as the light of Swar world and repose with the other luminaries for your support.

The earth compromises trillions of bacteria that support life on this earth, the same bacteria that produce fertile crops and create beautiful forms. When a man dies and disintegrates, his physical body reverts back to bacterial form. To be peaceful, the bacteria should not get contaminated, hence cremation and not burial as per ancient Hindu custom. The mass less part of the manifestation leaves the body as photons and revert back to its origin, which is the abode of all light dependant phenomena in nature.

वाज्यसि वाजिनेना सुवेनीः सुवितः स्तोमं सुवितो दिवं गाः ।

सुवितो धर्म प्रथमानु सत्या सुवितो देवान् त्सुवितोऽनु पत्म ॥३॥

Meaning: O Vajin, you are like a strong and swift bird. Go happily in the path of the luminous region; the path that is natural law of truth. The path traced by other luminaries and light of Sun (Swar world).

The natural law of the universal order is one of sacrifice. All the phenomenon in nature are related to the Virat Purusha (unifying force) in this spirit of sacrifice, even like the limbs of human body that coordinate with the overall purpose of our body. This Virat Purusha is in Hiranya Garba (the golden womb), source of all light Or Swar Loka. It is from this region, all luminaries emenate, led by Mahavishnu (Electromagnetic Force).

महिम्न एषां पितरश्चनेशिरे देवा देवेष्वदधुरपि क्रतुम् ।

समविव्यचुरुत यान्यत्विषुः आ एषां तनूषु नि विविशुः पुनः ॥४॥

Meaning: Such was the grace of our ancestors (the Angirasa Rishis) that they first become the masters of the world of forefathers and then attained the status of luminaries by the grace of other luminaries. Among the luminaries they harmoniously established their mighty intelligence, such that they were able to transcend all radiances (and comprehend the Eternal Truth). Later they again entered their own bodies.

Here is a postulate which is yet to be established by modern science. Even though there are many experiments afoot in this direction, Dr. William Tiller's ongoing research immediately comes to mind. The Vedas postulate that the individual consciousness will lead us to universal consciousness if we follow the path of natural law (path of sacrifice and love, which all natural phenomena follow). Have any human being proceed in the path and returned to narrate the experience? The Vedas say that the Angirasa Rishis were such persons. The word Angirasa itself means those who have tasted the essence of consciousness (Ang means Agni or consciousness, and Rasa means essence). Some of these Rishis narrate their experience in, what is called Apri suktas.

सहोभिर्विश्वं परि चक्रमू रजः पूर्वा धामान्यमिता मिमानाः ।

तनूषु विश्वा भुवना नि येमिरे प्रासारयन्त पुरुध प्रजा अनु ॥५॥

Meaning: (The Angirasa Rishis) circulated the entire cosmos by their inner potential. They transcended not only the existing dimensions but all other dimensions in this universe. Appropriate to the level of progress achieved by all beings towards the ultimate goal, they refurbished the form. They instilled an awareness of the light of consciousness appropriate to the individual.

Once the Individual Consciousness merges with Universal Consciousness, the brave one (Vira) achieving this ultimate goal of existence becomes Universal Consciousness. He would have traversed the entire cosmos and transcended all dimensions. He therefore is inalienable part of the Universal consciousness. He becomes the creator. Angirasa Rishis were such persons. Could we say they are dead and gone? No. Such are the great ones

240

who sit in judgement to review the progress and help others in reaching the goal. They assume the form of Agni in the universe.

द्विधा सूनवोऽसुरं स्वर्विदम् आस्थापयन्त तृतीयेन कर्मणा ।

स्वां प्रजां पितरः पित्र्यं सह आवरेष्वदधुः तन्तुमाततम् ॥६ ॥

Meaning: In the previous mantra three actions of Angirasa Rishis were delineated. The third action as mentors is explained here. They not only established the Swar world (photons) as Agni (fire) in this universe, but they also created Agni (fire) as father for the lineage.

Once the Angirasa Rishis become the Universal Consciousness, there is no such concept as past and future. There is only the present. Thus whatever action the creator effectuates, these Rishis also are part of that action.

नावा न क्षोदः प्रदिशः प्रुथिव्याः स्वस्तिभिरिति दुर्गाणि विश्वा ।

स्वां प्रजां बृहदुक्थो महित्वाऽऽवरेष्वदधात् आ परेषु ॥७ ॥

Meaning: As mentioned in mantra 5 above, this journey towards consciousness calls for great bravery. An example is given. A sailor is exposed to many dangers in the open seas when travelling from one part of the earth to another. Similarly, there are many obstacles in achieving the state of bliss. The Rishi of the mantras also makes a declaration: out of his many children, some were satisfied with the allurement of the material world, but others took to the path of eternal bliss.

Rishi Bharadwajah Barhaspatyah implies in Rig Veda Mandala 6 Sukta 22 Mantra 2 that Navagwas and Dasagwas are otherwise known as Angirasa Rishis in Rig Veda. They helped Indra (Atoms) to retrieve the Surya (Sun) from the dark matter or a black hole? Originally there were only nine of them (Navagwas) as per Rishi Sadaprna Atreyah in Rig Veda Mandala 5 Sukta 45 Mantras 7 and 11. Perhaps their efforts did not meet with success. In Rig Veda

Mandala 10 Sukta 108 Mantra 8 we are introduced to another Angirasa Rishi Ayasyah. The nine Angirasa rishis sought the help of the tenth Angirasa, Ayasyah Angirasa who had discovered the Swar world (the region for the genesis of photons). Then they were able to retrieve the Sun.

Glossary of Sanskrit Words

Abhipratarin—an ancient scholar

Abhram—clouds

Achamana—sipping water in a ritual

Aditi or Durga or Shive—dynamic energy as the Universal Consciousness

Aditya(s)—solar emanations

Aghora—subsidiary religious text

Agni—fire flame Consciousness

Aham—("I") ego

Ahanviya Yajna—a fire ritual

Aitaraya Brahmana—subsidiary ritual text to Rig Veda

Aitareya Upanishad—subsidiary ritual text to Rig Veda

Ajna Chakra—At the top of the spinal column

Akasa—vast empty space sky

Aklishta Vritte—perceptive act

Akshiyamana—imperishable

Amruta—ambrosia/nectar

Anahata Chakra—cardiac plexus

Ananda—supreme bliss

Angirasa Rishis—rishis who were essence of fire

Anna—food matter

Antariksha or Matari—vast inter-planetary space Anugraha—grace

Anvaharyapachana Yajna—a fire ritual

Apana—exhalation

Apas—water

Apri Hymns—extraordinary hymns of revelation

Apurva—an invisible reaction produced by vibration on environment

Arjuna, Dhananjaya—a heroic character in the epic Mahabratha

Aryaman—a ray of sun

Ashwin Twins—protons & neutrons

Astanga Sarira—a medieval text

Astitva—the existence

Asuras—inimical forces demonic forces

Asvapati—an ancient king

Atharva—One of four Vedas

Atma-Vichara—self contemplation

Aum or OM or Pranava—a holy word

Avaranas—attractive ornaments

Avidya—transactional knowledge

Barathi (Mahi)—a name for divine inspiration

Bhaga—a ray of sun

Bhagawan—a divine soul

Bhagwat Geeta—a medieval composition of spiritual poems

Bhu Loka or Bhu—earth

Bhudevi—the luminary earth.

Bhuvar Loka or Bhuvah—the intermediary between earth and outer space

Bijaksharas—seed syllables

Bindu—point

Brahma Loka—event horizon

Brahma or Brahmanaspati or Brihaspati—repository of all energies and forces in universe

Brahma Yajna—meditation of convergence

Brahmachari (n)—a bachelor on spiritual path

Brahmana or Brahmin(s)—a person who has chosen Consciousness as goal of his life

Brahmanas—ritual prescriptions

Brahmanda—the universal egg

Brahmanda Purana—one of the 18 purana texts

Brhadaranyaka Upanishad—an earliest spiritual guide book

Brhat—the large or vast

Buddhi—intellect

Chakra (s)—power points in our body

Chandra—moon

Channdas Chhandamshi—poetic metre

Chhandogya Upanishad—an earliest spiritual guide book

Chit Cit-Shakti—consciousness

Chitta—memory

Daksha—a ray of the sun

Daksha Yajna—a ritual performed by an ancient king

Devadatta—a breathe that induces yawning and sleep

Devatas—luminaries

Devi Mahatmya or Sat-Chandi—the saga of dynamic energy

Dharma—natural law

Dhvani—noise-unlettered sound

Dig Devataas—luminaries of directions

Dirtharashtra—king of Kuru Clan of Hastinapura

Disha—quarters

Diti—indifferent to consciousness

Draupadi's Swayamvara—princess Draupadi's choice of a spouse

Durga Suktam—hymns addressed to dynamic energy

Dwaparayuga—the second era

Dwaraka—a medieval kingdom

Dwija—twise born

Dyau—heaven

Ganapathi or Ganesha—the individual consciousness

Gandha—smell

Ganesha Atharva Sirsha or Ganesha Upanishad—a eulogy of individual consciousness

Garhapatya Yajna—a fire ritual

Gautama—an ancient spiritual student

Gayatri Gayatri-Mantra—an invocation of consciousness

Gokul—a tribal town where Lord Krishna grew-up

Govardan Hill—a hill

Gow—cow or symbol of light

Grahasta—householder

Grishma—summer

Gyanaindriyas—sense organs 96 97

Halahala—a poison

Hari Harayah Hari—one who takes away ignorance

Hari-Om—be dispelled of the ignorance of consciousness

Hatha Yoga—one of the branches of yoga

Havis—sacrificial material in a ritual

Hiranyagarba—the golden womb

Ida (Nadi)—an invisible nerve in our body

Idam—this

Ila—the inspiring word

Indra—atoms

Isavasya Upanishad—a spiritual guide

Jagat—the universe that is in constant movement

Jai Ramjiji—victory be to consciousness

Jain Religion's Concept-Pudgal—matter

Janah Loka or Janah—the populated upper region

Janaka—an ancient king

Janasruti—an ancient king

Janmas—rebirths

Jathavedas—knowledge of past present and future

Jaya—victory

Jaya Tirtha Swami—an authority on Rig Veda

Jivatma—the finite body

Jyotisha Shastra—astrology and allied sciences

Kailasa—the abode of gravitational force

Kaliyuga—the current era

Kanda Presta—the seat of pandava kingdom

Kapila Muni—an ancient sage

Karana Sarira—causal body

Karmaindriyas—physical organs of action

Karthikaya or Kumara—an epitome of sacrifice

Katha Upanishad—a spiritual guide

Kaushitaki Brahmana Upanishad—a spiritual guide

Kavi—poet

Klishta Vritte—the exercise of choice

Kretayuga—the first era

Krikala—a breathe that induces hunger thirst sneezing and cough

Krishna Lord—the principle character in the purana Mahabhagavatam

Krishna Yajur Ved a Taittiriya Samhita—a part of Yajur Veda

Kundalini Yoga—a branch of yoga

Kunti—Queen mother of Pandavas

Kurma—a breathe that lubricates the eyes by blinking

Kurukshetra—the great battle field where kuru clan was anihilated

Kutas—highest a heap mass or most excellent

Lalitha Pancharatnam—the necklace of five gems to the play of dynamic energy

Lalitha Sahasranama—thousand names of dynamic energy

Lalithambika—mother energy

Laxmi or Mahalaxmi or Narayani—the sustaining dynamic energy

Loka—layers of the world

Loka Mata—the universe as mother

Lopamudra—extraordinary wife of Rishi Agastya

Madhu Vidya—a vision of knowledge with honey as basis

Madhyama—the middle of subtle and gross sound

Madyama Kuta—the middle peak

Mahabhagavatha Purana—one of the 18 Purana texts

Mahanaraya Upanishad—a spiritual guide

Mahar Loka or Mahaha—the layer of galactic space

Maharishi Vyasa or Veda Vyasa—a medieval Rishi

Mahayugas—the four great eras

Manas—mind

Mandala—a cosmogram

Mandukya Upanishad—a spiritual guide book

Manipura Chakra—solar plexus

Manma—a imaginative constructive of meaning of a word

Mantra—a verse in Rig Veda a potent combination of seed syllables

Mantra Drashta—a visionary of mantra

Mantrartha Manjari—a compendium of mantras

Manvantaras or Kalpas—a period of 14 fourfold eras

Markandaya Purana—one of the 18 Purana texts

Marthanda—eight ray of the sun

Maruts—tachyons

Matarishvan—galactic wind

Matsya Purana—one of the 18 Puranas

Maya—illusion

Mayavi—magician or illusionist

Mitra—bonding

Mitra-Varuna—bonded hydrogen (H2)

Mrtyu—mortality

Muladhara or Muladhara Chakra—foundation coccyx plexus

Mundaka Upanishad—a spiritual guide book

Nachiketas—an ancient child who has a dialogue with the Lord of Death

Nada—primordial sound

Nadi—neurons

Naga—a breathe that induces hiccups and belching

Naivedya or Bhog—offerings in worship

Nama Rupa—name and form

Narada—an ancient sage

Narakasura—a demon

Nataraja—kind of the art of dancing

Navagwas or Dasagwas—nine or ten Angirasa Rishis

Nisha or Ratri—night

Nyaya System—Indian logic system

Nyaya Vartika—a treatise on logic

Oshadhi—herbs medicines thoughts of love

Padartha—material substance

Panchagni Vidya—the knowledge of the five fires

Pancha-Indriyas—the five sense organs

Pancha-Pranas—the five kinds of breathe

Pandavas—Sons of Queen Kunti through Luminaries

Para Vak—the subtle form of sound

Para-Brahman or Paramatma—consciousness

Paramanu—particle of an atom

Parasiva—gravitational force

Parijatha Parijatha Tree—a flower plant

Parijman—going round or spin

Parjanya—rain

Parthiva—concrete

Parvati—the dynamic energy of gravity

Pasu(s)—beings in bondage

Pasyanti—the third stage of sound movement from subtle to gross

Patanjali's Yoga Sutras—a well known treatise on yoga

Pathala Lokas—the nether worlds

Pindanda—earth the lumpy egg

Pingala—neuron

Prajapati—Lord of Genesis

Prakriti—nature

Pralaya and Mahapralaya—catastrophe

Prana—the vital breathe

Prana-Agnihotra Vidya—a fire ritual

Pranamaya Kosha—the encasement of breathe in our body

Pranavayu—oxygen

Pranayama—regulation of breathe

Prapancha-Sara-Tantra—a tantra text

Pravahana Jaivali—an ancient king

Puja—formal worship

Pura—in front of facing

Puranas—ancient lore in 18 books

Purna-Madhuna—a mead of honey and water

Purohit—a priest

Purusha—man

Purusha Suktam—hymn on consciousness

Purushottama Purusha—supreme consciousness

Pushana—growth of consciousness

Raja Yoga—a branch of yoga

Rajanya—king

Rakshasas—demons

Rama—an ancient king in the epic Ramayana

Ramayana—an epic

Rasa—essence

Rik(s)—eulogy

Rishi—a contemplative visionary

Rtam—natural order

Rudradhyaya—a study of gravitational force

Rukmini—wife of Lord Krishna

Rupa—form

Sabda Brahman—sound as energy

Sadana—spiritual practice

Sadhyas—those who have spiritual perfection

Sadyojata—a spiritual treatise

Sahasraara—the core region of countless petals

Saivagamas—texts related to gravitational force in nature

Sakuni—an ancient king of Afganisthan

Saman—hymns of Sama Veda

Samana—time gap between inhalation and exhalation

Sambhava Yoga—a branch of yoga

Samhara—transformation

Samit—faggot

Samkhya System—one of the six systems of Vedanta

Samrat—perpetually shining

Samsara Sagara—the ocean of mortal living

Samvarga Vidya—knowledge regarding all absorbing one

Samvatsara—year

Sanatana Dharma—the timeless law of nature

Sandhya—the three twilight prayers of a brahmana

Sanskar—tradition or establishment

Sanskrit—a language that is pure

Sanyasi—a monk

Saraswati—inspiration arising out of convergence of energies and forces in nature

Satapatha Brahmana—a text of rituals

Sat-Chit-Ananda—Truth-Consciousness-Bliss

Satya Loka—The ultimate destination

Satyabhama—another wife of Lord Krishna

Satyam—truth

Saunaka—an ancient scholar

Savitur Brahman—universal consciousness

Shad-Vaishnavyah—Six key verses related to Electromagnetic force

Shakti Cult Shakti Tantras—pertaining to dynamic energy in nature

Shakti Kuta—the third mass of energy

Shakti Para Shakti—dynamic energy in nature

Shantipaathah—peace invocation

Sharat—autumnal season

Shastras—repository of traditional lore

Shiva or Rudra or Maheshwara—gravitational force

Shodasa Upachara—sixteen ritual steps in worship

Shudra—a foot soldier

Shvetasvatara—upanishad a spiritual guide

Siddha Vaidya—knowledge leading to revelation

Siddhas Siddhi—enlightented souls and enlightenment

Soma—eternal and universal love

Spanda Shastra—science relating to spin

Sparsa—touch

Sri Chakra—a cosmogram of dynamic energy

Sri Suktam—hymns on dynamic energy

Srutis—Vedic exposition

Sthiti—sustenance

Sthula Sarira—gross body

Sudarshana Chakra—the armour wielded by electromagnetic force

Sukhsma Sarira—subtle body

Suras—enlightened ones

Surya—sun

Sushumna (Nadi)—an invisible nerve that passes through spinal chord

Suta—a medieval narrator

Sutantuh—the auspicious thread

Suvar Loka or Svah—the upper layer of atmosphere

Svarat (self-luminous) Swar World—world of photons

Svayambhu—self generated

Svetavaraha Kalpa or Vivasvata Manvantara—period of fourteen of the fourfold eras

Swadistana Chakra—one of the power vortices in our body

Swara Yoga or Swara—a branch of yoga

Swarga—heaven

Taittiriya Aranyaka—a portion of Yajur Veda

Taittiriya Upanishad—a spiritual guide book

Talas—layers below earth

Tandava Shiva Tandava—vigorous dance form

Tantra Shastra—science of tantra

Tantra-Raja—a treatise on tantra

Tapas—meditation

Tapoh Loka or Tapah—the flaming layer in universe

Tat Twam Asi—that though are

Tatpurusha—a treatise on gravitational force

Thretayuga—third of the four eras

Tirobhava—concealment

Trini Locana—three luminous realms of pure mind

Tripura Sundari—the dazzling reality that confronts us

Tulsi—holy basil leaves

Turiya—the fourth state of consciousness

Tvashtr—carbon

Udana—a type of breathe

Upaagamas—spiritual texts

Upanishad(s)—spiritual guide books

Upa-pranas—subordinate breathes

Upasaka—a spiritual practitioner

Upaveda—Ayurveda—science of medicine

Usha(s)—dawn

Vagbhava Kuta—one of three masses of cells in our body

Vaidyanatha—the authority on medicine

Vaikhari—gross sound normal speech

Vaisesika—a spiritual school (600 BCE)

Vaishya—trader

Vajasaneyi Samhita—a part of Yajur Veda

Vajin—name of a youth

Vajra Astra (Ayuda)—electron(s)

Varna—phonetics

Varuna—hydrogen

Vasanas—impressions

Vasanta—spring season

Vasus—gravitons

Vayu—wind air

Veda (s) Vedic—knowledge relating to knowledge

Vedanta—towards the end of knowledge

Vidya—learning

Vidya-Avidya Upasana—the practice of learning and accumulation of knowledge

Vidyut—lightning

Vijnana—higher or fundamental physics

Vipascit—the clarity of perception

Vipra(s)—persons with insight intuition and transcendental vision

Virat—manifoldly shining

Visana—a spiritual text

Vishaya-Chaitanya—objective

Vishnu or Mahavishnu—electromagnetic Force

Vishnu-Sahasra-Namas—thousand identifications of electromagnetic force

Vishwakarma—the divine architect

Vishwanara Vaishvanara Atman Virat Purusha—universal man

Visshudha Chakra—Cervial plexus

Visva-Sara-Tantra—a treatise on tantra

Visvedevas—all light dependant particles in nature

Vivasvan—a ray of the sun

Viveka—discrimination

Viveka Chudamani—a treatise on discrimination

Vritra and other Dhanavas—dark forces

Vyahriti (es)—the seven layers in the body as well as the universe

Vyakarna—Karika—a treatise on grammar

Vyana—one of the principle breathes

Yajamana—the organiser

Yajna—sacrifice journey

Yajna Purusha—personification of convergence

Yajnopavitam—sacred thread

Yajurveda—one of the four Vedas

Yajus—contents of the Yajur Veda

Yama—the lord of death

Yantra—cosmogram

Yaska—a compiler of an ancient lexicon on Rig Veda

Yoga—science of convergence

Yogeshwara—the lord of convergence

Bibliography

RgVeda Darshana Vol 1-16	S.K. Ramachandra Rao	Kalpataru Research Academy Bengluru. India	1998-2005
Rig Veda Samhita Vol 1-11	R.L. Kashyap	SAKSI Bengluru. India	2003-2009
The Secret of Veda	Sri Aurobindo	Sri Aurobindo Ashram, Puduchery. India	1956
Sakti And Sakta	Sir John Woodroffe	Ganesh & Co. Chennai. India.	1918
The Garland of Letters	Sir John Woodroffe	Ganesh & Co., Chennai. India.	1922
Principles of Tantra Part 1-2	Sir John Woodroffe	Ganesh & Co., Chennai. India.	1913-14
Brhadaranyaaka Upanishad	Swami Krishnananda	The Divine Life Trust Society, Shivanandnagar, India.	1984
Chhandogya Upanishad	Swami Krishnananda	The Divine Life Trust Society, Shivanandnagar, India.	1984

Mahanarayanopanishad	Swami Vimalananda	The Ramakrishna Math, Chennai, India.	1957
Isavasya Upanishad	Swami Chinmayananda	Central Chinmaya Mission Trust, Mumbai, India.	1980
The Tao of Physics	Fritjof Capra	Fontana/Collins, UK.	1975
A Short History of Nearly Everything	Bill Bryson	Black Swan, UK	2003
Cosmos	Carl Sagan	Ballantine Books, New York, US	1980
The Trouble with Physics	Lee Smolin	Penguin Books, London, UK.	2006
Microcosmos	Lynn Margulis and Dorion Sagan	University of California Press, London, UK.	1997
50 Physics Ideas	Joanne Baker	Quercus, London, UK.	2007
A Brief History of Time	Stephen Hawking	Bantam Books, London, UK.	1988
The Eye of Shiva	Amoury de Riencourt	William Morrow & Co., New York, US	1981
The Cosmic Code	Heinz R. Pagel	Bantam Books Inc., New York, US.	1982
Swara Yoga	Swami Muktibodananda	Bihar School of Yoga, Munger, India.	1983

Philosophy of Religion	Swami Krishnananda	The Divine Life Trust Society, Shivanandnagar, India.	1985
Essays in Life and Eternity	Swami Krishnananda	The Divine Life Trust Society, Shivanandnagar, India.	1990
The Holy Geeta	Swami Chinmayananda	Central Chinmaya Mission Trust, Mumbai, India.	—
Freedom from the Known	J. Krishnamurti	B. I. Publications Pvt. Ltd., New Delhi, India.	1969
The light in Oneself	J. Krishnamurti	Shambhala Publications, Inc., Boston, US.	1999
Facets of Brahman	Swami Chidbhavananda	Sri Ramakrishna Tapovanam, Tirupparaitturai, Tamil Nadu.	1971
The Purusha Sukta	Swami Harshananda	Ramakrishna Math, Bangalore, India.	1996
Gayatri	I. K. Taimni	Theosophical Publishing House., Adyar, Chennai, India.	1974
The Bond	Lynne McTaggart	Free Press (The Simon & Schuster Inc), New York	2011

Mr. C. S. Moorthy was born in the year 1938 in Kanchipuram, Tamil Nadu in December 1938. He grew up in Mumbai where he did his schooling. He was elected as Associate Member of Chartered Institute of Management Accountants, UK in May 1978. He was conferred Master's Degree in English by Mysore University in February 1981. He retired as Chief Manager Finance of Southern Petrochemical Industries Corporation in December 1998.

He came in close association with Swami Chinmayananda and became ardent follower between the years 1959 and 1969. He was mentored by Swami Chinmayananda's then principle disciple Sri Brahmachari Natarajan, who later on became Swami Dayananda Saraswati on his own right. Mr. Brahmachari Natarajan encouraged Sri C.S. Moorthy to read Sri Jiddu Krishnamurti's books. In the year 1970, Sri C.S. Moorthy had a chance to attend the public lecture by Mr. J. Krishnamurti.

This lecture inspired Sri. C.S. Moorthy and he became a great admirer.

After the demise of Mr. J.Krishnamurti in 1986, Mr. C.S. Moorthy commenced his independent research on scientific and spiritual aspects of ancient scriptures. He wrote many essays on diverse subjects. Gleanings of Rig Veda is his first book, a concentrated extract of many years of avid thoughts, readings and his deep understanding on sacred scriptures written by Rishis.